AF412683

Palgrave Macmillan Studies in Banking and Financial Institutions

Series Editor: **Professor Philip Molyneux**

The Palgrave Macmillan Studies in Banking and Financial Institutions will be international in orientation and include studies of banking within particular countries or regions, and studies of particular themes such as Corporate Banking, Risk Management, Mergers and Acquisitions, etc. The books will be focused upon research and practice, and include up-to-date and innovative studies on contemporary topics in banking that will have global impact and influence.

Titles include:

Yener Altunbaş, Blaise Gadanecz and Alper Kara
SYNDICATED LOANS
A Hybrid of Relationship Lending and Publicly Traded Debt

Yener Altunbaş, Alper Kara and Öslem Olgu
TURKISH BANKING
Banking under Political Instability and Chronic High Inflation

Elena Beccalli
IT AND EUROPEAN BANK PERFORMANCE

Paola Bongini, Stefano Chiarlone and Giovanni Ferri *(editors)*
EMERGING BANKING SYSTEMS

Santiago Carbó, Edward P.M. Gardener and Philip Molyneux
FINANCIAL EXCLUSION

Allessandro Carretta, Franco Fiordelisi and Gianluca Mattarocci *(editors)*
NEW DRIVERS OF PERFORMANCE IN A CHANGING FINANCIAL WORLD

Violaine Cousin
BANKING IN CHINA

Franco Fiordelisi and Philip Molyneux
SHAREHOLDER VALUE IN BANKING

Hans Genberg and Cho-Hoi Hui
THE BANKING CENTRE IN HONG KONG
Competition, Efficiency, Performance and Risk

Carlo Gola and Alessandro Roselli
THE UK BANKING SYSTEM AND ITS REGULATORY AND
SUPERVISORY FRAMEWORK

Elisabetta Gualandri and Valeria Venturelli *(editors)*
BRIDGING THE EQUITY GAP FOR INNOVATIVE SMEs

Munawar Iqbal and Philip Molyneux
THIRTY YEARS OF ISLAMIC BANKING
History, Performance and Prospects

Kimio Kase and Tanguy Jacopin
CEOs AS LEADERS AND STRATEGY DESIGNERS
Explaining the Success of Spanish Banks

M. Mansoor Khan and M. Ishaq Bhatti
DEVELOPMENTS IN ISLAMIC BANKING
The Case of Pakistan

Mario La Torre and Gianfranco A. Vento
MICROFINANCE

Philip Molyneux and Munawar Iqbal
BANKING AND FINANCIAL SYSTEMS IN THE ARAB WORLD

Philip Molyneux and Eleuterio Vallelado (*editors*)
FRONTIERS OF BANKS IN A GLOBAL WORLD

Anastasia Nesvetailova
FRAGILE FINANCE
Debt, Speculation and Crisis in the Age of Global Credit

Dominique Rambure and Alec Nacamuli
PAYMENT SYSTEMS
From the Salt Mines to the Board Room

Andrea Schertler
THE VENTURE CAPITAL INDUSTRY IN EUROPE

Alfred Slager
THE INTERNATIONALIZATION OF BANKS

Noel K. Tshiani
BUILDING CREDIBLE CENTRAL BANKS
Policy Lessons for Emerging Economies

Palgrave Macmillan Studies in Banking and Financial Institutions

Series Standing Order ISBN 978–1–4039–4872–4

You can receive future titles in this series as they are published by placing a standing order. Please contact your bookseller or, in case of difficulty, write to us at the address below with your name and address, the title of the series and the ISBN quoted above.

Customer Services Department, Macmillan Distribution Ltd, Houndmills, Basingstoke, Hampshire RG21 6XS, England

Emerging Banking Systems

Edited by

Paola Bongini, Stefano Chiarlone and Giovanni Ferri

First published 2009 by
PALGRAVE MACMILLAN

Palgrave Macmillan in the UK is an imprint of Macmillan Publishers Limited, registered in England, company number 785998, of Houndmills, Basingstoke, Hampshire RG21 6XS.

Palgrave Macmillan in the US is a division of St Martin's Press LLC, 175 Fifth Avenue, New York, NY 10010.

Palgrave Macmillan is the global academic imprint of the above companies and has companies and representatives throughout the world.

Palgrave® and Macmillan® are registered trademarks in the United States, the United Kingdom, Europe and other countries.

ISBN-13: 978–0–230–57434–2   hardback
ISBN-10: 0–230–57434–3   hardback

This book is printed on paper suitable for recycling and made from fully managed and sustained forest sources. Logging, pulping and manufacturing processes are expected to conform to the environmental regulations of the country of origin.

A catalogue record for this book is available from the British Library.

Library of Congress Cataloging-in-Publication Data

Emerging banking systems / [edited by] Paola Bongini, Stefano
   Chiarlone, Giovanni Ferri.
      p. cm. — (Palgrave Macmillan studies in banking and financial
   institutions)
   Includes bibliographical references and index.
   ISBN 978–0–230–57434–2 (alk. paper)
   1. Banks and banking—Developing countries.   2. Finance—Developing
   countries.   I. Bongini, Paola.   II. Chiarlone, Stefano, 1970–
   III. Ferri, Giovanni, 1957–
HG3550.E44 2008
332.109172′4—dc22   2008029957

10   9   8   7   6   5   4   3   2   1
18   17   16   15   14   13   12   11   10   09

Printed and bound in Great Britain by
CPI Antony Rowe, Chippenham and Eastbourne

Contents

List of Tables

List of Figures

Foreword

The emerging countries on which this book focuses are not typical emerging countries. As far as their population is concerned they are all large, ranging from the huge (India and China) to the very large (Brazil and Russia) to the just large (Turkey). Their GNPs are also much bigger than those of the average emerging country. Only when GNP per head is considered do they fall back into the picture of typical developing countries – Turkey and Russia slightly looking down on the rest of the group.

Their banking systems, however, are much more like those of average emerging countries. They have developed from initial conditions that in some cases may appear very idiosyncratic. This is, however, superficial: if one looks more closely at each individual case study contained in this book, one soon realises that similar patterns emerge among all of them. One could say that starting from a socialist banking experience, as was the case of Russia and China, is very different from the experience of the others, of other emerging countries, of developed countries. But, is it really so? We could say that in the recent experience of the US and UK, for instance, to quote two countries that superficially looked as if they had purely private banking systems run for profit, substantial state involvement was present even before the current financial crisis, where it came back into fashion with avengeance: suffice it to quote the mortgage sector in the US since the second world war and the remarkable Bank of England involvement in industrial banking in the 1920s and 1930s (a little-known subject, which is currently receiving some attention on the part of economic historians). We do not have to remind readers of course of F. D. Roosevelt's Reconstruction Finance Corporation or of the much more recent Resolution Trust Corporation, which was given the task of solving the Savings and Loans Crisis in the 1980s.

Looking at a more distant past, is there much difference between the size and role of famous banks of issue like the Banque de France and the Bank of England in their respective credit markets at the start of the nineteenth century and that of monobanks like the Russian Central Bank or the People's Bank in China? As far as long-term 'special banks' are concerned, developed countries' banking history is even more similar to that of the countries analysed in this book. *A fortiori*, this book's case studies overlap even more with one another.

There is, however, enough idiosyncrasy left in the individual cases studied by the authors to make reading their chapters a very worthwhile and intellectually challenging pursuit. Let us take Russia and China to begin with. The fragmentation process that occurred in both countries' banking systems after the demise of the monobank created very different results, as far as the banking systems' liabilities are concerned. In China individuals and families, not having experienced runaway inflation for several decades, keep their hard-earned savings almost exclusively with banks. There is a lot of cash under mattresses, but no more than is common in other countries at China's stage of development, and especially personal income level. Wise behaviour on the part of the governing class has spared economic turmoil and hardship. Prices have increased at quite a moderate pace, if we consider the speed at which the country has grown. The exchange rate's relative stability since 1995 is, of course, an important part of the explanation. The demise of the welfare state, which has occurred at the same time, has emphasised the need for private savings, and fast growth under stable conditions has given many people in China the chance of accumulating savings in the form of bank deposits.

Not a very sophisticated portfolio allocation, we might say. Let us, however, keep in mind what Italians and Germans used to do until only too recently: they spread their eggs in very few baskets, owner-occupied houses, bank deposits, post-office savings accounts and treasury bonds. Direct share ownership, for instance, was not very popular in these two countries with anyone except the affluent, at least until recently. Nor did Germans and Italians (nor, for that matter, the Japanese), have much money invested in pension and investment funds. Marvelling at Chinese portfolio selection is therefore inappropriate.

The Russian case is altogether different. Runaway inflation, the destruction of manufacturing industry, giant financial swindles and extreme rent-seeking behaviour on the part of a few individuals who are now among the world's richest men and women, followed the demise of the Soviet Union. Banks, for a number of years, rightly became, in the minds of ordinary citizens, places where financial swindles are hatched rather than bona fide keepers of people's savings.

After a modicum of economic stability and a long worldwide raw materials boom, the Russian banking system now looks like a more primitive version of that of Germany, Italy and the US in the two decades before and after the First World War. Banks are the financial arms of industrial empires, which make their profits mainly by the mining and transformation of raw materials. They are not interested in ordinary citizens' savings. They provide financial resources to the industrial companies of their groups, and get the latter's shares as guarantee. Russian banks are also very active in the international financial markets, where in normal times they lend short and borrow long to fund their industrial offshoots. In troubled times, they tend to become massive net short-term borrowers.

Given these stark differences in the two countries' recent economic history one must agree with the authors here when they realistically suggest greater financial sophistication to the Chinese, while their advice to the Russians is much more subdued and circumspect. The fact is that, after two decades of transition, China has an economy that has become the workshop of the world and a financial system only burdened by the lingering debt of state-owned industries, a problem that the central government is determined to get rid of with the smallest political risk, i.e. at a snail's pace. Thus, in financial matters, the Chinese leadership seems to abhor the 'cold turkey' approach, which they are periodically invited to adopt. Understandably, we may say, as Russia tries painfully to emerge from massive doses of that approach their leaders meted out in the 1990s with tragic results.

Russia seems to have much the more fragile economic and financial system even today, when its leaders proudly exhibit their massive foreign exchange reserves. They do not seem to have been able to fend off another danger, the raw material producers' curse, also called 'Dutch disease'. Their economy managed to be exempt from that only for a few years after the massive devaluation of the rouble, in 1998. Through the 'high rouble' they have managed a very peculiar sort of 'trickle down' by which even ordinary citizens can afford sophisticated consumer products and foreign holidays. It is however rather odd that a very large country like Russia now imports most of its automotive products (it is the largest importer of cars in Europe) and household appliances, relying on extremely volatile raw material exports and short-term capital imports to finance even its domestic payments system.

The other banking systems studied in this book belong to more traditional developing countries, although, as I have said before, they are huge, very large, or just large. Two of them are former colonies, one was always independent. Nonetheless, the growth of their banking systems seems to have gone through similar stages, with huge publicly owned special banks dedicated to long-term finance and, in some cases, even publicly owned commercial banks, dedicated to gathering private deposits and lending out short-term commercial lending.

All three countries have seen, much more than China has, the growth of private banks, some of them extremely successful in developing lines of business that imitate best practice in developed countries. All three now permit a measure of involvement by foreign banks in their domestic markets, as does China, which, however, is even more careful than the others in allowing only a minority foreign shareholding in its largest banks. The other three do allow free-standing foreign banks to operate in their domestic markets, but try to keep their operations under close scrutiny. Most of all they seem keen to avoid big name, strong foreign banks monopolising the deposits of the local monied classes. Under the circumstances in which these countries still find themselves, this approach appears reasonable: Italians, for instance, know that allowing foreign banks into the domestic retail market has meant that often not the best foreign banking practices have been exported to Italy. More often foreign banks have practised deposit skimming and resorted to 'what the market will bear' pricing, maximising profits because of lower operational and funding costs rather than aggressively trying to increase market shares by price or service competition.

If we look at all the cases analysed by the authors in this book, only in one of them, Russia, have soft budget constraints and financial repression typical of socialist banking been completely destroyed. What has replaced them is admittedly very different but not particularly positive for the Russian economy or for the Russian saver. Soft budget constraints and extensive financial repression are a prominent part of the other countries' recent past, too. The latters' governing elites, however, have decided to choose a path to financial liberalisation which, prudent and moderate as it is, reminds us much more of what has happened and is still happening in Europe.

MARCELLO DE CECCO

Acknowledgements

The editors are grateful to the authors of the chapters for the effort and the passion they put in to this project. Moreover, they are heavily obliged to many friends and colleagues for ideas, support and advice received while thinking about and editing this volume. It is impossible to cite all of them but we cannot refrain from a few special mentions. First of all, we wish to thank Donato Masciandaro: the idea of this book was born thanks to a seminar on the Chinese banking system that he organised at Bocconi University. We are also indebted to Nicola Forti and Bancaria Editrice, who published the original Italian edition of this book and allowed us to go for this expanded English edition. A special thanks goes to UniCredit Group, and in particular to Francesco Giordano, Elena Belli and the Research and Strategy team. Obviously any errors or omissions are not their responsibility.

Alessia, Antonella, Luca and our children did not complain too much for the nights and weekends dedicated to the book instead of to them.

Notes on Contributors

P. Bongini is Associate Professor of Banking and Finance at the University of Milan-Bicocca, Faculty of Economics, where she teaches Portfolio Management and Market Microstructure. Her research interests and publications include financial systems' regulation, financial fragility, bank management and organisation.

A. Cicogna a senior officer with Banca d'Italia, is currently working in the International Economic Analysis and Relations Department. From 2001 to 2007, he was seconded to the Embassy of Italy in Cairo, Egypt, as Financial Attaché. In 2006–2007, he was also the Coordinator of a Eurosystem technical cooperation programme on banking supervision with the Central Bank of Egypt. He has written publications on Euro-Mediterranean economic relations and Mediterranean banking systems.

S. Chiarlone is a senior economist in the Research and Strategy Unit of UniCredit Group. He was previously an economist at the United Nations and he has previously been a researcher at Bocconi University and an Adjunct Professor of Economics at the Catholic University of Milan. His research focus ranges from international competitiveness to the economics of China and India and to financial globalisation.

A. Cimenoglu is the Head of Strategic Planning and Research at Yapi Kredi Bank, where he has been working since 1995. He holds a PhD in economics from Istanbul Technical University. He has been teaching on a part-time basis at various universities in Istanbul for 6 years, on banking sector and financial institutions, and fundamentals of economics. His main areas of research are mostly related to open economy macroeconomics, such as interaction between capital inflows, investments, savings and growth. He is also working on issues related to banking and financial institutions.

G. Ferri is Full Professor of Economics at the University of Bari, where he also chairs the Department of Economics. Previously, he worked at the World Bank and the Banca d'Italia. He was Visiting Fellow at Princeton University and the University of Tokyo. He holds a PhD in Economics from New York University and has published extensively on money and credit economics.

M. Ferrazzi is an economist at the Research Department of UniCredit Group, where he works on macroeconomic forecasts, foreign trade issues and corporate internationalisation, following Central and Eastern European countries. He was formerly a researcher in the Italian economic think tank Prometeia and lecturer for the Master's degree course in Corporate Internationalisation in Faenza; he also has experience as a professional journalist.

S. Ghosh is working at the middle management level in the Reserve Bank of India with job responsibilities in the areas of financial stability. He has published extensively in journals such as *Review of Financial Economics, Economic Notes, Managerial and Decision Economics, Emerging Market Review, Journal of Banking Regulation* and *International Journal of Auditing*.

M. Lossani is Full Professor of Economics at the Catholic University of Milan where he teaches International Economics. He holds an MA in International and Development Economics from Yale University (1988) and a PhD in Economics from the University of Milan. He was Visiting Fellow at the Economic Growth Centre at Yale University (1995) and Visiting Professor at Universitad Catolica Argentina in Buenos Aires (1999), Chulalongkorn University at Bangkok (2001) and National University at Hanoi (Vietnam).

A. Marra studied and worked both in Italy and abroad and joined Banca d'Italia in 1992. Till 2002 she was involved in banking regulation and supervision. From 2003 to February 2008 she was on secondment to the Italian Embassy in Moscow as Financial Attaché. At present she works in Rome and is responsible for the management and development of Banca d'Italia foreign network. She is author of several papers on the Russian banking system.

D. Revoltella is the CEE Chief economist for UniCredit Group. She is the coordinator of the New Europe Research Network, involving all the research departments in UniCredit banks in the region. She holds a MA in Economics from Bocconi University and a PhD in Economics from the University of Ancona.

L. Ruggerone is currently Head of Country Risk and Foreign Subsidiaries at the Risk Management Department of Banca Intesa San Paolo, which he joined in 2003, after serving as Head of Emerging Markets Economics at the Research Department of Banca Intesa. In addition to his role with Banca Intesa San Paolo, where he is responsible for risk policies and procedures at the Group level coordinating the ICAAP for all foreign subsidiaries, Luigi also teaches International Economics at Università Cattolica del S.C. He received his economics degree at Università Cattolica del S.C. of Milan and completed an MSc and an MPhil. in Economics at the University of Warwick; he is the author and co-author of various scientific works published in distinguished journals.

M. Zaninelli is Country Risk Analyst in the Risk Management Department of Intesa Sanpaolo SpA with previous experience in the Research Department of Unicredit SpA. and in the Authority for Electricity Energy and Gas (Italian regulator). He has BA in Economics from the Università Cattolica of Milan and MSc in Economics and Econometrics from the University of Southampton (UK).

Disclaimer: the views expressed in this volume are those of the authors and do not necessarily represent those of their institutions.

Introduction

P. Bongini, S. Chiarlone and G. Ferri

Over the last 25 years, breathtaking global economic integration has taken place as a result of reductions in transaction costs (transportation and ITC, mainly) and the removal of relevant obstacles to international trade and investment. Such a context has helped emerging economies integrate within the global economy: this integration involves both their real and financial sectors.

On the real economy side, such inclusion has been more pronounced in Asia and for transition economies. As world trade has been outpacing other forms of growth – global trade has grown at an average annual rate of 5.5 per cent between 1960 and 2006, e.g. 2.4 percentage point higher than world GDP – emerging economies have increased their exports-to-GDP ratio, which has risen from 20 per cent in 1984 to 35 per cent in 2004 (World Bank, Global Economic Prospects 2007, Managing the Next Wave of Globalization). An important role has been played by growing amounts of foreign direct investments (FDIs) in emerging countries, mainly connected to production offshoring by highly industrialised countries. FDI flows rose from US$20 billion in 1990 to more than US$200 billion by mid-2000. As a consequence, emerging economies have been included in global production networks and, in many cases, have been transformed in crucial crossroad of global manufacturing systems.

Reliable forecasts suggest that global growth will increasingly depend upon emerging markets. IMF estimates for 2008 and 2009 show that most of the world economic growth will depend on China's and India's buoyancy. Moreover, according to the World Bank (World Bank, 2006), over the next 25 years, emerging economies will represent 33 per cent of global GDP. Even if that does not immediately mean that emerging countries will become rich in 25 years' time, their per-capita GDP, adjusted for purchasing power, is estimated to rise from the current 16 per cent to 23 per cent with respect to the rich countries' average, while China is expected to reach 42 per cent. At the same time new middle and upper classes will emerge, increasing business opportunities for financial and corporate firms.

On the financial sector side, high saving rates and declining fertility rates should significantly boost emerging economies' total savings, thus amplifying the demand for an efficient intermediation and opening new market opportunities for banks and financial institutions in general. In particular, as a consequence of globalisation-related competitive pressures, foreign banks have become increasingly eager to extend their operations to emerging markets to exploit their product portfolios and competitive advantages. These new banking markets are likely to represent the profit pools of tomorrow. Moreover, their ballooning foreign reserves and the growing relevance of their sovereign wealth funds hint at an increasingly active role for emerging countries as financial players in the global arena.

This scenario suggests that world economy prospects increasingly depend on emerging economies. However, in spite of their success, emerging economies exhibit various fragilities. Their chief inefficiency lies in the financial system, especially banking, and such inefficiency has historically posed serious constraints to their growth. Moreover, given the increased global interdependence of financial markets and institutions, it has repeatedly led to centripetal financial crises, bursting in the emerging countries and draining investments from the periphery to the core of the world financial markets, with additional negative effects on their growth prospects.

For instance, after the mid-1990s several emerging markets were severely affected by financial crises. Asian markets were most severely hit: Indonesia, Thailand, Korea, Malaysia, and the Philippines experienced systemic crises curtailing their GDP and shaking their financial systems. Thereafter, crises hit Russia (1998), Brazil (1999) and later on Turkey and Argentina (2001). At the heart of these events lies the 'twin crises' mechanism, which links banking and exchange rate crises: the banking systems were part of the problem, because it sustained the credit boom before the crisis, either taking enormous exchange rate risk on its balance sheet or transferring it to firms. As a consequence, after the burst of the crisis the affected economies featured pervasive bank distress and closures and a widespread credit crunch negatively impinging on investment and output.

In the absence of a mechanism to manage systemic crises – e.g. even the mild Krueger proposal of 2001 was rapidly shelved – emerging economies unilaterally reduced their potential exposure to systemic crises via increased reliance on domestic capital markets for financing investment and by deeply restructuring their international position. Hence, they accumulated enormous amounts of foreign exchange reserves and switched from net borrowers to net lenders on international capital markets. However, such strategy has its own limits and drawbacks. First, the remedy might not be entirely effective, e.g. though the most recent sub-prime crisis, originates from the US, it may affect emerging economies as well, via reduced liquidity in the markets hitting banks' funding and slowing down credit growth or via reduced economic growth worldwide. Secondly, foregoing foreign capital inflows and accumulating excessive reserves is costing emerging economies (and the entire world) a lower growth.

By and large, most emerging markets have also embarked on banking restructuring after such crises. The crucial hotspot they faced was how to reduce the negative interferences either of state ownership (when government-owned banks were dominant players) or of influential vested interests (where banks were controlled by large private industrial/commercial conglomerates) in order to bestow financial institutions higher operational independence. Consolidation and privatisation are, indeed, fundamental pillars of banking reforms in emerging economies so far. In many cases, introducing international banking expertise and allowing foreign banks' entry – aimed at improving the loan supply process, at supporting banks' recapitalisation and at applying modern risk management techniques – was also crucial.

Since the end of the 1990s' consolidation in most emerging economies has led to a decrease in the number of national banks. Market-driven bank consolidation prevailed in Central and Eastern Europe as well as in Latin America, while governments piloted consolidation in Asia.

Privatisation was mainly motivated by the growing awareness that government ownership induced bank inefficiency and represented an obstacle to financial market development. The privatisation process is rather advanced in many emerging countries, even though governments often remain significant shareholders. It is worth noticing that, contrary to what prevails in most smaller-sized emerging economies, government control still prevails in China, India and Russia.

Pervasive entry revealed a growing interest in emerging economies motivated by foreign banks' drive to unfold their own comparative advantage (e.g. innovative products and services), as well as owing to foreign banks' strategic shift from servicing their multinational customers through cross-border operations to dealing with them via local subsidiaries. This switch helps make foreign banks' interests, e.g. locating in markets with high growth potential – converge with emerging economies' interests – attracting efficient foreign players. In such a scenario, foreign banks may contribute to modernising emerging banking systems in a context of reciprocal advantages. Their presence is by far the largest in Central and Eastern Europe and in Latin America. On the contrary, their penetration was much less intense in Asia, possibly because high national savings (e.g. in China) and government bail outs reduced the need for bank recapitalisation with private funding. Nevertheless, we have noticed a recent rapid intensification of (minority) foreign bank presence in China and (yet controversial) signals of openness to foreign investors in India.

Such a reform path was directed to achieve more resilient banking systems and a better credit allocation, both conducive to healthier growth prospects (banks should play a key role in reducing the risk of excess lending to overheating sectors and in granting credit to projects showing better risk/return ratios) and to easier access to international financial markets. Moreover, the restructuring of the banking system plays a crucial role in the development of the domestic financial markets for mainly two reasons: banks are key bond issuers and they may promote their customers' tapping financial markets.

Today, the key issue is whether such reforms path have been successful in making emerging countries more resilient to potential new crises. In fact, ten years after the Asian crisis, the world economy has been shaken by a deep financial crisis started in the US sub-prime mortgage lending market, whose extent cannot as yet be fully quantified but whose ramifications for the global economy are considerable.

Some of the features of the US sub-prime event are not so distant from the twin-crisis setting that hit many major emerging economies ten years ago. First, the event is marked by a deep banking crisis, where excessive bank lending had generated soft budget constraints, especially in the real estate sector. As a consequence, the US is experiencing a credit crunch and its economy is undergoing substantive deleveraging, even though more on the part of households rather than the company sector, at the time of writing. Secondly, the value of the US dollar plummeted against most currencies, particularly *vis-à-vis* the euro. However, there is a major difference as well. Namely, even though overlending in the US was fuelled by capital inflows, it was dollar-denominated. Thus, the depreciation of the US dollar is not hurting borrowers directly, as domestic currencies' devaluation invariably did during emerging economies' financial crises for domestic borrowers indebted in foreign hard currency. The other side of the coin is that the weakening of the dollar and the problems experienced by major US banks may be somewhat denting both the role of the dollar as a reserve currency and the dominance of Wall Street within the world financial market. For instance the increasing role of Sovereign Wealth Funds resident in emerging markets as 'recapitalis-ers of last resort' hints at a eastward rotation of the centre of gravity of the world financial market that has geopolitical consequences yet to be understood.

Notwithstanding the fact that the repetition of a grave systemic crisis exactly ten years after the Asian crises can lead to thinking of a kind of Juglar Cycle, the lesson we should perhaps learn is that systemic crises are the inevitable thorns that grow on the rose of financial liberalisation. Financial liberalisation is a beautiful flower with a heady perfume, but if you handle it without gloves there are times when you'll get pricked. Nonetheless, in order to understand lessons for emerging banking systems, it seems worth to further analyse whether there is anything in common between the current crisis and the 1997–98 Asian crisis.

Among the differences it is important to underline that the current crisis is spreading outwards from the centre and not originating in the periphery. In addition, unlike the sub-prime mortgage crisis, the one in Asia involved few financial innovations. But there are also two remarkable similarities. In the first place, in both the Asian and the sub-prime mortgage crises, credit was granted to subjects who should not have received it (at least not to such an extent): the *NINJA loans – no verification of Income, Job status or Assets* – instrumental in the sub-prime crisis mirror the excessive reckless lending of the major credit institutions from the industrialised countries when they extended credit to the Asian tigers on the eve of the 1997–98 crash. Secondly, just as the explosion of the Asian crisis shrivelled the emerging markets, today the crisis has dried up many segments of the global financial markets, including the interbank market.

Hence, the main common way out of the crisis refers to risk re-pricing in the concerned sectors. Today, what can be seen as a problem of lack of liquidity really comes down to the extreme difficulty of assessing counterparty exposure. We saw it in the summer of 2007 and during the first semester of 2008, with the huge cash injections by the Fed, the European Central Bank and the Bank of England, which nonetheless failed to produce as great a reduction in inter-bank lending rates as they would have done under normal circumstances. That is because, in the flurry of the crisis, each individual creditor bank is unable to establish with any real certainty the debtor counterpart's exposure to sub-prime losses. So, banks preferred to hold on to liquidity, either as cash or as government securities, which are now 'worth their weight in gold', exactly as it happened in 1998, when the escalation of the flight to quality into government securities was one of the principal causes of the LTCM débâcle. In the

United States on October 2007, under pressure from the Treasury, a super-fund of US$75 billion has been devised – Master Liquidity Enhancement Conduit (MLEC) – to help big banks restore liquidity to those structured investment vehicles (SIVs) that, because of the crisis, cannot manage to issue commercial papers to raise short-term funds while they wait to place asset-backed securities. A significantly titled article ('*The End of Sivilisation*' – a play on words between the 'end of civilisation' and 'the end of the SIV') warns that MLEC may not be enough to deal with unfinished asset-backing operations amounting to around US$400 billion. Moreover, also in the UK, the Central Bank has moved to accept structured products as collateral in order to ease banks' difficulties, while helping them to recapitalise. In such a context, we still cannot exclude that a second leg of the crisis could infect the most fragile emerging markets in the near future.

Emerging banks' direct exposure to domestic structured products was low at the onset of the crisis. Asset backed securities (ABS) issues amounted to around US$29.3 billion in 2006 for emerging markets (as compared to a global value of US$1.3 trillion), and mortgage backed securities (MBS) issues were US$7.3 billion (compared to a global value of US$1.1 trillion). Less sophisticated products (and an 'originate and hold' banking model) should spare emerging markets from domestic problems related to such assets. Anyway, ABSs, and especially MBSs, are on the rise: the annual averages were, US$20 billion and US$0.9 billion respectively, in 1998–2003. Further, we cannot exclude contagion through exposure to structured products issued by global banks. In general, the risk is limited, as buoyant domestic economies pushed banks into aggressive domestic lending, preventing them from looking for attractive investment overseas, but this possibility cannot be ruled out completely.

As for traditional lending, the pace of domestic credit growth has been extremely high in many emerging markets. Liquidity has remained available in many emerging markets; however, the potential consequences of the liquidity hoarding triggered by advanced markets' peers may eventually hit various emerging banks as well. Therefore some credit slowdown may be on the cards. Moreover, such an aggressive lending profile could be conducive to a rise in non-performing loans (NPLs), if corporate profits are to slow down. On the positive side, the above-mentioned restructuring efforts strengthened emerging banking systems before the current crisis (better capitalised and provisioned and with lower NPLs). Nonetheless, stringent monitoring is extremely important to ensure that vulnerabilities do not become systemic problems.

Hence, a full understanding of contemporary issues facing banking systems in emerging economies is particularly needed. This book's in-depth analysis provides insight into the main features and specificities of various emerging banking systems, ranging from the post-Asian crisis restructuring to the apparent resiliency to the current sub-prime crisis.

The banking systems covered include major emerging economies for each global regional area. Our sample of banking systems comprises: China, India and Indonesia for Emerging Asia; Brazil for Latina America; Turkey for Emerging Europe, the countries on the Southern brink of the Mediterranean Sea for Africa, and Russia for the Commonwealth of Independent States (CIS). Thus, we cover the BRICs plus Indonesia – the third largest country in Asia – Turkey, the largest emerging country neighbouring the European Union, and the largest Southern Mediterranean countries. The volume is organised as follows.

The first chapter highlights the main development paths and relevant issues pertaining to the restructuring of emerging banking systems. It starts by focusing on the key characteristics of the financial crises of the 1990s, highlighting the triggering role played by financial market imperfections. It subsequently shows that the heavy tolls imposed by such financial crises – and the lack of a global response for strengthening the international financial architecture – have pushed emerging markets towards a strategy of external de-leveraging as a safeguard measure. Such a strategy, argues the chapter, has considerable implications, related to: (i) the rationale and sustainability of a flows-of-funds scenario where money travels from emerging to advanced markets; and (ii) the fact that such lower international leveraging puts the onus of investment support on the domestic financial system of emerging markets. The chapter moves on to study the recent evolution of the financial systems of emerging markets. It shows that the banking system still plays, with very limited exceptions, a central role in their domestic financial markets. Then, it discusses the most recent three-pillar strategies followed by emerging countries to reform their banks, based on privatisation consolidation and increased access of foreign banks. Finally, given their increasing role, the chapter discusses in depth the role that foreign banks can play in the restructuring of the banking system.

Each of Chapters 2 to 8 examines the national emerging banking system in the countries above. The volume adopts a research template that guarantees consistency of the sample countries' analyses as regards basic information on both the real and financial economy, such as: (a) characteristics of the country's real economy and its recent evolution; (b) structure and recent development of the banking system; (c) recent regulatory and supervisory reforms, following transition and/or crisis; (d) bank consolidation trends; (e) main aspects of fragility; and (f) role of state-owned banks and foreign-owned banks and their importance in the intermediation process. All the above-mentioned topics are investigated in depth according to the specificities of each domestic banking system.

Besides providing a wide geographical span, the emerging economies considered in this book represent different models of integration. China and India are by far the largest countries and have a strong unresolved legacy of state intervention in the banking sector. China and India were quite untouched by the twin crises of the mid 1990s–early 2000s; however the public-sector involvement in the banking sector has heavily hit the efficiency of their banks. Both countries have eventually embarked in efficiency-spurring reforms and there is evidence of improvements of their banking systems, which seems supportive of resilience to the crisis. Notwithstanding reforms and huge interest by most major global banks, these markets are still quite closed to foreign penetration, posing a delay in the modernisation of their banking systems. Brazil, Indonesia, Russia and Turkey were heavily hit by the crises of the mid-1990s–early 2000s. They have reacted in very different ways to the crises and have achieved rather different success in attracting foreign investors. Hence, the analysis of their reform paths is instructive of alternative approaches to banks' restructuring, featuring different degrees of intervention of the public sector and of foreign players. North Africa's banking systems, finally, are clearly laggards in terms of development and size, while representing extremely promising markets for foreign banks in terms of growth potential and limited number of competitive domestic financial institution. It is, hence, quite interesting to look at their reform path to check whether they are conforming to the best practices developed elsewhere and how are they opening to foreign players. The limited progress made so far in bringing the region's institutional frameworks in line with conditions supportive of financial sector stability and sustainable growth may explain why the topic of financial liberalisation was not included in the agenda of recent Euro-Mediterranean Association Agreements (Euro-Med agreements).

This book was completed on the basis of information available up to May 2008.

As the volume goes to press the US sub-prime crisis has mushroomed into a global systemic crisis. European banks have suffered serious contagion. Also some emerging economies along with their banking systems have faced tensions. It is too soon to tell whether the contagion will sweep away the progress achieved in the past decade by emerging banking systems. What we can definitely assert is that the situation would have been much worse had that progress not been achieved.

1
Emerging Banking Systems

P. Bongini, S. Chiarlone and G. Ferri

Introduction

As the process of global economic integration moves irreversibly ahead, the increasing role of emerging countries is often undervalued and/or put at risk by the weakness of their banking systems. In parallel to inefficiencies arising from the misallocation of resources, the weaknesses in the national banking systems of emerging countries have contributed to the increasingly frequent systemic crises that occurred from the mid 1990s until only a few years ago.[1]

In fact, at the heart of these systemic crises lies the mechanism of the well-known 'twin crises', that is crises linked by the insidious tangled web formed by the exchange rate and the banking system. The first to study the phenomenon were Kaminsky and Reinhart (1999), who found that problems in the banking sector usually precede an exchange rate crisis. That exacerbates the banking crisis, triggering a vicious circle. Increased financial freedom also often precedes a banking crisis. The anatomy of twin crises suggests that they occur when the economy goes into recession following a prolonged economic boom nourished by credit, inflows of capital and over-valued exchange rates.

As banks are at the heart of emerging countries' financial systems, their inefficiency represents not only a direct brake to growth – via suboptimal allocation of credit – but also exerts an indirect negative effect, by increasing the likelihood of systemic crises, with their negative fallout. Therefore, the strengthening of emerging countries' banking systems is a key condition for the proper working of the global economy. It has to be said that in recent years something has already been done. As we will see in this book, there has been some bolstering of emerging banking systems thanks to a combination of regulatory reforms and banking supervision, privatisation, consolidation and entry of foreign players. The partial strengthening of these countries' banking systems has helped to create the conditions for the parallel growth of their financial markets. This evolution has improved the allocation of resources and has helped, at least in part, to reduce currency-risk exposure and the risk of systemic crises that this brings. However, much still has to be done to guarantee a better banking system for emerging economies, which is a necessary condition for sustainable global economic growth.

This chapter will address in more detail some of these issues. In the case of a crisis, we will examine how it was managed; where a systemic crisis did not ensue, we will analyse the measures adopted to improve the structure of the national banking system. We end this chapter with a look at the future prospects for banking in emerging countries and the possible role of foreign banks.

Systemic financial crises of the 1990s

As is implicit from the comments made above, certain distinctions have to be made when analysing the banking systems of emerging countries. We have already mentioned the principal one: it is important to distinguish between systemic financial crises, on one hand, and other crises or problems affecting domestic banking systems, on the other.

Another important distinction is between the problems typically associated with countries moving from planned to market economies, predominantly ex-Communist countries, and the problems of emerging countries whose economies were already market-based.

Two further distinctions should be borne in mind between: (i) countries where there is a strong presence of the state in the banking system; (ii) countries where there are strong ownership links between private industrial groups, often family owned, and private banks.

Finally, it is important to realise that the problems and criticalities of a domestic banking system will differ according to the level of development and maturity of the national financial market.

Distinctive features are often intertwined. For example, the share of state ownership in banks is usually higher in transition economies and other emerging economies where development has been principally in the form of government-sponsored industrial policies, e.g. Asia in general. Also, the presence of cross-ownerships amongst private industrial groups is often a primary cause of allocative distortions within economies with limited domestic competition and/or relative closure to foreign trade, a scenario typically accompanied by comparative immaturity of financial markets (Rajan and Zingales, 2003). What is more, the combination of these allocative distortions with the limited development of financial markets heightens the risk of boom–bust cycles triggered by volatility in international capital flows. A common feature of these conditions is to create fragilities, which, if not directly responsible for financial crises, certainly contribute to making them, once started, worse.

The increased globalisation of financial flows has brought about fundamental changes. In addition to the positive effects relating to the support that international capital provided to emerging markets' growth, some problem areas exist. Probably the most worrying is the occurrence of systemic financial crises in the form of a sudden retreat of international capital. The reduction in these resources, which had contributed so much during the prior phase of intense development, sets off or at least worsens the burgeoning macroeconomic crisis. In all such cases a loss of trust occurs in the prospects and/or solvency of the national economy in crisis, which inevitably leads to a stampede on the part of international investors.

An initial negative event – for example, an unexpected slowdown in growth, the emergence of heavy imbalances in foreign accounts accompanied by losses in competitiveness, or a large national financial institution finding itself in trouble – acts as the detonator of an explosive charge that has built up gradually in the meantime. Thus, many emerging markets found themselves falling from heaven down to hell: only a little earlier, international investors had thought it a 'must' to hold assets there, when a little later, the risks were considered so high that it was thought better to give the country a wide berth. During the Asian crisis, one of the editors of this book worked for the World Bank, and he witnessed the – apparently irreversible – lack of confidence shown by major Wall Street investment institutions in the economies in crisis when, in early September 1998, with the Asian crisis already raging and unresolved for over a year, another formidable broadside was felt, in the form of the Russian default and the prospect of a crisis in Brazil. Well, there they were, these investors who for many years had competed frantically to send the world's savings to the Asian tigers and who, in fact, until only a little earlier had paid scant heed to frequent warnings. Now they came begging on their knees to ask the international financial institutions, which they had previously considered totally irrelevant, to do something to restore confidence in the international markets, lest they implode. And, in fact, what, if not a structural breakdown of such massive proportions, would have brought a mythical beast like Long Term Capital Management (LTCM), the hedge fund created with the involvement and finely-honed economic and financial talents of two Nobel prize-winners, to (technical) bankruptcy? For the first time since the Great Crisis in the 1930s, the market makers went crawling to the Institutions.

So what could have happened? What had happened was that the markets had lost their bearings between 1997 and 1998 and, with benefit of hindsight, the international institutions had inadvertently helped to aggravate the problems, by applying deflationary remedies to a generalised debt crisis. Thus, the original crisis in Thailand spread like a contagion to Korea and Indonesia and, in somewhat smaller measure, to Malaysia and the Philippines; the effects were felt as far away as Hong Kong, Singapore and Taiwan, and – slightly – in Japan and even China, then still protected by controls totally blocking any movement of financial capital. Almost all the normal statistics previously observed in relation to the price of assets in emerging nations were shot to pieces in the stampede that took place. The system had ended up in a 'fat tail', the situation outfoxed the Merton and Scholes formulae and only Greenspan's liquidity injection saved LTCM and damped down the fire, which was extinguished some time later.[2]

Everything had started a few years earlier with the crisis in Mexico. Driven by the prospects of the NAFTA agreement – the free trade pact between Canada, Mexico and the United States – since the very beginning of the 1990s there had been an amazing increase in the capital inflowing into Mexico. The squeaks issuing from a twin (public and foreign) debt problem had led the foreign investors to turn on their heels and bring the capital they had earlier proffered in abundance back home. The Mexican crisis was the first systemic crisis in the globalised financial system and it was very different from the debt crises experienced in some Latin American countries in the early 1980s. In fact, in the early eighties, finance to those countries was coming through the reliance on loans from the banking syndicates, whereas in the case of Mexico, it was private capital that led the way.

The Mexican crisis drove even more money to Asia, then reaping the benefit of the idea of the *East Asian Miracle*: the title of a World Bank publication. But then, only shortly afterward, the Asian crisis blew up and what happened to Asia was the greatest systemic international financial crisis since the Great Depression of the 1930s. In the five countries hardest hit by the crisis growth of the ten preceding years had been close to 10 per cent per annum in real terms, with extremely high investment rates – over 30 per cent in relation to GDP – and their public accounts were in order, with State deficits below 2 per cent of GDP and quite moderate inflation rates of around 5 per cent. In 1998, the systemic crisis that had gradually worsened since mid-1997 caused GDP to drop by around 15 per cent in Indonesia, 10 per cent in Thailand, 7 per cent in Korea and Malaysia and 1 per cent in the Philippines. The economists racked their brains as to the reasons for this crisis, which could be explained neither by the theories relating to first generation financial crises, based on excess public sector spending (Krugman, 1979), nor by those about second generation crises, which state that a speculative attack can occur if a country loses its incentives to defend the preset exchange rate (Obstfeld, 1996). Alternative explanations were sought and two directly opposing schools of thought emerged. One put forward an interpretation based entirely on the existence of poor fundamentals (e.g. Krugman, 1998; Goldstein, 1998), the other stressed the part played by contagion and market irrationality (e.g. Furman and Stiglitz, 1998; Radelet and Sachs, 1998 Stiglitz, 1999). Then there's a middle view that leaves room for poor fundamentals as well as contagion and relates, in a way, to the famous 'twin crises' theory (e.g. Corsetti *et al.*, 1999). Furthermore, there is the position that assumes the possibility of contagion amongst countries (Masson, 1999) as an explanation for why the crisis spread so quickly from one country to another.

The crisis in Asia, which in Spring 1998 seemed about to be resolved, took another turn for the worse in subsequent months as tensions over Russia and Brazil increased. The strain reached a breaking point in August 1998 when Russia went into default. Brazil was still hanging on, but its crisis came about nonetheless, in 1999. The string of financial crises came to a halt in 2001, the year of reckoning for Argentina and Turkey.

Both countries had been only a few months previously regarded as the best examples by international financial institutions, described by Eichengreen (2001) as 'the poster boys of the Washington consensus'. After long periods of economic and monetary turbulence, both had been able to implement disinflationary measures and had been able to enjoy, over a certain period of time, accelerated growth. In retrospect, weaknesses appeared, that institutional investors during the honeymoon period had tended to pay little attention to. First, both in Argentina and in Turkey fiscal reforms were incomplete. Secondly, the disinflationary currency peg negatively hit international competitiveness with any change likely to seriously damage governments' credibility as well as the stability of the domestic banking systems, entangled with vast foreign currency mismatch. Finally, the funding of current accounts' imbalances was assured by substantial inflows of capital which, when foreign investor confidence began to drain, took the form of increasingly shorter term credits, thereby raising the risk of non-renewal. As a result,

Argentina and Turkey were particularly exposed to a worsening of international conditions. With the Asian crisis and Russia's default, investors' interest spreads widened. Further shocks took place: Argentina's competitiveness abroad was seriously affected by Brazil's devaluation at the start of 1999 and a strengthening of the US dollar, whilst in Turkey, the country was struck by a catastrophic earthquake; the prospects for both countries' export capacities were adversely affected by rising oil prices and weaker global economic growth. Against this backdrop, simply the hint of a government's flagging enthusiasm for fiscal reform was enough to push both countries' economies over the edge. In this way, Turkey paid the price of friction between the head of the government and the head of state over the way to face the question of corruption in the public sector, whilst Argentina suffered from a loss of consensus over tax cuts proposed by the government. Rising levels of future risk pushed up interest rates which in turn weakened growth and raised doubts as to the sustainability of both countries' debt. The IMF intervened immediately in the case of Turkey and a few months' later in support of Argentina, offering new loan facilities. However, the writing was on the wall and the systemic crisis was underway with particularly disastrous results for Argentina, which defaulted on a large part of its foreign liabilities.

Ten years on, the Asian crisis may appear to be only an unhappy memory but its costs were enormous. It's true that all the affected economies, sooner or later, began to grow again at high speed but the crisis struck deeply at the confidence rooted in the Asian tigers as they pursued what had seemed an unstoppable course. Despite the fact that attention concentrated more on its effects on capital flows, one of the most representative examples of the far-reaching consequences of the Asian crisis has been the impact on migration in the region.[3] In fact, systemic financial crises are dangerous and costly as they tend to turn into social and sometimes political crises involving the population at large.

Common characteristics of recent financial crises

There is firm evidence that at the heart of recent financial crises lies the mechanism of exchange-rate and banking crises ('twin crises') described by Kaminsky and Reinhart (1999). Consequently, the banking system of all emerging countries facing a crisis is part of the problem. Banks contribute to the pre-crisis boom, taking on their books exchange-rate risk – building up debts in US dollars and lending in overvalued domestic

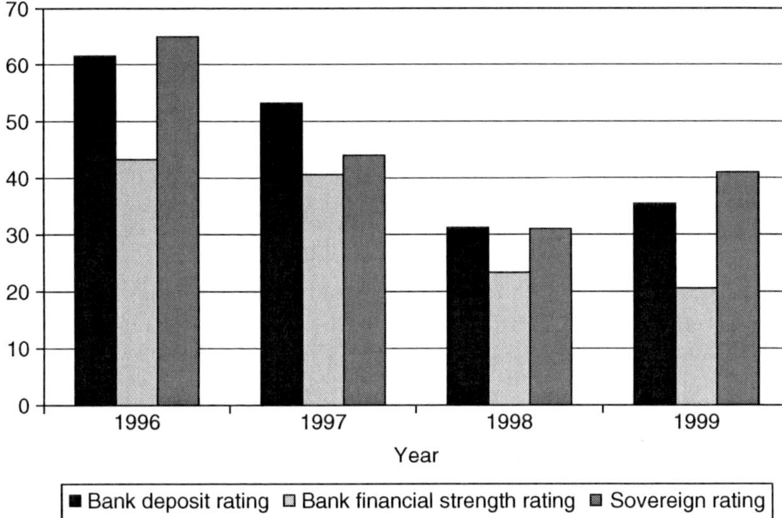

Source: authors' calculations based on Moody's ratings.

Figure 1.1   Sovereign and bank ratings during the Asian crisis

currencies – or transferring such risk onto firms – lending in dollars, but then having to write off the bad loans of the countless number of firms that went bankrupt when the crisis pushed up the exchange rate and made it impossible for them to pay back their debts.

It is no coincidence that a crisis leads to a downgrading in the banking system's rating which is generally sharper than that applied to a country's sovereign rating. This is apparent in the case of the Asian crisis, but similar results can be seen in other situations. Figure 1.1 illustrates the average value for the five countries involved – Korea, the Philippines, Indonesia, Malaysia and Thailand – of the three rating types at year end 1996 (before the crisis) and at year end 1999. The first, bank deposit rating, approximates the probability of default by banks taking into account potential bail outs by the authorities; the second, bank financial strength rating, approximates the probability of default by banks without considering any external institutional aid, whilst the third, sovereign rating, approximates the probability of default by a government.[4] During a crisis, all three ratings drop considerably.

Of more interest here is that, on examining both the pre-crisis (1996) and post-crisis (1999) situations, the reduction in the rating is relatively greater for banks than for the sovereign. This is clearly shown

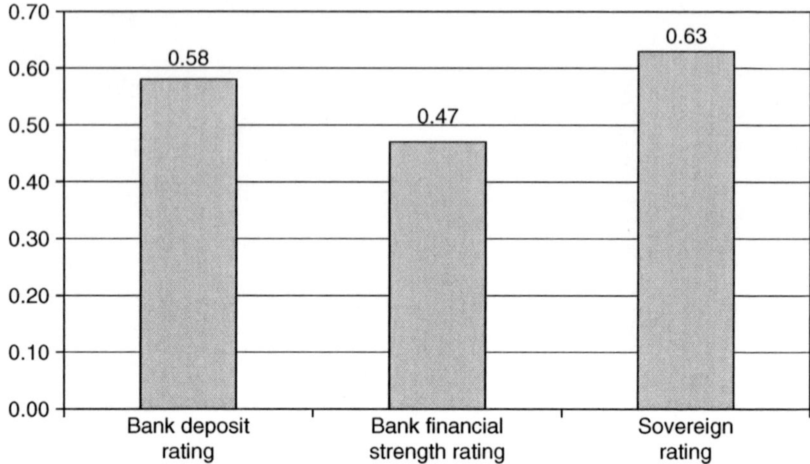

Source: authors' calculations based on Moody's ratings.

Figure 1.2   The Asian crisis: ratio between rating values at year end 1999 and 1996

in Figure 1.2: at the end of 1999, the average sovereign rating for the five countries was 63 per cent of that recorded at the end of 1996, whilst the drop in bank ratings is higher. In particular, the ratio between rating values at year end 1999 and 1996 is much lower for bank financial strength rating (47 per cent) than bank deposit rating (58 per cent).

The implications of the systemic crisis for the banking system are clear also from an analysis of bank collapses. In the Asian crisis, Bongini *et al.* (2001) show that between the end of 1996 and July 1999, the share of distressed (closed) banks reached respectively 65.6 per cent (23.7 per cent) in Thailand, 53.5 per cent (17.2 per cent) in Korea, 50.6 per cent (19.5 per cent) in Indonesia, 24.2 per cent (0.0 per cent) in Malaysia and 11.1 per cent (5.6 per cent) in the Philippines (Figure 1.3).

In turn, the worsening banks' health during a systemic crisis can have negative effects on the economy with an ensuing credit crunch.[5] A generalised tightening in the supply of credit was found during the Asian crisis on the basis of a variety of indicators (Domaç *et al.*, 1999): (i) increase in the real interest rate; (ii) increase in the spread between lending rates and risk free rates; (iii) fall in the real growth rate of lending; (iv) depositors' flight to quality in favour of those banks perceived as more solid, both domestic and foreign; (v) banks' flight to quality, for instance from lending to government stock; (vi) disproportionate

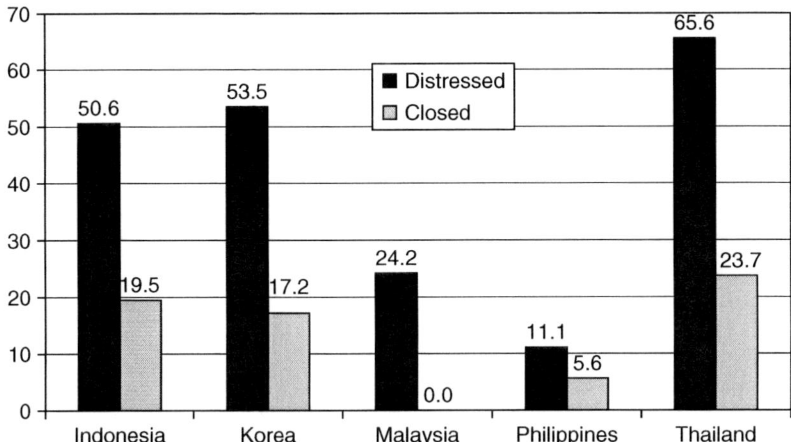

Source: Bongini *et al.*, (2001).
Figure 1.3   Bank failures and closures: December 1996–July 1999 (%)

contraction in lending to SMEs; (vii) increase in the rate of rejections of loan applications; (viii) shortening of lending maturities; (ix) contraction in 'pre-committed' credit lines, the first lending forms to feel the effect of a change in banks' credit policies.

A credit crunch can have extremely damaging effects on the economy hit by a crisis and cripple its potential for recovery. In particular, the crunch affects also 'good' firms, either by making them go bust or severely limiting their productive capacity. On this point, Bongini *et al.* (2000) illustrate how, in Korea, the crisis led to the failure not only of the worst firms, but also of some of the best (inefficient failures) which had grown considerably in the pre-crisis period, though accumulating large debts. What is more, SMEs are the most damaged segment as their only funding source, in addition to internally generated resources, is loans from banks. Staying in Korea, not surprisingly as Domaç and Ferri (1999) show, the fall in productive levels was far greater for SMEs.

Naturally, emerging countries' authorities became increasingly aware of the fragility of their national banking systems and consequently took various steps to improve efficiency and stability levels.

Recovery strategies followed by emerging countries

The next stage following a systemic crisis is characterised by an economic recovery held back by debt overhang – excessive levels of private sector

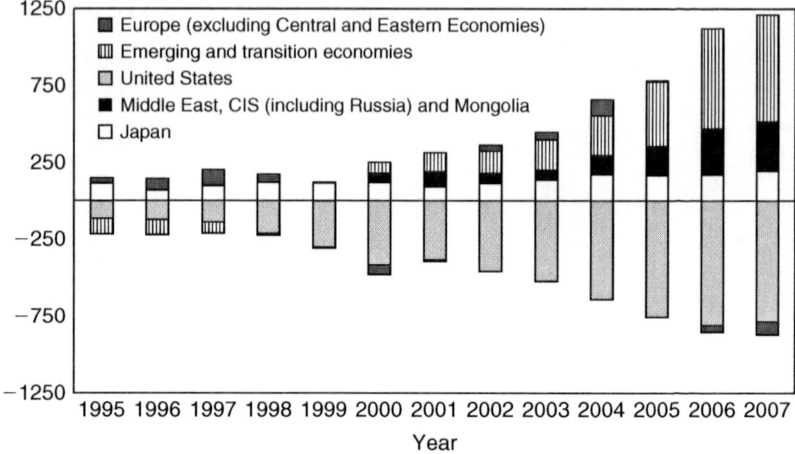

Source: World Economic Outlook, October 2007 Database.

Figure 1.4   Current account balances (US$bn)

debt – and widespread bank failures, which led to deep bank restructuring programmes, including consolidation and foreign banks' entry. Before analysing these features in detail, it is useful to review the recovery measures adopted by emerging economies to prevent further crises.

Prior to 2000, emerging economies were net capital importers and had current account balances in the red with funding substantially guaranteed by inflows of private capital, which peaked at US$294 billion in 1997 before slipping to US$134 billion in 1998 and US$166 billion in 1999.[6] The lion's share was made up by FDI which, in truth, had remained relatively stable even during the Asian crisis and the years of recovery that followed,[7] albeit recording volatility in those countries hit by the crisis. The sharp drop in net capital inflows to emerging countries following the Asian crisis was due above all to a marked reduction in foreign bank loans, which fell from a value of US$61 billion in 1997 to negative values of US$59 billion in 1998 and US$43 billion in 1999 on the back of worsening balance of payments and increased investors' risk aversion (IMF, 2003a). In addition, foreign banks tended to finance firms directly on local markets thanks to their increased penetration in emerging economies.

Following the effects of the Asian crisis, the emerging economies became net capital exporters. The main reason for this can be found directly in those countries that had suffered financial crises. The reduction in these countries' exposure to shocks originating from the international capital markets stems from two factors. The first is *corporate external deleveraging* aimed at reducing exposure to currency risk. The second is the accumulation of net foreign assets by the private sector of emerging economies and, later on, of currency reserves by these countries' central banks. The combination of both actions turned emerging economies from net capital importers to net capital exporters. This phenomenon was particularly apparent in crisis-hit countries.[8] Although only eight in number, they had average capital outflows amounting to US$48.5 billion in the period 2000–2004, almost the same as the average figure (US$45.8 billion) recorded by those countries – quantitatively higher in number – which were not directly hit by the crisis.

In more detail, we can see that this transformation into net creditors occurred over two phases. The five years from 1997 to 2001 were dominated by the flight of foreign private investors (private flows dropping from US$210 to US$140 billion) leading to a *corporate external deleveraging*,[9] which was accompanied by the accumulation of net foreign assets on the part of residents (capital outflows). The fall in corporate external leveraging implied a simultaneous rising demand for domestic financial sources in the context of expansionary monetary policies adopted in the post-crisis period. The reasons for this can be found on both the demand and supply side. In fact, on one hand, there had been a fall in the availability of resources to fund these countries' firms, whilst, on the other, the economic slowdown had reduced the demand for investments by these countries' corporate sector.

Since 2002, however, the transformation of emerging countries into capital exporters was dominated by the accumulation of currency reserves by governments (rising from US$500 to US$2,500 billion in the ten years from 1996 to 2006 according to IIF figures), which more than offset increased private capital inflows (peaking at US$350 billion in 2005).

This transformation is at odds with the conventional view that postulates capital flows from rich to emerging countries and necessarily requires a more detailed explanation. Initially, in order to avoid further financial crises, crisis-hit emerging economies began to restructure their international positions. However, emerging economies that were not affected took the precautionary step of following suit and became the major accumulators of currency reserves in order to equip themselves with the resources necessary to avoid further disastrous crises as well as keeping exchange levels low enough to sustain their export-led strategies. In fact, international reserves are an extremely important lifeline in the event of a sudden interruption in foreign capital flows (Tweedie, 2000) and help to reduce related real costs. Chan-Lau (2004) shows that the probability of a debt crisis falls as foreign reserves grow and several studies have also shown that foreign reserves reduce borrowing costs.[10] Nevertheless, an excess of foreign reserves may have its costs. In fact, the accumulation of excess reserves can generate excess liquidity – which may lead to inappropriately permissive credit policies – or lead to costly sterilisations (IMF, 2003b). Edison (2003) points out that already in 2002 the level of reserves accumulated in Asia had exceeded those necessary or justified by economic fundamentals, but excessively low opportunity costs prevented any change in this trend. On his part, Rodrik (2006) estimates that earnings equivalent to around 1 per cent of developing countries' GDP are lost due to excessively-high currency reserve balances. Finally, the backwardness of financial markets plays an important role in raising the demand for currency reserves.

The question of excess currency reserves does not have only macroeconomic implications, but is closely connected to the workings of financial markets in emerging countries and highlights the crucial need for their modernisation as a condition for a stable integration in the global economy. Indeed, on one hand, the immaturity of local financial markets generates inefficiencies in the intermediation of domestic savings, which in turn are less likely to replace foreign indebtedness. Additionally, firms operating in countries with imperfect financial markets tend to underestimate the positive cushioning effects of local currency-denominated debt (Caballero and Krishnamurthy, 2003) therefore exposing themselves to excessive foreign currency debt levels with the added danger of exchange-rate risk. On the other hand, the need to sterilise currency inflows arising from excess currency reserves encourages the issue of public sector bonds, which in turn contributes to the increased depth of domestic capital markets. This can act as an incentive for growth in the corporate bond market: for instance, the development of the yield curve of government bonds can provide a benchmark for determining market yields. In other words, if the excess of currency reserves is simply a temporary phenomenon, it may help to promote the development of market-financed debt and the modernisation of emerging countries' financial markets. At the same time, the presence of an adequately efficient banking system is also a prerequisite for the growth of a local corporate bond market. It is for this reason that emerging countries should take rapid steps to restructure their banking systems so as to better exploit the potential of temporary excesses in currency reserves and then, after having finalised the complete overhaul of the domestic financial system, bring them down to levels in line with the countries' economic fundamentals.

The reform of the banking systems of emerging countries

Since the mid-1990s, emerging countries have addressed the question of strengthening their banking systems in order to increase their stability and profitability as well as broadening the array of financial products and services offered and raising the allocative efficiency of both public and private sector banks. These reforms have typically followed a three-legged approach: consolidation, privatisation, and the entry of foreign players (Mihaljek, 2006).

At the end of the 1990s, according to Mihaljek (2006), the banking systems of many emerging countries were extremely fragmented, with a limited number of large-sized commercial banks very often coexisting alongside a large number of small privately (often owned by family-run companies) or publicly-controlled banks. In addition, small banks very often faced serious capital adequacy problems. Finally, only a few banks, generally the biggest, were listed. In order to strengthen their banking systems in the wake of the financial crises of the 1990s, many emerging countries adopted consolidation as a major strategy for banking reform. Starting from 2000, the total value of merged assets went beyond the US$270 billion mark in comparison to US$170 billion for the period 1995–2000. Since 1999, the number of banks has increased only in China (thanks to the transformation of Urban Credit Cooperatives into City Commercial Banks), Saudi Arabia and Colombia, whilst in other countries the process of consolidation has benefited of M&As and liquidation activities thereby bringing the number of banks down by between 10 per cent and 30 per cent. In those countries hit by a financial crisis, bank mergers were also seen as a form of exit strategy for the weakest banks, whereas in the other countries, governments attempted to enlarge the size of their banks to provide them with enough ammunition to compete with larger foreign banks entering their domestic markets. Two approaches to consolidation can be seen: market led or government led. The first prevailed in Central Eastern Europe, via Western bank buyouts, and in Latin America; government-led consolidation, on the contrary, was the dominant approach adopted in Asia, where many of the smallest banks were owned by private investors, who sold out only after receiving government incentives. For instance, in Indonesia, M&A activity was limited as very often the owners of small banks were reluctant to sell without special incentives (Goeltom, 2006).

The question of privatisation of emerging countries' banking systems is linked to the fact that state-ownership of banks is the conduit for the distortions present in domestic economies. The principal driver for privatisation, therefore, was a heightened awareness that the development of the financial system was a condition for increasing the potential for growth and that public ownership was often a hindrance to the full development of the financial market. In other words, the attempt to complete the restructuring of banks and transform them into economically sustainable organisations is based on the paradigm that private banks, in general, give greater priority to value creation and this should lead to more efficient credit allocation[11] and greater opposition to political interference.[12] Empirical evidence appears to support such position. Amongst important cross-country studies, La Porta *et al.* (2002) show that following an increase in state ownership levels in the banking system, the development of the national financial market, pro capita GDP and productivity in general all drop.[13]

The most evident case of distortions caused by public ownership is perhaps China, where the main factor of distortion is linked to the existence of a spurious type of relationship lending in which state owned banks have long been under political pressure to grant credits with little business logic to state owned enterprises with low profitability profiles. This serious conflict of interest has led to, on one hand, a substantial quantity of uncollectible loans that have threatened to destabilise the Chinese banking system in addition to the presence of a speculative bubble in many sectors, whilst on the other, a reduction in the financing of private firms which are, in many cases, better run and more profitable.

This is, however, not the only way in which political interference can influence the workings of the banking system. In the case of India, not only are the largest Indian banks state-owned, but political directives regarding the allocative choices of the banking system are enforced by law. In fact, Indian banks are subject to the mandatory so-called 'priority sector lending rule', which obliges both Indian and foreign banks to reserve shares of their lending volumes – 40 per cent for Indian banks and 32 per cent for foreign financial institutions – to specific economic areas (e.g., farming, rural economies, small and medium-sized enterprises). Furthermore, since 1949 a law has been in force that limits Indian banks' choices regarding their distribution network: for every new branch to be opened in areas already served by bank outlets, the bank has to open four branches in areas that are not. Clearly, such rules generate excessive costs and have negative effects on the profitability and efficiency of the Indian banking system.

It is not surprising that, growing awareness of these politically induced inefficiencies, has favoured a general move towards reducing state-ownership in banks in developing countries as such ownership

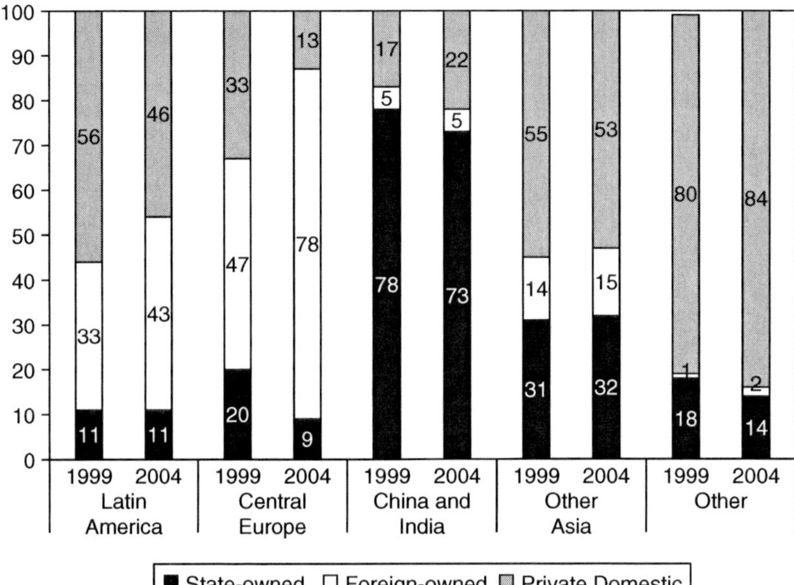

Source: Mihaljek (2006) and Central Banks bulletins.

Figure 1.5 The weight of different ownership forms in emerging countries' banking systems

negatively affects efficiency, the development of financial markets and, via these channels, economic growth. Needless to say, some justifications for public ownership can be found (Megginson 2005).

The process of privatisation is relatively advanced in many emerging countries, even though Boehmer *et al.* (2005) suggest that during this process governments often tend to maintain control and not to dis-invest completely (Figure 1.5). Privatisation has taken different paths: public sell offs also via competitive tender (such as in Mexico), pri-vate deals with strategic investors, IPOs (such as the first-time listing of large Chinese banks), voucher privatisations (the issue of free or low cost vouchers distributed to citizens and used in Eastern Central Europe). Clarke *et al.* (2005) show that there is no evidence suggesting the exis-tence of a standard privatisation method, whilst Mihaljek (2006) reports that since 2000 the main privatisations have taken place in Indonesia, Korea, Thailand and Central Eastern Europe. In Indonesia, 70 per cent of banking assets were sold via public offerings and in Korea between 1997 and 1998 the four of the country's top banks were privatised. In

Thailand, public authorities reduced their position in the banking system in three of the country's five major publicly-owned banks that were bought by the Financial Institutions Development Fund in 1997. Privatisations have been more or less completed also in the Czech Republic and in Hungary, whilst in Poland the government continues to keep a significant stake in PKO BP, the country's biggest bank. Elsewhere, such as in Turkey, the situation is at an intermediate stage.

The public sector remains the dominant player in other major emerging countries such as Russia, India and China. Governments of these three countries seem reluctant to follow the privatisation trend of their counterparts and continue to maintain control over their national, public-sector champions. China is currently diversifying ownership of its state-owned banks (SOB and JSCB) without necessarily preparing the ground for a full transfer of ownership into private hands. This ownership diversification strategy includes the sale of minority holdings to foreign banks in order to attract them as strategic investors both in large national and second-level banks. In India, following the reopening of bank asset sales to the private sector at the beginning of the 1990s, the authorities have recently authorised public banks to sell parts of their capital to private investors, though significant limits on voting rights remain in place (a ceiling of 10 per cent). A progressive increase in openings to foreign banks is also forecasted for 2009. In Russia, government strategy to reduce the public sector's presence in the banking industry has as yet to define any precise moves and the gradual reduction in the weight of Sberbank (the share of household deposits dropped from 75 per cent in 2000 to 60 per cent in 2004) has been counterbalanced by expansion of other state-controlled banks.

The third leg of banking reform in emerging countries has been the entry of foreign banks and very often privatisations have been instrumental in the sale of local banks to foreign banking groups. These groups have, in fact, contributed to the recapitalisation of the banking systems of many emerging countries, particularly after the banking crises of the 1990s. This was also made possible by the growing interest on the part of foreign banks in emerging markets. First, foreign banks adopted a strategy to optimally exploit their competitive advantages, that is product and service innovation, in emerging markets. Second, foreign banks increasingly targeted emerging countries through local networks: on one hand, to reduce cross-border risk exposures, local lending replaced cross-border lending (Moreno and Villar, 2005), on the other hand, this move was functional to exploit the advantages offered by the growth of emerging economies. There was therefore a meeting of interests: local banking

Table 1.1 Banks in principal emerging and transition economies

	Share of total assets of	
	Top 5 foreign banks	*Islamic banks*
	Latest available data	
China	. . .	–
India	5.5	4
South Korea	22.4	n.a.
Indonesia	23.2	1,42
Malaysia	18.3	11.8
Philippines	11.7	0.002
Thailand	11.2	n.a.
Vietnam	0.0	n.a.
Bulgaria	59.0	–
Croatia	72.6	–
Czech Republic	64.7	–
Hungary	54.4	–
Poland	41.3	–
Romania	61.8	–
Russia	4.8	–
Serbia	43.8	–
Slovakia	70.5	–
Slovenia	24.5	–
Turkey^	38.3	n.a.
Ukraine	29.4	–

Notes: ^: foreign banks refers to joint ventures banks;
–: non applicable;
. . . = negligible.
Source: Various national sources.

systems needed foreign banks to provide support in the modernisation process and foreign banks were happy to follow suit in order to exploit further opportunities for growth.

With reference to data in Table 1.1, and Figure 1.5, the presence of foreign banks is extremely high in Central Eastern Europe (accounting for 96 per cent of total assets of the Czech banking system, for instance) and in Latin America, but lower in Asia (above all in China and India). In Central Eastern Europe and Latin America this transformation was closely linked to the need to recapitalise the local banking industry. In particular, in Central Eastern Europe the presence of foreign banks is above 70 per cent (except in Russia, where it is lower) and, in many cases, major domestic banks are under foreign control. In Asia, in contrast, the

Table 1.2   Banking systems: non-performing loans/total loans ratio and return on equity

	NPL ratio		ROE	
	2001	*2007*	*2001*	*2007*
Argentina	13.1	2.9	−0.2	9.7
Brazil	5.6	3.1	−1.2	27.8
Chile	1.6	0.8	17.7	16.2
Colombia	9.7	3.4	1.1	19.8
Mexico	5.1	2.5	8.6	20.2
Venezuela	7	1.2	20.3	32.4
Bulgaria	3.3	1.7	21.9	25.4
Czech Republic	13.7	3.0	16.6	23.1
Hungary	2.7	2.5	15.9	22.9
Poland***	21.1	3.1	12.4	25.6
Romania	3.3	9.1	15.8	11.5
Russia	6.2	2.6	19.4	21.1
Slovakia	11.1	3.1	8	9.7
Slovenia*, ****	7	2.5	4.8	15.1
Turkey	29.3	3.6	−69.4	24.4
Ukraine	25.1	13.2	7.5	12.7
China**	29.8	6.6	13.7	19.9
India*	11.4	2.8	10.4	12.7
Indonesia	31.9	10.9	12	14.6
Malaysia	17.8	6.6	13.3	18.2
Philippines	27.7	5.7	3.2	11.6
Thailand	11.5	8.6	4.2	7.3
Egypt****	16.9	24.7	12.4	14.3
Morocco	16.8	9.5	10.2	21.6
Tunisia*, ****	19.2	19.2	13.2	9.1
South Africa	3.1	1.2	8.9	18.4

Notes: * = ROE, 2006 in stead of 2007, ** = ROE, 2003 instead of 2001, *** = NPL 2002 instead of 2001, **** = NPL 2006 instead of 2007.
Source: IMF (2003b, 2006, 2008).

penetration of foreign banks has been quantitatively lower, probably due to much higher levels of domestic savings, which have kept banks liquid (China is a good case in point) and public bail outs have made foreign capital less needed. However, there has been a strong recent increase in foreign banks (with minority shareholder status as described above) and the road map in India appears to be in place for greater openness to foreign investors. The crucial role of foreign banks will be discussed in greater detail on page 21 below.

In conclusion, thanks to reforms, the state of emerging countries' banking systems appears, as Table 1.2 shows, to be healthier, with a generalised improvement in non performing/total loans ratios and ROE, with the only exceptions of Romania and North African countries. What is not shown, however, is whether this improvement stems solely from the restructuring of the banking system or whether it is the result of the high levels of liquidity and economic growth of the last few years that have considerably raised demand for credit, which in turn has likely biased downward the ratio of non performing to total loan while boosting ROE. The distinction between the causes for improvement is significant. The first explanation, in fact, would lend support to the view that the chances of further financial crises starting from emerging economies are considerably lower than in the recent past, whilst the second would suggest that the absence of financial crises in the last few years is due solely to a generally positive macroeconomic climate.

The financial sector of emerging countries

Fragilities of emerging countries' banking systems have not always been the cause of system-wide financial crises. However, such fragilities hamper growth in those countries not hit by systemic crisis. This is particularly the case in those countries that have limited openness to international financial flows.

An inefficient financial system in fact may have significant negative impacts on these countries' economies. Firstly, the lack of adequate development of equity and bond markets diminishes the capacity on the part of these economies to cope with credit crunches[14] and to distribute the risk represented by complex transactions in a scenario of disintermediation. Data confirm that, in the emerging economies, the banking system is a primary component of domestic financial markets.

The size of the bond market is, in fact, smaller in emerging economies than in the most advanced countries. At year end 2006, the value of bonds amounted to 42.4 per cent of GDP in emerging countries in comparison to 169 per cent for the European Union and 205 per cent in the United States due to the under-representation of all possible issuer segments (IMF, 2006). Besides, the corporate bonds segment of the market is particularly small. In Asia, on average, in 2005 it accounted for 6.9 per cent of GDP. Malaysia and Korea are the only countries in which the corporate bond market is of significant size (38 per cent and 21 per cent of GDP, respectively), whilst in China the figure does not go beyond 1 per cent and in India is only slightly higher. In Latin America the share represented by corporate bonds is 2.6 per cent of GDP, with only Chile having a significantly higher figure (11 per cent of GDP). The growth of these markets in Central Eastern Europe has been less significant (1 per cent of GDP with a peak of 3.5 per cent only in the Czech Republic) as a result of the high levels of bank credit available, also following the entry of many foreign banks. In addition to a generalised underdevelopment of the financial system, the limited role of the corporate bond market stems from the fact that only the largest firms can operate as issuers, with small and medium-sized enterprises being excluded. A further problem for SMEs is the lack of interest shown by institutional investors in less liquid and more opaque securities which are often also of sub-investment grade. To favour the development of these markets, the IMF (2005b) suggests improving the business fundamentals of these firms and facilitating their access to credit rating systems.

On the other hand, the equity markets do not provide a stable alternative funding source for firms. In fact, these markets tend to be highly reactive to international economic cycles. Put in another way, they reflect more the trends in global investors' risk appetite than the fundamentals of the listed companies and this condition may trigger liquidity drains not justified by the state of the domestic economy. Evidence of this lies in the sharp falls recorded in stock markets[15] and new share issues[16] between 2000 and 2003, both of which gradually recovered in 2004–2006 as a result of events on advanced markets and, after the gloom of post 9/11, a return to optimism marked by abundant liquidity and heightened risk appetite on the part of market operators. At the end of 2006, in spite of these upturns, the average capitalisation of emerging countries was the equivalent to 89 per cent of GDP, whilst capitalisations in the United States and the European Union represented, respectively, 148 per cent and 95 per cent. Emerging countries' markets with the highest levels of capitalisation were Asia (109 per cent of GDP, thanks above all to the Singapore, Hong Kong, Malaysia, India and the recent upsurge in China) and Central and Eastern Europe (89 per cent of GDP). The IMF (2006) also measured that the ratio between market and book value was much lower (50 per cent) in emerging markets in comparison to advanced markets, which appears to suggest a reluctance on the part of firms to enter share markets. Additionally, the cost of capital in emerging markets is much higher than that recorded on advanced markets, a fact due to both the scarceness of liquidity on capital markets (Mathieson *et al.*, 2004) and poor governance and disclosure practices (IMF, 2005). In fact, emerging countries' stock exchanges are often marked by issuers' severe corporate governance problems which discourage long-term savers and investors and fuel speculative behaviour.

The role of foreign banks

As we have already seen, one of the pillars in the restructuring process of emerging banking systems has been the attraction, with the exceptions mentioned, of foreign banks, which now in certain countries account for significant shares of national total assets. The presence of foreign banks by means of local branches, can be an important incentive for modernisation and stability as the competition these foreign players create forces domestic banks to quicken their restructuring. To an even greater extent, the acquisition of local banks has the dual effect of speeding up the restructuring of existing market players and allowing foreign banks to exert greater competitive pressure thanks to the wider presence in emerging economies' domestic markets achieved via bank acquisitions.

The opening up of emerging markets to foreign banks began only recently[17] with the gradual dismantling of restrictions and limits on what foreign players could do. This choice was an obvious consequence of increasing openness to and integration with the international economy and represents just one of the many phases to wider liberalisation (Eichengreen and Mussa, 1998). However, it was only after the crises of the second half of the 1990s that the opening up to foreign banks started to have any practical effect. The quickening of reforms in those years depended, in part, on the fact that, in addition to the initial objective of liberalisation (i.e., a more efficient and stable banking system), another contingency could no longer be postponed: the need for the rapid restructuring of banking systems after the crisis (utilising the know-how of prime international banks) and for the reduction of costs (selling off banks in difficulty to foreign banks). In fact, as the IMF reported (IMF, 2000), authorities in many emerging countries realised that in order to reduce the sensitivity of their banking systems to economic and financial shocks, both domestic and international, in addition to strengthening prudential regulation, steps had to be taken to reduce vulnerability of the system represented by the large number of small banks with non-diversified credit portfolios and almost inexistent risk management capabilities. This awareness led not only to the process of consolidation discussed in the previous paragraph, but above all to the opening up to foreign banks so as to reduce concurrently the costs of restructuring and the vulnerability of the system through the integration of the weakest local banks into international ones with globally diversified portfolios.

In the light of these events, an important question is whether the growing presence of foreign banks in emerging markets acts as a driver for the growth and development of emerging banking systems. In deciding to open their systems to foreign banks, the authorities of many emerging countries (above all the smallest) would clearly see the presence of foreign banks in their countries as beneficial.

The literature has analysed in detail the impact of foreign banks' presence in emerging systems.

On the negative side, foreign banks may generate criticalities to supervisory authorities as they tend to cream-skim domestic customers, with negative consequences on domestic banks' portfolios, or they may lead to capital outflows and excessive credit restrictions. In particular, a negative consequence of foreign banks' presence is 'cherry picking' on their part, thanks to risk management techniques in no way comparable to those available to their domestic rivals, thus leaving local banks with the riskiest borrowers.[18] It should be said that such techniques powered by sophisticated credit scoring models, may, however, be less effective in environments dominated by severe informational asymmetries which make the relational information available to local banks extremely valuable. This concentration of lower quality borrowers amongst local banks could lead to a worsening of the stability of emerging banking systems. In fact, if local banks are inefficient and have insufficient capital adequacy levels, this move towards the riskiest borrowers without appropriate risk management and valuation capabilities can cause an increase in non performing loans and, over time, excessive capital absorption and subsequent collapse.[19] Foreign banks may also concentrate lending to larger local businesses and focus less on small and medium-sized enterprises and, in general, on more opaque borrowers (Berger *et al.*, 2001). In a similar way, the domestic banking system could be badly hit by the decision on the part of a large foreign bank to close local branches which have a marginal role in its overall strategy, but which for the emerging country involved are strategically significant. Moreover, in case of a banking crisis, an excessive share of foreign banks might impose critical decisions to the regulators regarding its lender-of-last-resort role and the use of public money to save foreign banks. Finally, the process of consolidation currently underway in advanced markets could cause excessive concentration on some emerging markets which would require effective antitrust provisions at the local level to prevent reduced competition.

On the positive side, foreign banks contribute to raising efficiency and stability of emerging banking systems, particularly if foreign access is accompanied by liberalisation of financial services.

On the question of the efficiency[20] of emerging banking systems, an increased presence of foreign banks should generate improvements in the quality and availability of financial services, as well as – thanks to greater competition – bringing down prices. Additionally, the raising of technical and professional skills amongst local staff employed by foreign banks should have positive effects on the local banking system as a whole via the physiological shift of employees from foreign or foreign-controlled banks to locally owned ones. Another line of research suggests that the entry of foreign banks is beneficial above all in the retail segment, whilst a foreign presence in the wholesale segment is thought to increase systemic crisis. Operationally, this possibility is linked to the fact that foreign banks have access and know-how of advanced risk management techniques and tend to make quantitatively higher levels of prudential provisioning. What is more, better management represents greater protection in the event of negative shocks.[21] The growing presence of foreign banks also reduces the macroeconomic cost of regulatory restrictions (Chiuri *et al.*, 2002). These last two factors appear to suggest that a strong presence of foreign banks may prevent the twin crises of the exchange-rate and the banking system (Kaminsky and Reinhart, 1999).

One of the reasons that has limited, in Asia, the opening up of domestic systems to foreign banks is the fear of 'cut and run' effects on the supply of credit during a crisis. Even though cross-border lending was effectively reduced during the crises of the mid-1990s, there are signs that foreign banks shifted lending to local-based funding (Moreno and Villar, 2005). Foreign banks with a local presence should be less susceptible to financial crises thanks to their access to cross-border lending transactions, which stabilise market share and provide borrowers with funds in the event of temporary liquidity shortages, their access to funding sources from the parent company[22] or to global financial markets thanks to the globally diversified portfolio of the parent company or the group as a whole. Another factor that reduces susceptibility to financial crisis is that, since the foreign bank's local business volume in an emerging country is small in comparison to total group volumes, exposure to local risk is lower (Dages *et al.*, 2000). Foreign banks, therefore, having access to the liquidity necessary to support enterprises during a credit crunch, should reduce the costs of domestic crises by containing the possible domino effects of cross-defaults. Finally, the presence of foreign banks could reduce the likelihood of capital flights: when there are doubts regarding the stability of the domestic banking system, residents could transfer their deposits to foreign banks present in the country, thereby limiting the negative effects on credit supply arising from the transfer of funds abroad.

With regards to the questions of stability and prudential regulation, foreign bank penetration corresponds, in part, to importing higher levels of prudential supervision than those available locally thanks to both consolidated supervision on foreign banks' branches and internal control carried out by the parent company over its local branches. Furthermore, branches of international banks may be equipped with reporting and disclosure procedures in line with international best practices, which could push local banks to seek the reputational gains associated with disclosure and financial robustness. The fact also that foreign banks' activities are typically more sophisticated pushes market watchdogs for improvements in the competences of both domestic and foreign banks. However, seen from an opposite viewpoint, both home country and host country supervisors may not be able to monitor and control completely the complex financial transactions carried out by international banks present on more than one market. As international banks tend to look for equilibrium in their portfolios at international level, some local branches could, therefore, find themselves with excessive exposures to certain segments and with subsequent difficulties that national regulators may not be adequately informed of. What is more, if the acquisition of local banks implies their delisting, an important source for the oversight of performance is lost.

Results supplied in empirical literature show that, since positive effects outweigh negative ones, access on the part of foreign banks is beneficial to emerging countries. Barth *et al.* (2001) find that more stringent entry restrictions for foreign banks is correlated to less efficient banking (higher margins and costs). Claessens *et al.* (2001), in a study of eighty emerging and advanced countries, find that foreign banks are more efficient (in terms of profitability and interest margins) than local banks in emerging markets, whilst the opposite holds for advanced countries. In addition, the entry of foreign banks tends to reduce banking sector profit margins and costs[23] and this effect does not depend on the size of banks' market shares. Demirgüc-Kunt *et al.* (2003) reveal that greater concentration in the banking sector is associated with less efficiency in emerging countries. Claessens and Laeven (2003) report that a higher number of foreign banks allied to no entry restrictions are associated with greater levels of competition. Further evidence suggests that competition is more vibrant in contexts where foreign banks operate. Moreno and Villar (2005), for example, suggest that the rationalisation that followed the entry of foreign banks benefited the banking system in the form of reduced general costs and increased profits, both of which contributed to greater stability. An opposite position is offered by Levy and Micco (2003) who find that the penetration of foreign banks reduced competition in several Latin American countries. However, other studies tend to suggest that in Argentina (Clarke *et al.*, 1999), Colombia (Barajas, *et al.*, 1999), Turkey (Denizer, 1999) and eight Asian countries (Claessens and Glaessner, 1999) the increase in the number of foreign banks brought with it greater efficiency to the banking system.

Few studies have investigated the connections between the entry of foreign banks and the likelihood of banking crises. Levine (1999) shows that, after having checked for other factors that can influence the probability of a systemic banking crisis, the presence of foreign banks emerges as a factor of stabilisation. Martinez Peria *et al.* (2002), on the other hand, report that whilst foreign banks transmit external shocks to the countries in which they are located, the same banks react more to positive local shocks than negative ones. Lastly, Laeven (1999) shows that from 1992 to 1996 foreign banks had run fewer risks than domestic banks and that banks owned by family groups and by businesses had portfolios with higher risk levels. It comes as no surprise that these last two categories of bank included the highest number of financial institutions requiring restructuring, whereas there was no foreign bank in the same condition.

On the subject of credit supply, however, during the period 1996–99, the IMF (IMF, 2000) shows that even though there had been a sharp fall in cross border lending, the contraction in lending in emerging countries was only slightly more intense on the part of foreign banks (−40 per cent) in comparison to that of domestic banks (−35 per cent). Palmer (2000) shows that during the Asian crisis, the reaction by US banks present in the area was influenced by strategic considerations relating to a long-term commitment on the basis of the significance of the market and future business prospects. Martinez Peria *et al.* (2002) show that foreign banks did not reduce their lending during the crises and, according to Detragiache and Gupta (2004), foreign banks did not exit Malaysia during the 1997–98 crisis and their credit activities continued at a more sustained pace than domestic banks during the Argentine and Mexican crises of 1994–95 (Goldberg *et al.*, 2000). Goldberg *et al.* (2000) reveal a close similarity between the composition of private foreign and domestic banks' portfolios on one hand and the volatility of their loans on the other and suggest that the fundamental factor in conditioning the growth and volatility of credit is a bank's financial health rather than its nationality. No evidence, lastly, is available to show that foreign banks in effect concentrate their lending on the largest local businesses at the expense of SMEs (Giannetti and Ongena, 2005, de Haas and Naaborg 2005).[24]

With regards to the stability of deposit bases, during the Asian crisis, customers shifted considerable quantities of funds from financial companies and domestic banks to both larger domestic banks and foreign institutions (IMF, 2000). For example, foreign banks recorded large increases in market shares in Korea, Indonesia and Thailand between 1997 and 1998 (Domaç *et al.*, 1999). Also during the crisis in Argentina in March 1980, foreign banks were the primary beneficiaries of a flight to quality (Baliño, 1991), whilst in 1994 doubts concerning the capacity of Argentine banks to meet depositors' requests led to a flow of funds towards foreign banks (IMF, 2005).

In conclusion, evidence regarding the effect of foreign banks' entry into emerging countries appears to support the position that competition tends to improve the efficiency of domestic banking systems; evidence as to the effects entry has on stability, though still limited, also appears to be supportive.

Conclusions

In this chapter, we have attempted to show that the improved solidity and performance of emerging banking systems will play a significant role in future world economic growth.

We have seen that there are two specific areas that require reform. On one hand, credit misallocation is a long-standing problem in emerging economies which reduces their potential for growth. On the other, the fragility of emerging banking systems means that these economies are inevitably more liable to systemic crises. Consequently, an emerging country that is able to make its banking system more solid not only improves its prospects of development directly, in the form of improved credit allocation, but also indirectly, by accessing international markets for its domestic development programmes without the fear of being enmeshed in a systemic crisis.

On this point, the upgrading of the banking system has so far been a crucial component for the resilience of some emerging countries to the current systemic crisis. In this respect, observing that the subprime crisis has initially left banking systems in emerging countries rather unscathed provides no permanent relief: historical experience teaches, in fact, that crises are usually more likely at the periphery than at the core of the world financial system. A contagion cannot yet be excluded. Hence, the importance of running conservative external policies and promoting a healthier and adequately capitalised banking system is crystal clear for all economies.

Notes

1. The first systemic crisis hit Mexico (1994), later followed by other crises in Asia (1997–98), Russia (1998), (1999), Argentina and Turkey (2001–2002).
2. For an in depth analysis of the initial success and the later distress of LTCM, see Lowenstien (2001).
3. For instance, the *Asian and Pacific Migration Journal* devoted two issues (Nos. 2 and 3 of 1998, in volume 7) to study the impact of the crisis on migratory flows from/to Bangladesh, Hong Kong, Indonesia, Japan, Korea, Malaysia, Philippines, Singapore, Thailand and Taiwan..
4. The ratings are those issued by Moody's and have been converted into numerical values as follows:

   Bank deposits and sovereign ratings

   $$Aaa = 100; Aa1 = 95; Aa2 = 90; Aa3 = 85; A1 = 80; A2 = 75; A3 = 70;$$
   $$Baa1 = 65; Baa2 = 60; Baa3 = 55; Ba1 = 50; Ba2 = 45; Ba3 = 40; B1 = 35;$$
   $$B2 = 30; B3 = 25; Caa1 = 20; Caa2 = 15; Caa3 = 10; Ca = 5; C = 0.$$

   Bank financial strength rating

   $$A = 100; A- = 92, 5; B+ = 85; B = 77, 5; B- = 70; C+ = 62, 5;$$
   $$C = 55; C- = 47, 5; D+ = 40; D = 32, 5; D- = 25; E+ = 17, 5; E = 10.$$

5. The Council of Economic Advisors (1991) defines a credit crunch as 'a situation in which the supply of credit is kept below the level usually associated with prevailing markets rates and the profitability of investment projects'.
6. Figures provided by the Institute of International Finance.
7. FDI towards emerging countries amounted to US\$117bn in 1997 and continued to grow in 1998 and 1999 (US\$122bn and US\$154bn, respectively).
8. According to the IMF study referred to (IMF, 2004), the 'crisis countries' are Argentina, Brazil, Indonesia, Malaysia, Philippines, Russia, Thailand and Turkey.
9. The phenomenon of corporate external deleveraging had already started in 1997 for those countries affected by the Asian crisis.
10. Kamin and von Kleist (1999), Eichengreen and Mody (1998), and Ferrucci (2003).
11. Megginson (2005) points out that the potential lower efficiency of public banks is principally due to three reasons: (i) managers of public banks have fewer incentives to increase revenues and cut costs; (ii) collective action problems reduce monitoring and control on the part of governments; and (iii) governments as owners will probably not allow public-sector banks to fail or to suffer cost cutting so increasing moral hazard and operating inefficiencies.
12. Shleifer and Vishny (1994) show that public-owned banks are less efficient because political influence pushes them to favour non-economic objectives.
13. La Porta *et al.* (2002) use cross country data from 92 countries and find that public ownership of banks is particularly significant in poorer countries, where it holds back the development of the financial system and slows down

economic growth, as a result of the low productivity levels that typically stem from acting as a state monopoly.

14. For example, Davis and Stone (2004) have shown that bond issues significantly reduce the corporate sector's susceptibility to credit crunches.

15. The average value of emerging countries' share lists reported by the IMF (2006) was 333 at year end 2000, dropping to 292 at year end 2002, then recovering to 747 midway through 2006.

16. Share issues moved from US$46bn in 2000 to US$11bn the following year, after which they started an upward trend, moving to US$27bn in 2003 and to US$78bn in 2005.

17. For example, the IMF (2000) draws attention to the fact that, prior to the 1997–98 crises, many Asian countries had imposed operating restrictions on foreign banks which included severe limits to the number of branches (only one) and a long-running freeze on foreign bank licences. See also the following chapters for details of specific restrictions still in force in India, China, Russia and other emerging countries.

18. For an analysis of the Korean experience, see Kim and Lee, (2003).

19. This situation was worsened at times by local banks' lending portfolios that were characterised by an excess of regulated rate loans, whilst foreign banks had entered the market during a phase in which they could freely fix their borrowing and lending rates.

20. For a more detailed analysis of the positive and negative effects of the presence of foreign banks on the stability and efficiency of emerging bank systems, see IMF (2000).

21. There is, for instance, no evidence of foreign banks in difficulty during the Asian crisis (Bongini *et al.*, 2000).

22. We are, however, unaware of any studies documenting this form of support.

23. Focarelli and Pozzolo (2001) illustrate the same type of effect in mergers and acquisitions amongst OECD countries.

24. In their analysis of four Latin American countries, Clarke *et al.* (2005) find that foreign banks, in effect, lend less to SMEs.

References

Baliño, T. (1991), 'The Argentine Banking Crisis of 1980', in *Banking Crises: Cases and Issues*, ed. by V. Sundararajan and T. Baliño (Washington: International Monetary Fund), pp. 58–112.

Barajas, A., R. Steiner and N. Salazar (1999), 'Foreign Investment in Colombia's Financial Sector', IMF Working Paper 99/150 (Washington: International Monetary Fund, November).

Barth, J., G. Caprio and R. Levine (2001), 'Bank regulation and supervision: what works best?', World Bank Policy Research Working Paper No. 2775, August.

Berger, A. N., L. F. Klapper and G. F. Udell (2001), 'The Ability of Banks To Lend to Informationally Opaque Small Businesses', *Journal of Banking and Finance*, Vol. 25, 2001.

Boehmer, E., R.C. Nash and J.M. Netter (2005), 'Bank Privatization in Developing and Developed Countries: Cross-sectional Evidence on the Impact of Economic and Political Factors', *Journal of Banking and Finance*, vol. 29, issues 8–9, 1981–2013.

Bongini, P., G. Ferri and H. Hahm (2000), 'Corporate Bankruptcy in Korea: Only the Strong Survive?', *The Financial Review*.

Bongini, P., S. Claessens and G. Ferri (2001), 'The Political Economy of Distress in East Asian Financial Institutions', *Journal of Financial Services Research* 19(1): 5–25.

Brandt, L. and H. Li (2003), 'Bank Discrimination in Transition Economies: Ideology, Information, or Incentives?', *Journal of Comparative Economics* 31: 387–413.

Caballero, R. J. (2006), 'On the Macroeconomics of Asset Shortages', *NBER* Working Paper 12753, December 2006.

Caballero, R. J. and A. Krishnamurthy (2003), 'Excessive Dollar Debt: Financial Development and Underinsurance', *Journal of Finance*, Vol. 58, pp. 867–94.

Canals, Jordi (1997), *Universal Banking: International Comparisons and Theoretical Perspectives* (Oxford: Oxford University Press).

Chang, C. (2003), 'Progress and Peril in China's Modern Economy', *Federal Reserve Bank of Minneapolis: The Region*. 17(4): 26–30, Dec.

Chan-Lau, J. A. (2004), 'Reserve Holdings and Sovereign Default Risk,' unpublished; (Washington: IMF).

Chiuri, M.C., G. Ferri and G. Majnoni (2002), 'The Macroeconomic Impact of Bank Capital Requirements in Emerging Economies: Past Evidence to Assess the Future', *Journal of Banking and Finance* 26(5): 881–904.

Claessens, S. and T. Glaessner (1999), 'Internationalization of Financial Services in Asia', *Policy Research Working Paper Series 1911*, The World Bank, Washington.

Claessens, S and L. Laeven (2003), 'What Drives Bank Competition: Some International Evidence', mimeo, World Bank, February.

Claessens, S., A. Demirgüç-Kunt and H. Huizinga (2001), 'How Does Foreign Entry Affect Domestic Banking Markets?', *Journal of Banking and Finance* 25(5): 891–911.

Clarke, G., R. Cull and M. Shirley (2005), 'Bank Privatization in Developing Countries: A synthesis of Lessons and Findings, *Journal of Banking and Finance*, 2005, vol. 29, issues 8–9, pages 1905–30.

Clarke, G., R. Cull, L. D'Amato and A. Molinari (1999), 'The Effect of Foreign Entry on Argentina's Domestic Banking Sector', Policy Research Working Paper Series 2158, The World Bank, Washington.

Clarke, G., R. Cull, M.S. Martinez Peria and S.M. Sánchez (2005), 'Bank Lending to Small Businesses in Latin America: Does Bank Origin Matter?', *Journal of Money, Credit, and Banking*, Vol. 37/1: 83–118.

Corsetti, G., P. Pesenti and N. Roubini (1999), 'What Caused the Asian Currency and Financial Crises?', *Japan and the World Economy*, Vol. 11, No. 3: 305–13.

Council of Economic Advisors (1991), 'Economic Report of the President', Washington, DC.

Dages, B.G., L. Goldberg and D. Kinney (2000), 'Foreign and Domestic Bank Participation in Emerging Markets: Lessons from Mexico and Argentina', *NBER Working Paper* No. 7714.

Davis, E. P. and Mark R. Stone, (2004), 'Corporate Financial Structure and Financial Stability', *Journal of Financial Stability*, Vol. 1, No. 1: 65–91.

de Haas, R.T.A. and I. Naaborg (2005), 'Foreign Banks in Transition Economies: Small Business Lending and Internal Capital Markets', De Nederlandsche Bank, April.

Demirgüç-Kunt, A, L Laeven and R Levine (2003), 'Regulations, Market Structure, Institutions, and the Cost of Financial Intermediation', World Bank, mimeo, 22 July.

Denizer, C., 1999, 'Foreign Entry in Turkey's Banking System, 1980–1997', in Claessens, S. and M. Jansen (eds), *The Internationalization of Financial Services: Issues and Lesson for Developing Countries* (Boston: Kluwer Academic).

Detragiache, E. and P. Gupta (2004), 'Foreign Banks in Emerging Market Crises: Evidence from Malaysia', IMF Working Paper.

Domaç, I. and G. Ferri (1999), 'Did Financial Shocks Disproportionately Hit Small Businesses in Korea?', *Economic Notes*, No. 3: 403–29.

Domaç, I., G. Ferri and T.S. Kang (1999), 'The Credit Crunch in East Asia: Evidence from Field Findings on Bank Behavior and Policy Issues', World Bank.

Edison, H. 2003, 'Are Foreign Exchange Reserves in Asia Too High' *World Economic Outlook* (Washington: International Monetary Fund, September)

Eichengreen, B. (2001), 'Crisis Prevention and Management: Any New Lessons from Argentina and Turkey?', background paper for the World Bank's Global Development Finance 2002, October.

Eichengreen, B. and A. Mody (1998a), 'What Explains Changing Spreads on Emerging Market Debt?', NBER Working Paper No. 6408 (Cambridge, Mass.: National Bureau of Economic Research).

Eichengreen, B. and M. Mussa (1998b), 'Capital Account Liberalization–Theoretical and Practical Aspects', IMF Occasional Paper No. 172 (Washington: International Monetary Fund).

Ferri, G. (2002), 'Quali lezioni per il futuro dalle crisi argentina e turca?', Rapporto Monetario CER, Roma.

Ferrucci, G., 2003, 'Empirical Determinants of Emerging Market Economies' Sovereign Bond Spreads', Working Paper No. 205 (London: Bank of England).

Focarelli, D. and A.F. Pozzolo (2001), 'The Patterns of Cross-Border Bank Mergers and Shareholdings in OECD Countries', *Journal of Banking and Finance* 25(12): 2305–37.

Folkerts-Landau, D. and B. Chadha, 1999, 'The Evolving Role of Banks in International Capital Flows', in *International Capital Flows*, ed. By Martin Feldstein (Chicago; London: University of Chicago Press), pp. 191–234.

Furman, J. and J.E. Stiglitz (1998), 'Economic Crisis: Evidence and Insights from East Asia', Brookings Papers on Economic Activity.

Giannetti, M. and S. Ongena (2005), 'Financial Integration and Entrepreneurial Activity: Evidence From Foreign Bank Entry in Emerging Markets', ECB Working Paper no. 498.

Goeltom, M. (2006), 'Indonesia's Banking Industry: Progress To Date', in BIS Papers 28, 'The Banking System in Emerging Economies: How Much Progress Has Been Made?', August, 2006 (Basel: Bank of International Settlements).

Goldberg, L., G. Dages and D. Kinney (2000), 'Foreign and Domestic Bank Participation in Emerging Markets: Lessons from Mexico and Argentina', *Economic Policy Review*, 6(3), Federal Reserve Bank of New York.

Goldstein, M. (1998), 'The Asian Financial Crisis: Causes, Cures, and Systemic Implications', Policy Analysis in International Economics Institute for International Economics.

Hawkins, J., (2002), 'Bond Markets and Banks in Emerging Economies', in *The Development of Bond Markets in Emerging Economies*, BIS Papers No. 11 (Basel, Switzerland: Bank for International Settlements, June).

IMF (1995), 'International Capital Markets: Developments, Prospects, and Key Policy Issues', Washington, DC: World Economic and Financial Surveys.

IMF (2001), IMF Survey, Vol. 30, No. 23, 10 December.

IMF (2003a), 'Global Financial Stability', Report, September 2003 (Washington, DC: IMF, 2003a).

IMF (2003b), 'World Economic Outlook', September 2003 (Washington, DC: IMF, 2003b).

IMF (2004), 'Emerging Markets as Net Capital Exporters', in IMF, Global Financial Stability Report September 2004 (Washington, DC: IMF, 2004).

IMF (2005a), 'Corporate Finance in Emerging Markets', in IMF, Global Financial Stability Report April 2005, IMF, Washington DC.

IMF (2005b), 'Development of Corporate Bonds Markets in Emerging Markets Countries', in IMF, Global Financial Stability Report (Washington, DC: IMF, 2005b).

IMF (2006), 'Global Financial Stability Report', September 2006, (Washington, DC: IMF, 2006).

IMF (2008), 'Global Financial Stability Report', April 2008, (Washington, DC: IMF, 2008).

Kamin, S. and K. von Kleist (1999), 'The Evolution and Determinants of Emerging Market Credit Spreads in the 1990s', BIS Working Paper No. 68 (Basel: Bank for International Settlements).

Kaminsky, G. L. and C. M. Reinhart (1999), 'The Twin crises: the Causes of Banking and Balance-of-Payments Problems', *American Economic Review*: 473–500.

Kim, H. E. and B. Y. Lee (2003), 'The Effects of Foreign Bank Entry on the Performance of Private Domestic Banks in Korea', Central Bank papers submitted by Working Group members, 2003.

Krugman, P. (1979), 'A Model of Balance-of-Payments Crises', *Journal of Money, Credit and Banking*, Vol. 11, No. 3: 311–25

Krugman, P. (1998), 'What Happened to Asia', mimeo, MIT, 1998.

La Porta, R., F. López-de-Silanes and A. Shleifer (2002), 'Government Ownership of Banks', *Journal of Finance*, 57: 265–301.

Laeven, Luc (1999), 'Impact of Ownership Structure on Bank Performance in East Asia' (Washington: World Bank, September).

Levine, Ross, (1999), 'Foreign Bank Entry and Capital Control Liberalization: Effects on Growth and Stability', unpublished (Minneapolis, Minnesota: University of Minnesota, October).

Levy Yeyati, E. and A. Micco (2003), 'Concentration and Foreign Participation in Latin American Banking Sectors: Impact on Competition and Risk', Working Paper No 499, Inter-American Development Bank.

Lowenstien, R. (2001), *When Genius Failed: The Rise and Fall of Long-Term Capital Management*, (London: Fourth Estate).

Martinez Peria, M. S., A. Powell, and I. V. Hollar (2002), 'Banking on Foreigners: The Behavior of International Bank Lending to Latin America, 1985–2000'.

Masson, P. (1999), 'Contagion: Macroeconomic Models with Multiple Equilibria', *Journal of International Money and Finance*, Vol. 18, Issue 4: 587–602.

Mathieson, D. J., J. E. Roldos, R. Ramaswamy and A. Ilyina (2004), 'Emerging Local Securities and Derivatives Markets', *World Economic and Financial Surveys*, (Washington, DC: IMF, 2004).

Megginson, W. L. (2005), 'The Economics of Bank Privatization', *Journal of Banking and Finance*, vol. 29, issues 8–9: 1931–80.

Mihaljek, D. (2006), Privatisation, Consolidation and the Increased Role of Foreign Banks, in BIS Papers 28, 'The Banking System in Emerging Economies: How Much Progress Has Been Made?' (Basel: Bank of International Settlements, 2006).

Miller, M. H. and J. E. Stiglitz (1999), 'Bankruptcy Protection Against Macroeconomic Shocks: The Case for a Super-Chapter 11', presented at conference, Capital Flows, Financial Crisis and Policies', World Bank, Washington, DC, 15–16 April.

Mohanty, M. S., G. Schnabel and P. Garcia-Luna, D. (2006), Banks and Aggregate Credit: What is New?, in BIS Papers 28, 'The Banking System in Emerging Economies: How Much Progress Has Been Made?' (Basel: Bank of International Settlements, 2006).

Moreno, R. (2002), 'Reforming China's Banking System', FRBSF Economic Letter No. 2002–17, 31 May.

Moreno, R. and A. Villar (2005), 'The Increased Role of Foreign Bank Entry in Emerging Markets?, BIS Papers 23 (Basel: Bank of International Settlements).

Obstfeld M. (1996), 'Models of Currency Crises with Self-Fulfilling Features', *European Economic Review* 40: 1037–47.

Palmer, D. E. (2000), 'U.S. Bank Exposure to Emerging-Market Countries During Recent Financial Crises', Federal Reserve Bulletin, US Board of Governors of the Federal Reserve Board (February).

Park, A. and K. Sehrt (2001), 'Tests of Financial Intermediation and Banking Reform in China', *Journal of Comparative Economics* 29: 608–44.

Radelet, S. and J. Sachs (1998), 'The Onset of the East Asian Financial Crisis', NBER, Working Paper No. 6680.

Rajan, R. (2006), 'Investment Restraint, The Liquidity Glut, and Global Imbalances', remarks at the Conference on Global Imbalances organized by the Bank of Indonesia in Bali, 16 November.

Rajan, R. G., and L. Zingales, (2003a), 'Banks and Markets: The Changing Character of European Finance', NBER Working Paper No. 9595 (Cambridge, Mass.: National Bureau of Economic Research).

Rajan, R.G. and L. Zingales (2003b), *Saving Capitalism from the Capitalists. 'Unleashing the Power of Financial Markets To Create Wealth and Spread Opportunity* (New York: Random House; Crown Business – trad. it, 2003b).

Rodrik, D. (2006), 'The Social Cost of Foreign Exchange Reserves', NBER Working Paper No. 11952 (Cambridge, Mass.: National Bureau of Economic Research, 2006).

Schinasi, G. and T. Smith, (1998), 'Fixed-Income Markets in the United States, Europe, and Japan: Some Lessons for Emerging Markets', IMF Working Paper No. 98/173 (Washington, DC: IMF, 1998).

Shleifer, A. and R. W. Vishny (1994), 'Politicians and Firms', *The Quarterly Journal of Economics*, Vol. 109, No. 4 (November), pp. 995–1025.

Stiglitz, J.E. (1999), 'Introduction', Conference on 'The East Asian Crisis: Lessons for Today and for tomorrow', *Economic Notes*, No. 3: 249–54.

UNCTAD (2003), *Handbook of Statistics* (New York and Geneva: United Nations).

Vansetti, M. C., P. Guarco and G. W. Bauer (2000), 'The "Fall" of Bancomer and the Future of Indigenous Mega-Banks in Latin America', Moody's Investor Service, Global Credit Research (April).

Wei, S.J. and T. Wang (1997), 'The Siamese Twins: Do State-Owned Banks Favor State-Owned Enterprises in China?', *China Economic Review* 8(1): 19–29.

World Bank (1996), *The East Asian Miracle*, (Washington, DC: The World Bank, 1996).

Zhou, X. (2004), 'Some Issues Concerning the Reform of the State-owned Commercial Banks', Speech by the Governor of the People's Bank of China, at the IIF Spring Membership Conference, Shanghai, 16 April.

2
China

S. Chiarlone and G. Ferri

Introduction

The Chinese economy has been growing at a very sustained pace – approximately 10 per cent per year for over 25 years and has attracted large flows of international capital. Furthermore, the consensus suggests that such a scenario is probably going to persist.

In such a context of high liquidity, the efficiency of banking intermediation is crucial to avoid bubbles, whose bursting would affect the long-term sustainability of economic growth. Nonetheless, fragility has characterised the Chinese banking sector since the early 1980s. This is linked with the back of the medal of the gradual transition process: State-Owned Enterprises (SOEs) have survived the end of the planned economy becoming all too frequently loss-making entities (Opper, 2001; OECD, 2005). Also, state-ownership of banks is widespread in China and, consequently, banks have faced pressure to keep lending to SOEs, even when prudential credit risk management would have discouraged such practice.

Accordingly, a series of policy actions aimed at reducing Non-Performing Loans (NPL) (including the establishment of policy banks and asset management companies and various state recapitalisation of the large banks) has had limited success at strengthening banks' health because it did not cut the links between state banks and SOEs. At the end of 2003, NPLs still made up 21 per cent of total loans. Only since 2003 has the focus of the banking restructuring strategy switched from reducing existing NPLs to facing the roots of NPL generation (including the transformation of state banks in corporations and selling minority shares to foreign banks, and in the stock exchange to improve corporate governance). The drop of the NPL ratio to about 7 per cent at the end of 2006 showed strongly positive achievements, even though this was partly the result of overall credit growth. At the same time, the banking scenario has changed with an increasing relevance of smaller and better-managed Joint Stock Commercial Banks (JSCBs) and city commercial banks (CCBs). These banks represent a very positive add-up to the Chinese banking sector, though it seems that their better lending practices largely depend on the fact that most of their business is located in China's richer provinces (Ferri, 2008). In other words, they cannot offer, on their own, a solution to the problems of the Chinese banking sector, which demands an improvement of the big four SOCBs,[1] which still dominate the banking landscape in China.

So far, the health of the Chinese banking sector seems to be improving. The large banks are acquiring front-level positions in the world bank rankings, and even showing signs of an embryonic strategy to become global. Nonetheless, their shape remains to be monitored: risk management practices demand further improvement and loans to SOEs – also because of remaining public pressures – still exceed these companies' declining role in China's industry. Completing reform of the corporate sector (and streamlining the still excessive number of SOEs) is of utmost importance. Moreover, a liberalisation of the exchange rate and higher government spending (education, health care and pensions) would reduce the excess liquidity and, as a consequence, would require banks to be more efficient in managing their liabilities. Finally, a larger presence of foreign banks (increasingly possible after the December 2006 law, which allows foreign banks to establish wholly foreign owned subsidiaries with full operation in Renminbi) will probably trigger stronger competition. Such competitive pressure will force Chinese banks to rush for modernisation, in order not to lose market share.

The rest of the chapter is organised as follows. The following section is devoted to an overview of the Chinese economy. Next, the analysis of the structure of China's banking sector and its main reforms, increasingly focussed on transforming the intermediaries into profit making entities is discussed. This is followed by a section addressing the role played by the new breed of JSCBs and CCBs. Their increasing presence is expected to be beneficial because these banks are visibly outperforming SOCBs. The penultimate section tackles the issue of the international integration of the Chinese banking system where, alongside the increasing presence of foreign banks in China, the new phenomenon has recently emerged featuring the largest Chinese banks moving towards a global strategy. Finally, we present our conclusions.

The Chinese economy: an overview

China started its transition from planning to market economics in 1978. The transition has been extremely long because China, differently from Central and Eastern European countries, has followed a very gradual approach. There is a widespread consensus among economists (e.g. Lau, *et al.*, 2000; Stiglitz, 2002) that such a choice was right: (i) it has avoided the tensions linked with the *phasing out* of SOEs; and (ii) it has allowed a certain degree of *institution building* before the privatisation of many economic sectors. Gradual economic transition has allowed it to maintain a significant rate of growth and to smooth the private sector integration into the global economy.

So far, as for GDP growth, such strategy has been successful. GDP has increased by around 10 per cent annually (on average) for the last 25 years, pulled by domestic more than external triggers: saving is striking (45 per cent of GDP at end 2006) and investment (43 per cent of GDP at end 2006) is the main contributor to economic growth. On one hand, buoyant investment might be signalling a bubble in selected sectors. On the other hand, household consumption lags behind because of excessive precautionary saving (Blanchard and Giavazzi, 2006). Chinese households account for 41 per cent of total Chinese saving and the limited modernisation of the financial sector has historically channelled all such savings into banking deposits and – more recently – into the stock exchange, fuelling a potential credit and stock exchange bubble. For instance, new loans were roughly equal to US$443 billion in the first nine months of 2007, which corresponds to a US$26 billion increase for the whole of 2006, while the Shanghai and Shenzen composite index touched an historical record in mid-October (+176 per cent on October 2007). Hence, financial risks are still there for China.

Net export has started contributing significantly to growth only in the last few years, but foreign invested enterprises represent over 50 per cent of Chinese export. The booming trade surplus inflates liquidity and contributes to the excessive pickup in investment. This is partly linked to the Chinese exchange rate policy. The Renminbi's value against the US dollar had been fixed between 1995 and 2005, even resisting pressures for depreciation during the Asian crisis. In July 2005, the Renminbi was revalued by 2.1 per cent (from 8.28 to 8.11) and its value is now set with reference to a basket of currencies. In other words, the exchange rate is highly managed despite recent pro-market reforms, which allow banks and enterprises to hedge. This is confirmed by the limited appreciation versus the US dollar – while the latter was depreciating – which corresponds to a strongly managed depreciation against the euro. In order to slow down a natural appreciation process (which would, instead, be desirable in the presence of a trade surplus exceeding 7 per cent of GDP), the Chinese government is forced to buy huge amounts of foreign currencies (which partly explains the booming international foreign reserves exceeding US$1.4 trillion at the end of 2007). Less than full sterilisation of foreign exchange reserve accumulation has left substantial liquidity in the banking system, and credit growth appears to be accelerating (average credit growth exceeded 15 per cent in 2000–2006), with the likely effect of creating new NPLs in the near future and undoing some of the banking reform progress.

The current situation prompted the authorities to take monetary policy actions and administrative measures to try to contain credit and investment growth. What is peculiar about the Chinese economy is that such a lending boom mostly benefited the SOEs.

Since the mid-1990s the shape of the Chinese corporate sector has started to modify significantly. If we look at the SOEs and non-state-owned industrial enterprises, with sales above 5 million yen, as monitored by the National Bureau of Statistics of China, from 1998 to 2005 the share of private enterprises in the total number of enterprises has increased from 6.5 per cent to 45 per cent, and the share in total valued added from 2.6 per cent to 18 per cent (Figure 2.1). For SOEs the shares decreased, respectively, from 39.2 per cent to 10 per cent and from

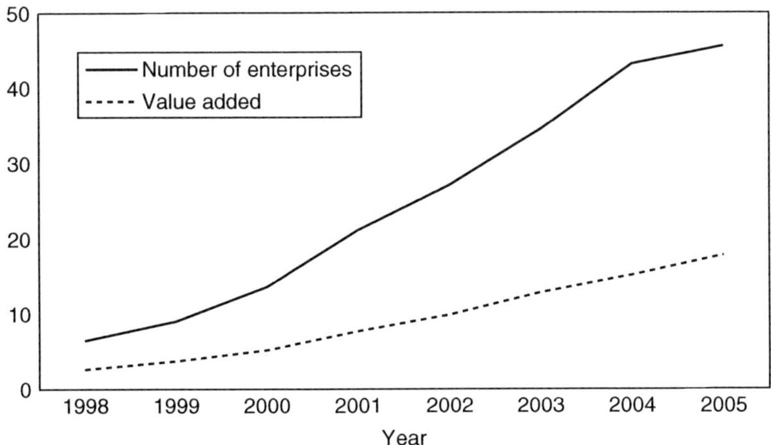

Source: National Bureau of Statistics China.

Figure 2.1 Chinese private enterprises (% of total industrial enterprises)

Table 2.1   Profitability of Chinese enterprises by ownership

	ROA		ROE	
	1998	*2003*	*1998*	*2003*
All enterprises	6.1	12.2	3.8	12.2
State-owned enterprises	4.8	10.2	2	10.2
Collective enterprises	11.2	16.5	10.8	16.5
Private enterprises	7.8	15	6	14.4

Source: OECD, economic surveys, China.

57 per cent to 37.6 per cent of the total. The OECD (2005) reports that according to pre-tax return on equity (ROE) and return on investment (ROA), private firms are more profitable than SOEs, even though profitability is on the rise also for the latter (see Table 2.1). Private firms have a lower level of indebtedness (as a percentage of their assets) and a lower debt/equity ratio as compared to state firms. Nonetheless, debt/equity ratios are decreasing for both private and state owned enterprises.

Notwithstanding such evolution, private companies continue to face difficulties in their access to bank credit, while being more profitable. According to a recent OECD survey (OECD, 2005), about 41 per cent of private enterprises have no access to credit and 56 per cent have no access to bank credit. Smaller private enterprises are more constrained than other firms. For private firms, lack of collateral and discrimination are reported to be the major hurdles. Even though their situation is improving, with a 67 per cent increase in lending between 1998 and 2003, private companies are financially constrained: public ownership in the banking and industrial sectors is one of the reasons behind the fragility of Chinese banking. Indeed, according to Pitsilis *et al.* (2004), SOEs were receiving about 65 per cent of total loans, even if their contribution to the Chinese GDP was around 25 per cent. For private companies, the relative figures are, respectively, 20 per cent and 45 per cent.

Such a lending pattern reflects a limited possibility to enforce rigorous credit standards: central and local governments forced banks to lend to unprofitable SOEs and they still do, albeit although to a lesser extent. State-backed borrowers were often allowed not to repay their debts, with a historically low bankruptcy rate. The political payoff for the government was to keep a low unemployment rate and a high production rate, albeit loss-making. The price was a very high level of NPLs (over 30 per cent of total loans in mid-1990s and around 21 per cent at the end of 2003) and low banks' profitability and competitiveness.

On the other hand, though, such policy can hardly be sustainable in the long run, as the government has to step in and bail out banks once the loans become non-performing.

In addition, this situation is incompatible with an increasing access by foreign players, because domestic banks are not competitive and risk losing market shares. WTO accession forced China to commit to a significant liberalisation of the market access opportunities for foreign banks by December 2006. Thus, the restructuring of the banking system is a crucial issue.

Structure of the Chinese banking system

As of 1978, China had a single bank (The People's Bank of China, PBOC) serving as a commercial bank and as the central bank. Since then, many reforms have changed the banking sector and the financial sector. The former reforms included the foundation of the four big SOCBs in 1978–82, which gave road to a traditional two-tier system and flashed the green light for smaller banks as the JSCBs and the CCBs. Reforms of the whole financial sector included the foundation of the Shenzen and Shanghai stock exchanges, their opening to foreign investors through the Qualified Foreign Institutional Investors schemes, the opening of the bond market to corporates and many others.

So far, the Chinese financial sector depends heavily on banks. Domestic banking credit is above 142.5 per cent of GDP. The total capitalisation of the Shenzen and Shanghai's stock markets, on the other hand, is growing from about 40 per cent of the GDP at the end of 2006, to around 120 per cent of the GDP at the end of 2007. Though, new equity capital raised by domestic companies in 2005 was around 0.22 per cent of the GDP. The corporate debt market is also very small: the outstanding domestic debt was about 11 per cent of GDP at the end of 2005, while international issues were slightly below 1 per cent (0.98 per cent). In short, the banking system provides for most of the financing of Chinese companies' needs. Moreover, China has a very high level of domestic saving, which is mainly generated by the household sector and is mostly deposited into the banking system for lack of alternative instruments (Kuijs, 2006). Therefore, the banking sector plays a crucial intermediation role in the Chinese economy.

In 2007, there were 131 major commercial banks in China. The dominant players are the SOCBs: in order of size, Industrial and Commercial Bank of China, Bank of China, China Construction Bank and Agricultural Bank of China. At the end of 2006, they accounted for 51.3 per cent

Table 2.2   Total assets end of 2006 (% distribution)

	2006
SOCBs	51.3
JSCBs	16.3
CCBs	5.9
Other banking institutions	26.6

Source: CBRC.

of China's total banking assets (Table 2.2). The number of banks recently increased as many urban credit cooperatives were turned into banks (CCBs) and a few new national JSCBs were established. The 115 CCBs and the 12 JSCBs account for 5.9 per cent and 16.3 per cent of the total banking assets respectively. Overall, the above-mentioned banks (SOCBs, JSCBs and CCBs) represent almost 73.5 per cent of the total banking assets.

State ownership is overwhelming if compared with other emerging markets and only India shows comparable figures. State control extends beyond SOCBs. According to the China Banking Regulatory Commission:

- The share of foreign and private ownership in JSCBs is, respectively, 14.3 per cent and 12.1 per cent at the end of 2005. Only Minsheng Bank and Zheshang Bank were still privately controlled at the end of 2006.
- As for the CCBs, foreign and private shares account for 4.2 per cent and 29.4 per cent, respectively, at the end of 2005.

The Chinese banking system has been very fragile for a long time because of the high incidence of NPLs, mostly due to political pressures and the poor commercial ability of many banks. The government made continuous attempts to improve this situation: in 1994, three Policy Banks were set up to free SOCBs from politically motivated lending; the Commercial Bank Law of 1995 established prudential ratios and made banks responsible for their P&L; and in 1998, the Central Bank applied a reserve requirement and encouraged SOCBs to reduce the weight of SOEs in their portfolio. The State was forced to recapitalise SOCBs to bring their capital adequacy ratios (CARs) over 8 per cent. In 1999, four asset-management companies were created to absorb and sell SOCB's NPLs. The results have been unsatisfactory. Notwithstanding such efforts, at the end of 2003 the NPL ratio of Chinese banks was still over 21 per cent of total loans. Many analysts suggest that this is strictly related to excessive links between SOCBs and SOEs as seen above.

Recent reforms in the Chinese banking sector

The institutional structure

Since 2003, the bank restructuring strategy has changed and refocused on transforming the banks in to efficient and listed corporations, while reducing the public support to state enterprises. Also, the institutional structure of the Chinese banking sector has been deeply modified.

Until 2003, the PBOC had many roles (central bank, regulator of the banking system, lender of last resort and ultimate shareholder of the SOCBs): this generated conflicts of interest that reduced PBOC's screening capacity. As a consequence the bank was split up in 2003, with its bank regulatory functions transferred to a new agency, the China Banking Regulatory Commission (CBRC).

PBOC retains interest rate-setting power and overall responsibility for the stability of the financial system. Since 2004, PBOC has largely focused on limiting the impact of high inflows of foreign exchange – driven by speculation over revaluation of the Renminbi – into the country. It has also worked hard to limit investment expansion in some over-heated sectors, such as construction and steel, by restricting the banks' ability to lend.

Monetary tightening started from mid-2004: In October 2004, PBOC raised the benchmark lending rate from 5.31 per cent to 5.58 per cent (in August 2006 the one-year lending base rate was adjusted to 6.12 per cent and the deposit rate to 2.52 per cent), reversing the downtrend of the previous nine years. At the same time, interest rates were liberalised while only lending interest rates in rural areas remain capped. Nonetheless, banks seem to use such pricing opportunity for loan rates (applying spreads on the reference rate), but they do not compete on deposits, applying the reference maximum rate. In 2005–2007, the policy of liberalising interest rates and the deeper use of market-driven instruments continued, with many rate hikes to face increasing inflation. Moreover, since March 2005, PBOC unveiled plans for the setting up of a national credit database. Finally, in order to facilitate liquidity management, PBOC set up a financing mechanism for financial institutions through which they could borrow against collateral, while interbank activity is to be enhanced by the new China interbank offered rate.

Establishment of the CBRC was designed to improve the quality of bank supervision. CBRC – the bank regulator – is charged with overseeing banks and other bank-like financial institutions. It also oversees the planned consolidation of rural credit co-operatives. In 2004, CBRC allowed commercial banks to issue subordinated bonds (followed by similar moves for hybrid bonds) and removed the preferential risk weights (for calculating risk-weighted assets) assigned to large SOEs. CBRC has tightened regulation in an effort to lower NPLs, and to improve risk management and corporate governance at all banks. CBRC issued directives to all of China's big SOCBs to develop internal rating systems in line with the Basel II accord and 'start collecting the necessary data as soon as possible'. Large commercial banks are expected to be Basel compliant by 2012. CBRC has continued to guide the restructuring and oversee listing of the big SOCBs, not only so that they could raise capital but also because they would then be pressurised by shareholders to improve their corporate governance. The introduction of foreign shareholders proceeded cautiously in response to local criticism that banks were being sold off too cheaply to foreigners.

The banking sector

A wave of reforms were also tackling the structure of the banking system. First of all, the Chinese government and supervisory authorities carried out a strategy to transform SOCBs into profit-oriented banks. The strategy relied heavily on: (a) converting the legal status of these state-owned banks into public corporations; (b) requiring banks to apply prudential lending and risk-management techniques; and (c) recapitalising three SOCBs[2] with further sales and write-offs of NPLs at market value as a preliminary step for initial public offerings (IPOs).

Secondly, in order to reduce the potential pressures to save ailing state companies, the State-Owned Assets Supervision and Administration Commission (SASAC) was founded, whose mandate was to consolidate the 196 most strategic SOEs and turn a subsample of them into global champions. Officially, all the other SOEs were left to their own destiny, even though local governments might step in and take some of the most relevant local SOEs under their protection. In 2006, moreover, a long-awaited Bankruptcy Law was introduced.

Last but not least, a more permissive attitude towards banks' listing was envisaged. This was allowed in order to put shareholders' pressure on managers: besides the IPOs by China Construction Bank (2005, US$9.2 billion), by Bank of China (2006, two tranches of US$9.7 billion and US$2.5 billion) and by Industrial and Commercial Bank of China (2006, US$21.9 billion), many other banks recently listed, such as China

Table 2.3 NPL ratios of Chinese banks by ownership

	end 2003	end 2006
SOCBs	20.4	9.2
JSCBs	7.9	2.8
CCBs	15	4.8

Source: CBRC.

Table 2.4 Special mention loans (% of total loans)

	2006
ICBC	9.03
BOC	8.15
CCB	9.25
Bank of Communications	8.06
China CITIC Bank	4.60*
China Merchants Bank	2.03
China Minsheng Banking Corp.	2.60*
Shanghai Pudong Development Bank	4.60*
Huaxia Bank	5.33
Shenzhen Development Bank	6.00*
Industrial Bank	3.30*

Note: * = 2005.
Source: Bank's Report, Fitch (2006).

Merchants Bank (2002), Huaxia Bank (2003) and Bank of Communications (2005) while several others declared to be pursuing the same path.

This new roadmap achieved swift results. While at the end of 2003 the NPL ratio of commercial banks (including rural ones) stood at 21 per cent (of which, 20.4 per cent for SOCBs, 7.9 per cent for JSCBs and 15 per cent for CCBs), it had dropped to 7.1 per cent three years later (9.2 per cent for SOCBs, 2.8 per cent for JSCBs and 4.7 per cent for CCBs; Table 2.3).

The decrease in NPL ratios, however, appears too rapid to be fully genuine and it probably hides potential fragilities.

Major problems can be detected on the accounting side. At the end of 2005, for instance, special mention loans, i.e. loans not yet non-performing, but very likely to become so, were extremely high for many banks (Table 2.4). According to FitchRatings (2006), the total special mention loans corresponded to US$156 billion of future NPLs. Moreover, NPLs might be underestimated as a result of incorrect accounting: a report by Ernst & Young[3] (released and immediately withdrawn under Chinese pressure[4]) estimated that bad debts, including special mention loans, amounted to US$911 billion, i.e. six times the official figure. Although the report's approximations might be excessive, as they are part of an attempt to estimate the potential size of the NPLs market in Asia, they do raise some concerns.

Finally, the economy is flourishing: assets increased by 45 per cent between 2004 and 2006, while GDP grew over 10 per cent year by year. It is extremely unlikely that in such buoyant conditions the NPL ratio could rise: total loans (denominator) grow strongly and their buoyancy helps weak enterprises to repay debts (capping the growth of the numerator). Nonetheless, the test will be a future economic slowdown, once the excessive liquidity dries up. In fact, it seems that excessive liquidity and old-fashioned lending practices triggered over-lending to SOEs and to sectors characterised by an overcapacity (e.g. real estate, where investment recorded a double-digit growth since 2000). So far, SOCBs estimate that less than 2 per cent of the loans made since 1999 are non-performing. However, average loan maturities increased and anecdotal evidence indicates that banks are already rolling over loans to fragile SOEs. In the presence of a more moderate growth pattern many of such loans might turn out to be non-performing.

Moreover, Chinese banks are among the few banks from emerging markets directly exposed to the recent sub-prime crisis (Chiarlone, 2007). Bank of China reported a significant exposure US$9.7 billion to US sub-prime mortgages, while ICBC and CCB aknowledged an exposure of over a billion dollars each. Dynamic earnings and the recent capital increases should allow them to absorb any such losses. A more widespread Chinese contagion is avoided by the fact that Chinese banks need a special licence to operate with financial derivatives and the holding of foreign securities is very limited beyond the big banks. Finally, the Chinese government has considerable funds available to save state banks, should any other problem arise.

All such risks imply that the restructuring process of Chinese banks is not yet over. It is important that it focuses on prudent lending and on modern risk-management techniques, including:

- proper credit evaluation and risk-management tools;
- improvement of staff quality through the training of existing personnel;
- development of better NPLs' management and debt restructuring capabilities.

Furthermore, an increasing competitive pressure on the main public banks by second-tier banks could trigger the SOCBs' faster modernisation and transformation into fully commercial entities. Also, the international competition from foreign banks entering the Chinese market and the cooperation with strategic foreign partners could also be an important push factor for Chinese banks to proceed swiftly towards modernisation. However, access by foreign banks is still not completely free.

The new breed of Joint Stock Commercial Banks and City Commercial Banks[5]

For the sake of simplicity, we will lable New Tigers the sum of the JSCBs and CCBs. The New Tigers are growing very rapidly. Even though truly private commercial banks have been largely absent from China, and in spite of belonging to different institutional categories, the New Tigers share a common trait distinguishing them from the SOCBs. Contrary to SOCBs, which – until their listing – have had the state as the single shareholder, the New Tigers have a plurality of shareholders. Some of these shareholders may themselves belong to the public sector, being part either of the public administration or of the SOE system, but none of them is in the position of a single shareholder in any of the New Tigers. As argued elsewhere (Ferri, 2003), the plurality of shareholders may significantly reduce political interference in banks' business, thus delivering better corporate governance and performance.

This conjecture seems consistent with what is observed over the years. Namely, the New Tigers are denting the SOCBs' market share more and more, and also the former visibly outperform the latter by conventional indicators. Between 1998 and 2005, the annual rate of growth of total assets of the New Tigers constantly outpaced that of the SOCBs, with the only exception of the first year – when the Asian crisis also caused in China a shift by depositors to the largest banks, possibly perceived as *too big to fail* – and in the latest year – when the SOCBs' rate of growth slighty overcame that of the New Tigers (Table 2.5). This gap produced a significant erosion for the SOCBs while the market share of the New Tigers, conversely, almost doubled from 12.8 per cent to 23.9 per cent. Even more importantly, the New Tigers made such significant gains in market share while achieving much higher returns than the SOCBs. Indeed, between 1998 and 2005 the ROA of SOCBs was always lower, usually much lower, than for the New Tigers: on average, the two groups of banks reached, respectively, 0.264 per cent and 0.611 per cent (Table 2.5). A similar indication may be derived by looking at the New Tigers' ability to generate remuneration on their own capital: between 1998 and 2005, in spite of

Table 2.5　Total assets, ROA and ROE: SOCBs vs New Tigers and CCBs

Year	Growth rate (%)			ROA (%)			ROE (%)			Market Share (%)	
	SOCBs	New Tigers	CCBs	SOCBs	New Tigers	CCBs	SOCBs	New Tigers	CCBs	New Tigers	CCBs
1998	16.3	12.6	19.2	0.096	0.807	1.673	2.211	7.949	5.948	12.8	1.9
1999	9.4	20.2	22.2	0.126	0.585	1.010	2.450	7.964	6.846	14.1	2.2
2000	11.3	28.4	29.7	0.182	0.542	0.815	3.639	8.583	6.133	15.7	2.5
2001	6.9	25.2	33.5	0.164	0.644	0.594	3.202	11.259	7.029	18.7	2.8
2002	11.1	29.1	39.5	0.182	0.547	0.464	3.682	9.003	7.037	21.5	3.0
2003	12.1	27.7	19.0	0.077	0.480	0.335	1.583	8.171	9.146	22.1	3.1
2004	6.8	19.4	13.5	0.662	0.554	0.313	7.452	11.463	6.342	23.8	3.2
2005	19.4	17.9	13.2	0.621	0.729	0.445	−2.071	13.949	6.922	23.9	3.3
Average	–	–	–	0.264	0.611	0.706	2.769	9.793	6.925	–	–

Source: authors' calculations from on Bankscope database.

their low capital, SOCBs' ROE kept on average at 2.769 per cent, while that of the New Tigers stood at 9.793 per cent.

As for the CCBs – which are part of the New Tigers – they also experienced high growth, resulting in an increase in their market share from 1.9 per cent to 3.3 per cent and displaying good performance both in terms of ROA (0.706 per cent) and in terms of ROE (6.925 per cent).

The issue that arises is whether the New Tigers offer China a 'growing out' option to overcome the difficulties in restructuring its SOCBs and, through this, bring better banking to China. Certainly, one might envisage a positive answer if the New Tigers were to continue the rapid growth of the latest decade (Ferri, 2005). However, there is no guarantee that this is based on solid economic reasoning. To be sure, the continuation of that growth postulates that the New Tigers really enjoy a competitive edge across the board *vis-à-vis* SOCBs. But is this really the case? One way to address this issue is assessing whether the better performance of the New Tigers is fully grounded in better governance. It is exactly at this juncture that we notice a second trait distinguishing the New Tigers from SOCBs. The New Tigers concentrate their business in the most developed part of China, its vibrant Eastern Belt, while on the other hand, SOCBs operate throughout the whole of the country.

As a result, it is not clear whether the New Tigers' better performance is owed entirely to better governance or whether geography plays a big part. For instance, according to Huang (2002), SOCBs generate 95 per cent of their profits from about half a dozen of the coastal cities, including Shenzhen, Guangzhou, Xiamen, Shanghai, Tianjin, and Beijing. If this is true, then doubts are cast on the possibility that the growth of the New Tigers can provide an effective solution to the banking problem outside the affluent Eastern Belt. As a consequence, to gauge how much of a solution the New Tigers may offer, we need to consider in more depth how far geography (i.e. favourable bank location) lies behind their strong performance.

By focusing on 20 CCBs – which share analogous corporate governance setups – that are located in three provinces with differing levels of development, Ferri (2008) is able to ascribe any significant difference in performance across provinces to their relative underlying prosperity. His results show that these banks' performance was systematically and positively related to the level of economic prosperity in their provinces.

The main result of the econometric analysis implies that the New Tigers may be unable by themselves to bring better banking to the whole of China. This suggests that authorities are right when they stress the need to restructure and rehabilitate the SOCBs. While the authorities'

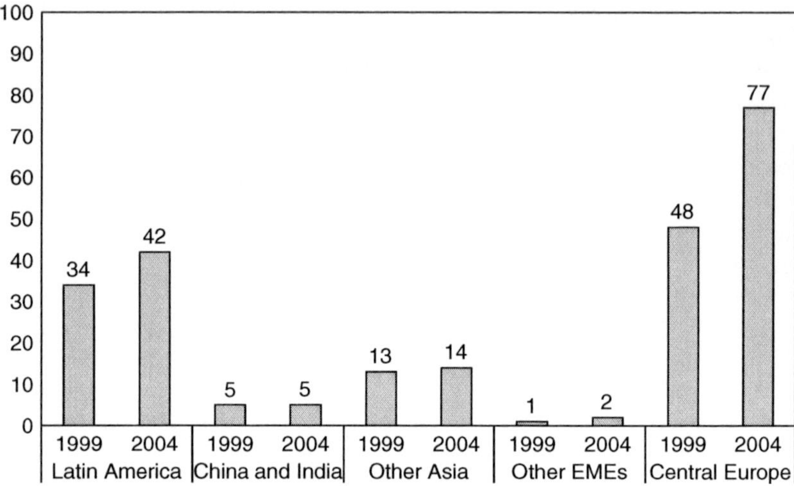

Source: Mihaljek, D. (2006).

Figure 2.2   Foreign-owned banks: share in total bank credit (%)

push to transform SOCBs into public companies goes in the right direction, it is not clear whether stock-exchange listing can really, per se, improve these banks' corporate governance. Given their size and considering that the government could continue to be the largest shareholder, doubts are legitimate. Perhaps, as suggested by Huang (2002), it would be advisable for China's authorities to consider breaking up SOCBs. Together with stock-exchange listing, this would help streamline SOCBs and could also facilitate the introduction of foreign strategic investors, thus contributing to improve their governance.

International integration of the Chinese banking system

So far, the presence of foreign banks is limited as compared to other emerging economies (Figure 2.2). In June 2006, foreign banks had 208 branches and sub-branches, plus 241 representative offices. Their total assets amounted to US$84.5 billion at the end of 2005 (1.9 per cent of the total banking assets) and posted an NPL ratio below 1 per cent. Major players are Asian and British banks, together with Citibank (Table 2.6).

There are many reasons behind such low penetration by foreign banks. The chief ones are the following:

- Independent operations were restricted until the end of 2001. The WTO-related liberalisation has been very gradual.
- Foreign buy-out was quite impossible until the early 2000s.

Table 2.6   Leading foreign banks in China

	Origin	Branches and sub-branches	Representative offices
HSBC	UK	13	3
Bank of East Asia	Hong Kong	12	5
Standard Chartered Bank	UK	8	7
Hang Seng Bank	Hong Kong	8	2
Citibank	US	7	3
Nanyang Commercial Bank	Hong Kong	6	0
Sumitomo Mitsui Banking Corp	Japan	5	4
OCBC	Singapore	5	3
Bank of Tokyo Mitsubishi	Japan	5	3
ABN AMRO Bank	Japan	5	3

Source: Almanac of China's Finance and Banking, 2005.

The government recognised recently that foreign competition is beneficial for the modernisation of the banking system; it also stated, however, that the control of domestic banks must stay in national hands. As a consequence, a full opening of the Chinese market to foreign capital can only take place on the condition that major domestic banks become competitive enough to survive as independent entities. By preventing foreign pressure from biting into Chinese banks' P&L, this strategy nevertheless discourages restructuring and delays the modernisation process.

The situation is slowly changing. Two key events are likely to bear an impact. First, according to the statements released by CBRC, no increase in the 20 per cent cap on individual foreign investment in local banks is in the pipeline (with a 25 per cent limit on total foreign holdings). Secondly, in accordance with China's WTO commitments, the Chinese State Council promulgated the new Regulations on the Administration of Foreign-Funded Banks (effective from 11 December 2006).

According to most analysts, the 20 per cent limit implies that the main road to a significant penetration of the Chinese market is a strategic minority cooperation with a domestic bank, waiting (and hoping) for an increase in the cap. In the short run, this option allows foreign banks to sell their products and, in the medium run, could provide a first-come first-serve advantage, should the privatisation of Chinese banks take place in the future. Nonetheless, no such increase is to be expected soon, because China will probably wait for its banks to be competitive before any further opening. There is some consensus on the fact that a majority ownership by foreign banks is more likely to be allowed, if ever,

Table 2.7   Foreign investment in Chinese banks

Invested bank	Foreign presence	(US$ m)
ICBC	Goldman Sachs (5.8%), Allianz (3.2%), and AmEx (0.8%)	3800.0
Bank of China	RBS (9.6%), Merryl Linch (2.5%), UBS (1.6%) and Temasek (4.8%)	6700.0
China Construction Bank	Bank of America (8.5%) and Tamasek (6%)	5500.0
Bank of Communications	HSBC (19.9%)	1750.0
Citic	BBVA (5% and may increase to 9.9%)	501.0
Shanghai Pudong Development Bank	Citibank (4.6%)	72.5
Minsheng Banking Corporation	IFC (1.1%) and Temasek (4.6%)	123.5
Industrial Bank	Hang Seng Bank (15.6%) and IFC (4%)	260.0
China Everbright Bank	ADB (3.3%)	20.0
Guangdong Development Bank	Citigroup (20%) and IBM (4.74%) plus local partners (60%)	3100.0
Shenzen Development Bank	Newbridge Capital (17.9%) and GE Consumer Finance (7%)	249.0
Hua xia Bank	Deutsche Bank (9.9% and may rise to 20%) and Sai Oppenheim (4.1%)	270.0
Bohai Bank	Standard Chartered (19.99)	123.0
Bank of Beijing	ING Bank (19.9%) and the IFC (5%)	270.0
Bank of Shanghai	HSBC (8%) and the IFC (7%)	112.9
Tianjin City Commercial Bank	ANZ Banking Group (19.9%)	120.0
Dalian City Commercial Bank	Rumours about Bank of Nova Scotia (20%) and the IFC (5%)	370.0
Hangzhou City Commercial Bank	Commonwealth Bank of Australia (19.9%) and ADB (5%)	106.0
Nanjing Commercial Bank	IFC (15%) and BNP Paribas (19.2%)	113.4
Jinan City Commercial Bank	Commonwealth Bank of Australia (11% and may rise to 20%)	17.3

Source: press and company reports.

in second-tier medium-sized Chinese banks only, while major banks are bound to stay public and Chinese. Some economists (e.g. Bottelier, 2005) suggest that, as some second-tier Chinese banks whose foreign ownership is close to 20 per cent are preparing for IPOs, this might imply that the limit will be dropped sooner of later. In this context, the US$23 billion-worth acquisitions by foreign banks (Table 2.7) might be an attempt to take position in Chinese banks with a national licence, in order to be ready to grow if and when the 20 per cent limit will be raised.

On the other hand, the new regulation provides a different strategy to tap the domestic customers in local currency (Table 2.8). In fact, banks that either turn their branches into wholly foreign-funded local banks (WFFB) or create a Sino-foreign joint venture (JV) will be allowed to carry out all the major activities in domestic currency; however, they will be fully subject to the Chinese regulation. If instead they keep running their activities through foreign branches, they will be prevented from dealing with local customers in renmimbi and will be submitted to tighter capitalisation rules. According to some analysts, this might represent an alternative path, albeit slower, to a stable and widespread presence in China. So far, altogether twelve foreign banks have been allowed to incorporate their Chinese branches into local subsidiaries: Citibank, Hang Seng Bank, Standard Chartered, HSBC, Mizuho Corporate Bank, Bank of Tokyo–Mitsubishi UFJ Ltd, DBS Bank, ABNAMRO, Wing Hang Bank, Oversea-Chinese Banking Corp., JPMorgan Chase Bank and the Bank of East Asia. Among these, JPMorgan Chase Bank will register its local subsidiaries in Beijing, Wing Hang Bank in Shenzhen and the other ten in Shanghai.

Most recent developments relate also to the increasing growth of Foreign Direct Investment (FDI) by Chinese banks. They might, indeed, be feeling pressure to expand their business overseas amid official efforts to cool down the economy. In the latest round of tightening measures, the banking authority has reportedly ordered domestic banks to freeze new loans and maintain overall lending at mid-October levels for the rest of the year.

So far, the Chinese flows of outward FDI was US$3.5 billion in 2006, among which the banking industry invested US$2.5 billion.[6] By the end of 2006, the accumulated stock of outward FDI was US$15.6 billion, among which US$12.3 billion originated from the banking industry alone. By the end of 2006, the Chinese SOCBs had established 47 branch offices, 31 affiliated institutions and 12 representative offices in 19 countries (regions) including the United States, Japan and Britain, etc. hiring more than 20,000 local staff. This is definitely only the start of the game. In fact, also boosted by growing capitalisation, while that of Western banks is dented by the sub-prime crisis, Chinese banks are starting to look at M&A operations as buyers. For instance, in 2006, CCB agreed to buy Bank of America's Hong Kong and Macau unit for US$1.24 billion, the largest overseas acquisition by a Chinese lender. CCB defined the purchase is a step toward creating a leading international lender.

More operations surfaced in 2007 totalling a reported value of US$10.7 billion. The deals include China Development Bank's injection

Table 2.8 Main rules according to the new regulation

WFFB and JV	*Not locally incorporated foreign banks*
Only commercial banks which have assets over US$10 billion and have had a representative office for at least 2 years can control WFFB	Can establish branches only where a representative office has been established for at least 2 years, provided total assets are over US$20 billion
Only commercial banks which have assets over US$10 billion and have had a representative office for at least 2 years can form a JV	If more than one branch is established, one branch must be designated for the overall management of all branches
Every branch must have a working capital of RMB 100m (US$12.5m) (Total branches' working capital must be below 60% of the bank's capital)	Every branch must receive a working capital amounting to no less than RMB200m (about US$25m)
Minimum paid-up registered capital is RMB 1 billion (US$125m)	Every branch must have: 30% of its operating capital in interest banking assets. RMB operating capital and reserves equal to no less than 8% of its RMB risk assets; a current ratio of no less than 25% and no more total domestic liabilities
WFFB and JV which have been doing business in China for 3 years and have been profitable for two consecutive years may engage in almost all banking activities	Branches cannot carry out bank card and RMB business for PRC citizens. They may receive time deposits from them for an amount of no less than RMB 1m each.

of US\$3 billion into Barclays. In October, the Industrial and Commercial Bank of China announced an agreement to acquire 20 per cent of South Africa's Standard Bank for US\$5.46 billion; and to plan opening a subsidiary in the United States, as part of its going-global strategy that also involves Russia, Indonesia and the Middle East. In October 2007, Bear Stearns and China's Citic Securities revealed plans to invest US\$1 billion in each other and Minsheng Bank said that by 2009 it could become the biggest single shareholder of UCBH Holdings by acquiring a 20 per cent stake in three phases. UCBH Holdings is the holding company of United Commercial Bank, a leading bank in the US serving Chinese communities and American companies doing business in China. The deal is the first strategic investment in a banking institution in the United States by a Chinese bank. Finally, in November 2007 there have been rumours that Industrial and Commercial Bank of China, Bank of China and China Construction Bank approached – with negative results – the Singaporean state investment agency Temasek, seeking to buy its 17 per cent equity of Standard Chartered, which makes 90 per cent of its profits from emerging markets.

Conclusions

The Chinese financial system is still not completely restructured, as NPLs remain at uncomfortable levels. The presence of foreign banks is low, but is likely to increase in the near future. A greater role for foreign banks could contribute to the modernisation of the Chinese financial system and push domestic players towards higher competitiveness and prudential lending, with positive impacts on the overall stability. Nonetheless, it is unlikely that foreign banks will acquire in China the level of control that they have in Central and Eastern Europe. A possible outcome is that China might become a continental banking area with a few strong state national champions (few of which could gain international relevance in line with the Chinese go global policy), many mid-sized domestic banks (even privatised or foreign controlled) and an increasing role for the major foreign global players, through either M&A or organic growth.

Notes

1. For simplicity, throughout the chapter we will keep calling the big four as State Owned Commercial Banks. Though this is correct in practice – as the state still

holds majority – the definition is not formally tight for the three of them which have been listed.
2. Bank of China and China Construction Bank were injected US$22.5 billion each in 2004, whereas the Industrial and Commercial Bank of China received US$15 billion in 2005. Agricultural Bank of China, the weakest one, is expected to receive similar assistance.
3. McGregor (2006), 'China Bad Loans May Reach Total of $900 billion', *The Financial Times*, 3 May.
4. McGregor (2006), 'Beijing Attacks E&Y Report on Bad Debt as "ridiculous"', *The Financial Times*, 13 May.
5. This section draws partly on Ferri, (forthcoming), 'Are New Tigers Supplanting Old Mammoths in China's Banking System?: Evidence from a Sample of City Commercial Banks', *Journal of Banking and Finance*.
6. Ministry of Foreign Commerce of the People Republic of China (2007), '2006 Statistical Bulletin of China's Outward Foreign Direct Investment'.

References

Blanchard, O. and Giavazzi, F. (2006) 'Rebalancing Growth in China: A Three Handed Approach', MIT Department of Economics Working Paper No. 05-32.

Bottelier, P. (2005) 'Testimony to the 8/11/05 Hearing of the United States-China Economic and Security Review Commission on The General Health of China's Banking System'.

Chiarlone, S. (2007) 'An introduction to Potential Channel of Contagion to Emerging Markets', UniCredit Group, Banking and Finance Monitor No. 1.

Ferri, G. (2003) 'Corporate Governance in Banking and Economic Performance – Future Options for PRC', Asian Development Bank Institute Discussion Paper No. 3, August.

Ferri, G. (2005) 'Banking in the People's Republic of China: Are New Tigers Supplanting Old Mammoths?', Asian Development Bank Institute Discussion Paper No. 35, September.

Ferri, G. (forthcoming) 'Are New Tigers Supplanting Old Mammoths in China's Banking System?: Evidence from a Sample of City Commercial Banks', *Journal of Banking and Finance*.

FitchRatings (2006) *China: Taking Stock of Banking System NPLs*. (New York: Fitch, 2006).

Huang, Y. (2002) 'Is Meltdown of the Chinese Banks Inevitable?', *China Economic Review* 13, 382–7.

Kuijs, L. (2006) '*How Will China's Saving-Investment Balance Evolve?*' World Bank Policy Research Paper 3958.

Lau, L.J., Qian, Y. and Roland, G. (2000) 'Reform Without Losers: An Interpretation of China's Dual-Track Approach to Transition', *The Journal of Political Economy* 108-1, 120–43.

McGregor, R. (2006) 'Beijing Attacks E&Y Report on Bad Debt as "Ridiculous"', *The Financial Times*, 13, May.

McGregor, R. (2006) 'China Bad Loans May Reach Total of $900 billion', *The Financial Times*, 3 May.

Ministry of Foreign Commerce of the People Republic of China (2007), '2006 Statistical Bulletin of China's Outward Foreign Direct Investment'.

OECD (2005) *Economic Survey of China 2005*, (Paris: OECD).

Opper, S. (2001) 'Dual-Track Ownership Reforms: Lessons from Structural Change in China, 1978–1997', *Post Communist Economies* 13(2), 205–27.

Pitsilis, E.V., Woetzel, J.R. and Wong, J. (2004) 'Checking China's vital signs', *Mckinsey Quarterly*, Special Edition: China Today.

Stiglitz, J.E. (2002) *Globalization and Its Discontents*, (New York, London: W.W. Norton).

3
India

S. Chiarlone and S. Ghosh

Introduction

After three post-independence decades of inadequate progress, India grew at 6 per cent per annum from 1980 to 2002 and at 7.6 per cent from 2002 through 2007. Its rising path has been unique: rather than exporting labour-intensive, low-priced manufactured goods, India relied on its domestic market more than on exports, consumption more than investment, services more than industry and high-tech more than low-skilled manufacturing. Moreover, 30–40 per cent of GDP growth depends on rising productivity rather than on increases in the amount of capital or labour (Rodrik and Subramanium, 2005). Bosworth and Collins (2007) document that, over the period 1993–2004, 2.3 per cent of the growth (out of a total of 6.5 per cent) was accounted for by productivity changes. This suggests that India's reform processes has been able to obtain results in terms of better incentives and competition, inducing improvements in productivity.

As a result of to the stronger contribution by domestic demand, the economy has been relatively insulated from major global turmoil. Nonetheless, such features did not spare India from an external crisis in the early 1990s that triggered wide reforms. Moreover, the strong reliance on high-tech raises doubts about India's growth inclusiveness. While the consumption-driven model is people-friendly, in order to lift millions of households out of poverty and create jobs for its rapidly expanding working age population, India would need to strengthen its traditional manufacturing sector, although experts have questioned the validity of this proposition (See Rajan, 2008).[1]

As for Indian banking, it has lived through three phases, so far. The first one (before 1969), was dominated by private ownership. The government nationalised most banks in 1969 and in 1980, and imposed quantitative targets and tight administrative constraints. Financial liberalisation started in 1992, with reforms aimed at increasing stability and competitiveness. India is now on track to create a modern financial system. Skeptics, though, point to the still high weight of the public sector, the major remaining constraints relate to foreign ownership and statutory priority lending and the remaining indications of credit exclusion (the words 'credit' and 'advances' are used interchangeably).

From protectionism to liberalisation

Indian growth averaged 3.5 per cent from 1950 to 1980. In this so called 'Hindu' growth rate period, India adopted an import substitution and infant industry strategy. India pursued nationalisation in many sectors (including banking), high public investment in infrastructure and implemented a centralised planning strategy. Such an approach yielded good growth rates during 1951–64: about 4.3 per cent. Nonetheless, from 1965 to 1980, growth slowed down significantly (annual GDP growth averaged 2.9 per cent), in part due to the failure of the centralised planning strategy, other than to external factors such as drought and 'oil shocks'. The economy had, in fact, become overtly controlled and rigid, and largely closed to international trade and investment; such a development strategy implied that entrepreneurship was heavily constrained. That was no longer acceptable in a rapidly globalising world.

In the early 1980s, India embarked on a path of economic reforms in the so-called *Bharatiya* (meaning, Indian) growth period. Modest liberal reforms – especially lowering marginal tax rates and tariffs and providing some leeway to manufacturers – revived average growth to 5.6 per cent. A pro-active attitude towards the private sector contributed strongly to an improvement in the scenario. However, by the start of the 1990s, profligateness brought India to the brink of a balance of payments crisis with a realistic threat of sovereign default; fiscal deficits increased significantly, while inflation crept up to uncomfortable levels. These developments triggered wide-ranging pro-liberalisation reforms and much more attention to fiscal health. All such reforms laid the groundwork for increasingly high growth rates, averaging 6.2 per cent in 1993–2000 and over 7.5 per cent since 2003.

Financial sector reform was central. Introduction of some operational autonomy in state-owned banks, entry of new private and of a greater number of foreign banks, and (limited) permission for foreign investment in banking were some of the major measures. Besides, prudential regulation was strengthened, in line with international best practices. The capital market has been revived with policy reforms, financial infrastructure strengthened and an improved payment and settlement architecture developed. Among major interventions, we signal the 1992 abolition of the Controller of Capital Issues (CCI), which was in charge of both controlling the issuance of securities and administering their price; such reform liberalised the issuing of corporate bonds and the subsequent demutualisation of the stock exchange.

The bank nationalisation period

After independence, national savings were low and supplied mainly by households. The banking sector was invested of a very important intermediation role. By 1951, there were 566 banks in India. When so, many rural and semi-urban areas were not well serviced. Also, the bulk of credit was directed towards large corporates, at the expense of the agricultural and small and medium enterprises (SMEs). The All-India Rural Credit Survey Committee reported that out of the total borrowings of farmers of about Rs7.5 billion, commercial banks provided less than 1 per cent, while money lenders accounted for an overwhelming 70 per cent (Reserve Bank of India [RBI], 1954).

Such features were not in line with the national objective of achieving equitable allocation of credit. Therefore, the Reserve Bank of India[2] (RBI) was encouraged to promote credit, with special attention being paid to agriculture. Moreover, since 1967 a Bill imposed extensive social control over banks and banking policy. Banks were required to implement the government's objectives of improving banking access of rural areas and SMEs. These developments culminated in a two-stage bank nationalisation process, in 1969 and in 1980,[3] aimed at ensuring that financial intermediaries met the credit demands fully according to national priorities. In fact, political economy considerations and borrowers' needs gained primacy over the financial viability of the banking sector. Such choices were supported by an intensified public control over the financial system through various measures such as active mobilisation of savings through bank-dominated network, directed lending, interest rate regulation, etc. Moreover, we signal the separation between banks (allowed to receive deposits and extend short term credit) and Development Finance Institutions and Non Bank Financial Institutions (allowed to finance themselves in the capital market and extend medium and long term credit) (Mor *et al.*, 2006).

Table 3.1 Progress of commercial banking

	June 1969	Dec. 1980	Mar. 1991	Mar. 2000	Mar. 2006	Mar. 2007
No. of commercial banks	73	154	272	297	222	183
No. of bank offices in India	8262	34594	60570	67868	71685	73836
Of which						
Rural & semi urban	5175	23227	46115	47428	46247	47044
Population/bank office (000s)	64	16	14	15	16	16
Deposits (Rsbn)	46.5	404.4	2011.9	8515.9	21090.5	26083.1
Per capita deposit (Rs)	88	738	2368	8247	19130	23382
Credit (Rsbn)	35.9	250.8	1218.7	4540.7	15070.8	19289
Per capita credit (Rs)	68	457	1434	4705	13869	17541
Total asset (Rsbn)	68.4	710.8	3275.2	11516.2	27858.6	34634.1
Asset/GDP	0.18	0.59	0.58	0.59	0.86	0.93

Source: Reserve Bank of India, Annual Report, Report on Trend and Progress of Banking in India; statistical tables relating to banks in India, various issues.

Two important facets of banking during the post-nationalisation period deserve mention. The first was 'priority sector lending': both the State Bank of India, and the nationalised banks including private banks were required to lend at least a fixed percentage of credit to agriculture and small-scale industry (RBI, 1983). Such requirements, initially stipulated at 33 per cent of bank credit, were, over a period of time, raised to 40 per cent with sub-targets for agriculture and small-scale industry. Secondly, the branch licensing policy entailed banks to open four branches in unbanked locations for every branch opened elsewhere. Such policy increased the scope of banking in India to a scale unique to its level of development: by 2000, India had over 60,000 bank branches, spanning every district across the country. The compound growth rate of branch expansion, which was 8.7 per cent in the decade before nationalisation jumped to nearly 12 per cent in the following decades. Deposits and credit also witnessed concomitant increases, with growth rates of 21.3 per cent and 19 per cent, respectively, in the post-nationalisation period as compared with around 12 per cent in the preceding decade (Table 3.1), with a greater share of credit devoted to rural areas and agricultural uses. Burgess and Pande (2005) showed that the re-distributive nature of branch expansion led to a substantial decline in rural poverty.

The statutory control on banking business during the nationalisation phase was set to very high levels. Since their institution, scheduled banks[4] were required to maintain a minimum cash reserve ratio of 5 per cent of their demand liabilities and 5 per cent of their time liabilities on a daily basis. In 1962, RBI was empowered to vary the CRR between 3 per cent and 15 per cent of the total demand and time liabilities. In addition, banks had also to maintain liquid assets in cash, gold and government securities not less than 20 per cent of their net-demand-and-time-deposit liabilities (Statutory Liquidity Ratio, SLR). The RBI can still use the CRR to influence bank credit and system liquidity.[5] Besides, the RBI was empowered to decide minimum lending rates on various types of advances. In addition, RBI acquired extensive powers of supervision and control of commercial banks over the years. This was crucial since bank failures were a major problem during this and earlier periods (Desai, 1967).[6] The threat to risk sharing on account of financial stability underscored by the Diamond and Dybvig (1983) framework provided a rationale for a public deposit insurance scheme. In the face of bank runs in the 1960s, especially of two prominent banks of that time, the Palai Central Bank and the Laxmi Bank, a Deposit Insurance and Credit Guarantee Corporation was established as a fully-owned subsidiary of the RBI in 1962.[7]

Overall, by the end of the 1980s, the financial system was stretched and credit allocation schemes plus reserve requirements had severely restricted the freedom of intermediation: lending to unprofitable businesses with limited guarantee of recovery of funds raised costs, adversely impacted the quality of assets and strained profitability. Moreover inadequate prudential norms and risk management practices, contributed to growing non-performing loan (NPL) ratios. On the expenditure front, the quantitative restrictions (branch licensing and restrictions on new lines of business) and inflexible management structures severely constrained the functional autonomy of banks. As the quality of asset portfolio of banks rapidly deteriorated, it was evident that the profitability of the banking system was severely compromised.

The banking reforms

The unprecedented balance-of-payments crisis of the early 1990s, coupled with limited public resources for investment or provision of public services, rapidly brought forth the imperatives for financial sector strengthening. It was recognised that the success of the economy is contingent on a healthy financial system. India started a banking sector reform package in 1992. The thrust of the reforms was to promote a diversified, efficient and competitive financial system. Its first phase was guided by the recommendations of the Committee on the Financial System which proposed to bring about 'operational flexibility' and 'functional autonomy' so as to enhance 'efficiency, productivity and profitability' (Government of India, 1991). The second stage of the reforms paid more attention towards strengthening the foundations of the banking system and make it internationally competitive (Government of India, 1998).

The approach to reforms is based on five principles (Reddy, 2004): cautious and proper sequencing; mutually reinforcing measures; complementarities between reforms in banking sector and changes in fiscal, external and monetary policies; developing financial infrastructure; and developing financial markets. The reforms were carefully sequenced: prudential norms and supervisory strengthening were introduced early, followed by interest rate deregulation and gradual lowering of statutory preemption, while legal and accounting measures were ushered in only when the basic tenets of the reforms were already in place. Concurrently, a process of gradualism was pursued along with a process of continuous consultation with all stakeholders: such involvement enhanced the credibility of policies (Ahluwalia, 1993, 2002). Another positive feature has been the constant rebalancing of priorities according to evolution of the business environment, and its harmonisation with other policies: recognising the inter-linkages, wide-ranging reforms were also undertaken in the real sector so that financial intermediation kept pace with underlying economic activity. Finally, the reforms were characterised by non-reversals, taking on board the views of all stakeholders (Mohan, 2005).

Among the various reforms, it is worthwhile to highlight the reduction in the high levels of statutory pre-emption (i.e. CRR reduced to 7.5 per cent from 15.5 per cent in 1991 and SLR reduced to its statutory minimum of 25 per cent from 37.5 per cent in 1991) and rationalisation of the interest rate structure to make it market-determined, with few minor exceptions (e.g. savings deposits). The RBI has, also, progressively widened the definition of the priority sector to include more commercially viable lending options and brought the interest rates on such loans more in line with commercial lending practices, even if domestic banks must still devote at least 40 per cent of their loan portfolio to priority sectors (agriculture, small-scale industries, retail trade and small businesses) and foreign banks 32 per cent.

Since the onset of reforms, clear and transparent guidelines were laid down for the establishment of private banks and an easier access for foreign banks was allowed, in order to increase competitive pressures. Based on deposits and credit, the Herfindahl index of concentration, which were 0.081 and 0.104, respectively in 1992, have declined to 0.063 and 0.058, respectively, in 2004 (Mohan, 2006). A precondition for new banks was to be fully computerised, in order to infuse technological efficiency and push existing banks in the same direction.

At the same time, the weight of the public sector in banking has been reduced. Moreover, the ownership base in state-owned banks has been diversified. The regulations were amended to enable these banks to raise private capital, not exceeding 49 per cent of their equity, in order for the government to retain majority shareholding.[8] Equity sales in the market aggregating around Rs180 billion (US$4.5 billion) have been made by these banks, with several banks making subsequent follow-on offerings. Over the period 1993–2007, as many as 20 state-owned banks have accessed the capital market. At present, state-owned banks with 100 per cent government ownership comprise only around 10 per cent of commercial bank assets compared to around 90 per cent at the beginning of reforms.

A set of progressively tighter micro-prudential measures were instituted, with the objective of benchmarking against international best practices. Risk-based capital standards were hiked to 9 per cent, effective from March 2000. Asset classification into doubtful, sub-standard and standard assets and related provisioning requirements were strengthened (Table 3.2). Also rules on exposure limits for single and group borrowers, accounting rules, and investment valuation norms were improved. As part of such effort, the process of regulation and supervision has been strengthened with a strategy of on-site inspection and off-site surveillance, together with greater accountability of external auditors. In such a context, the RBI has been focusing on ensuring 'fit and proper' owners and directors of the bank (banks have been advised to ensure that a nomination committee screens the nominated and elected directors) and laying stress on diversified ownership.

As for Basel II, banks will initially adopt Standardised Approach for credit risk and Basic Indicator Approach for operational risk. After adequate skills are developed, some banks may be allowed to migrate to the Internal Rating Approach. From 2008, capital adequacy levels will be determined by a three-track approach. On the first track, commercial banks would be required to maintain capital for both credit and operational risks as per Basel II framework. The cooperative banks, on the second track, are required to maintain capital for credit risk as per Basel I framework and through surrogates for market risk; and the regional rural

Table 3.2 Evolution of prudential requirements from 1992–93 to 2006–2007

	1992–93	*1995–96*	*1999–2000*	*2001–2002*	*2003–2004*	*2006–2007*
1. CAR statutory minimum (% of risk weighted assets)						
Domestic banks with international business	4	8	9	9	9	9
Other domestic banks	4	8	9	9	9	9
Foreign banks	8	8	9	9	9	9
2. Number of quarters after which asset are defined as non-performing						
Sub-standard assets	4	2	2	2	1	1
Doubtful assets	8	8	8	6	6	4
3. Provisioning requirements (% of corresponding asset): statutory minimum						
Standard asset			0.25	0.25	0.25	0.4*
Sub-standard asset	10	10	10	10	10	10
Doubtful asset						
Secured portion #**	20–50	20–50	20–50	20–50	20–50	20–50
Unsecured portion	100	100	100	100	100	100
Loss asset	100	100	100	100	100	100

Notes: * General provisioning requirements in respect of specific sectors (e.g. residential housing loans beyond Rs0.2m) raised to 1% and in case of personal loans, including credit card receivables, loans and advances qualifying as capital market exposures and commercial real estate loans as also loans to non deposit-taking systemically important non-banking finance companies raised to 2%.
** 20% if doubtful asset (DA) = 1 year; 30% if DA of 1–3 years and 50% if DA > 3 years.
Source: Reserve Bank of India, Annual Report, Report on Trend and Progress of Banking in India and statistical tables relating to banks in India, various issues.

banks, on the third track, have a minimum capital requirement. There-fore, a major segment of systemic importance would be on a full Basel II framework. The banking system has also witnessed greater levels of trans-parency and standards of disclosure in order to promote greater market discipline in line with the envisaged Basel II Accord.

Institutional arrangement to improve supervision and to ensure integrity of payment and settlement systems has been put in place. Key measures include the institution of a Board for Financial Supervision (1994) in order to ensure an integrated approach to supervision. In order to address the issue of regulatory gaps and overlaps across major regulatory authorities, a High Level Co-ordination Committee on Financial and Capital Markets has been operational since 1999.[9] To minimise settlement risks, the Clearing Corporation of India Ltd was established in 2002. As well, a Board for Regulation and Supervision of Payment and Settlement Systems has been recently founded in order to set policies related to oversight of the relevant financial infrastructure. Finally, to address the systemic risks arising from growth of financial conglomerates, the RBI has put in place an oversight framework that envisages periodic sharing of information among the concerned regulatory bodies.

The legal infrastructure has also been strengthened. For instance, corporate debt restructuring process has been improved. Compromise settlements have been introduced to provide an opportunity to borrowers for settlement of their outstanding dues. These have been supplemented by Debt Recovery Tribunals (DRTs) and Lok Adalats (people's court) for settling limited banking disputes. Visaria (2006) reports that the establishment of DRTs significantly lowered loan delinquency. More recently, the Securitisation and Reconstruction of Financial Assets and Enforcement of Security Interest Act (2002) has allowed secured creditors to enforce their interests and take possess of secured assets, in order to improve loan-recovery rates. The Credit Information Companies (Regulation) Act (2004) is expected to make available credit histories of both individuals and small businesses, lower transactions costs and enhance the quality of credit decision making. The Act makes it mandatory for banks to share information about their borrowers with credit bureaus. The net effect of these measures has resulted in a significant reduction in ex-ante generation of problem loans over the reform period.

The net impact of these policy measures appears to have stood the country in good stead, especially in the wake of the global financial meltdown. India has been by and large spared the global financial contagion (Mohan, 2000), so far. Overall, efficiency and productivity

Table 3.3   Performance indicators of commercial banks (as % of total assets)

	1980–91	1992–96	1997–2001	2001–2002	2002–2003	2005–2006	2006–2007
Operating expense	2.53	2.74	2.64	2.19	2.24	2.11	1.97
Spread	1.90	2.94	2.87	2.57	2.77	2.78	2.78
Net Profit	0.15	−0.16	0.61	0.75	1.01	0.88	0.90

Source: Reserve Bank of India, Annual Report, Report on Trend and Progress of Banking in India and statistical tables relating to banks in India, various issues.

Table 3.4   NPL and CAR of bank groups: 1998–2007 (%)

	State Bank of India and nationalised banks		Old private banks		New private banks		Foreign banks	
	NPL/total loans	CAR	NPL/total loans	CAR	NPL/total loans	CAR	NPL/total loans	CAR
3/1998	16.0	11.6	10.9	12.3	3.5	13.2	6.4	10.3
3/2002	11.1	11.8	11.0	12.5	8.9	12.3	5.4	12.9
3/2007	2.7	12.4	3.1	12.1	1.9	12.0	1.8	12.4

Sources: Reserve Bank of India, Annual Report, Report on Trend and Progress of Banking in India and statistical tables relating to banks in India, various issues.

has improved by enhancing competition (Prasad and Ghosh, 2005). Moreover, Das and Ghosh (2006) report significant progress in the performance of state-owned banks, post liberalisation and a gradual convergence in their performance with foreign-owned and new private peers. The overall capital adequacy ratio (CAR) of commercial banks, which was 10.4 per cent in 1996–97 has since trended upwards to reach 12.3 per cent in 2006–2007. Similarly, improved recovery management and better risk assessment, has resulted in a steady decline in the NPLs ratio of banks, from 15.7 per cent in the mid-1990s to 2.7 per cent in 2006–2007 (Table 3.4). Such figures compare favorably with other emerging markets (Table 3.5).

The structure of the Indian banking system

India's financial system is broadly serviced by two major groups of intermediaries: banks (commercial and co-operative, Table 3.6) and financial

Table 3.5   Indicators of the banking sector – international comparison (%)

	CAR		ROA		NPL/Total loans		Provisions/NPL	
	2001	*2007*	*2001*	*2007*	*2001*	*2007*	*2001*	*2007*
China	–	–	–	0.9*	29.8	7.0	–	–
Brazil	14.8	18.5	−0.1	2.1	5.6	4.0*	126.6	153
Mexico	13.9	16.1	0.8	3.2	5.1	2.2	123.8	194.7
Korea	11.7	13.0	0.7	1.1	3.4	0.8	89.6**	177.7
India	11.4	12.3	0.5	0.9	11.4	2.5	43.7	56.1
South Africa	11.4	12.7	0.8	1.4	3.1	1.1	46	64.3***

Notes: * for 2006; ** for 2002; *** for 2005.
Sources: IMF Global Financial Stability Report, various issues.

Table 3.6   Structure of the Indian banking system*

Institution	*No. of institutions*	*Total asset (Rsbn)*	*% of total asset*
Banking Sector (1 + 2)	3117	38912	100.00
1. Commercial banks (a + b)	191	34658	89.07
(a) Scheduled commercial banks	187	34653	89.06
State Bank of India and			
Nationalised banks	28	23361	60.04
Private sector banks	26	7454	19.16
Foreign banks	29	2780	7.14
Regional rural banks	96	1058	2.72
(b) Local Area Banks	4	5	0.01
2. Cooperative banks	2926	4254	10.93

Note: * Figures as at end-March 2007.
Source: Reserve Bank of India, Annual Report, Report on Trend and Progress of Banking in India and statistical tables relating to banks in India, various issues.

institutions, which includes development banks and the broadly defined non-bank financial institutions. The focus of here is on commercial banks which account for over 85 per cent of banking assets. As of March 2007, there were 179 scheduled commercial banks, 96 of which were regional rural institutions. The present banking law makes limited distinction between universal and strictly commercial banks and most banks operate as universal banks.

India's scheduled commercial banks are the major depository institutions and mobilise most of the country's savings. They traditionally

Table 3.7 Basic statistics for different banking categories: 2006–2007 (%)

	SBI & associates	Nationalised banks	Private banks	Foreign banks	All banks
Offices	24.5 (26.7)	62.6 (64.3)	12.5 (8.7)	0.5 (0.3)	100 (100)
Employees	28.6 (32.7)	52.8 (59.9)	15.5 (6.1)	3.1 (1.4)	100 (100)
Deposits	23.9 (28.0)	49.6 (57.4)	20.8 (7.9)	5.7 (6.7)	100 (100)
Advances	25.1 (31.0)	46.7 (51.4)	21.6 (8.7)	6.6 (8.9)	100 (100)
RoA	0.82 (0.42)	0.85 (−0.36)	0.87 (1.06)	1.65 (1.58)	0.90 (0.13)

Note: Figures in brackets refer to 1995–96.
Source: Reserve Bank of India, Annual Report, Report on Trend and Progress of Banking in India and statistical tables relating to banks in India, various issues.

provide short-term credit to meet the working-capital needs of enterprises. Since deregulation, however, many of the larger banks have begun to target the medium-to-long-term corporate lending, the infrastructure debt market, and the retail sector. In the absence of a developed domestic long-term debt market (outstanding domestic and international debt issues accounted for less than 3 per cent of GDP in 2005), financial institutions maintain a specialist role in meeting corporates' long-term funding requirements. Over the past several years, the distinction between commercial banks and financial institutions has weakened anyway.

State-owned banks account for a share greater than 60 per cent of total asset. They have large branch networks and broad geographic coverage, accounting for over 77 per cent of bank offices. At the end of March 2007, about 35 per cent of commercial bank branches were located in rural regions, a further 23.5 per cent in semi-urban areas. This is obviously a by-product of the '4 for 1' branch opening policy. The State Bank of India (SBI) is by far the largest bank; it accounted for 17.0 per cent of advances in 2006/2007. Among the first ten large banks, eight are predominantly state-controlled (besides SBI, Canara Bank, Punjab National Bank, Bank of India, Bank of Baroda, Union Bank of India, IDBI Bank, Central Bank of India and HDFC Bank). Altogether, they account for over half of the lending market. Banking reforms have triggered a deep restructuring and increasing profitability for many of such banks (Table 3.7). Over the last decade, however, the share of public banks (SBI group and nationalised banks) in deposits and advances has declined, largely at the expense of new private banks. In response to competitive pressures, the former have reduced their operating costs by rationalising their manpower as also their branch networks.

Private banks[10] account for 19.2 per cent of total assets and over a fifth of total advances. Even before 1991, a few private banks have been operating in India: the 20 so-called 'old private banks' escaped nationalisation because they were considered too small. They exhibit many of the problems that earlier besieged the State Bank of India and the other nationalised banks, in particular relatively weaker asset quality and capital adequacy. The new private banks,[11] on the other hand, benefited from the lack of burdensome administrative controls and branch legacy, and have been able to establish a small but growing foothold in the market, leveraging on information technology and communications networking and focusing on high-net-worth companies and individuals (Standard & Poor's, 2005). ICICI Bank is the largest privately owned bank and the second Indian banks by total advances (roughly 10 per cent of total advances). It accounts for about half of the advances made by the private banking sector. It was a public-sector financial institution that was corporatised and later merged with its commercial bank subsidiary. It is now jointly owned by Indian and foreign banks, and by the shareholding public.

Foreign banks play a small but innovative role in India. At end of June 2007, 29 foreign banks with 268 branches from over 25 countries were operating in India (Table 3.8). They accounted for about 7.1 per cent of total commercial banking sector asset. Another 34 foreign banks had representative offices. India has traditionally been quite open to foreign banks, even if less to foreign acquisition of Indian banks. There is no restriction on the licensing of new foreign banks in India, although licensing may be restricted if the foreign banks' market share exceeds 15 per cent of the banking system. So far, foreign banks are allowed to either open up branches or set up wholly owned subsidiaries. Foreign banks are subject to the same prudential requirements as their domestic counterparts. Although their activity has historically been restricted (for example, they are permitted to open up to 12 branches per year), recent evidence suggests a gradual opening up of the financial sector: during calendar year 2007, the RBI issued 19 approvals for opening branches by foreign banks in india.

The traditional contribution of foreign banks has been to meet the banking needs of foreign companies operating in the country and they are dominant in the forex market and in the derivatives market.[12] In fact, traditionally, foreign banks focused on cross-border transactions involving trade finance with the larger Indian corporates. Recently, some of them have successfully tapped the middle-class and personal-banking markets. Their competitive advantage is based on their larger range of

Table 3.8 Foreign banks in India

Country	No. of banks	Branches in India
Belgium	1	1
Canada	1	5
France	3	15
Germany	1	8
Hong Kong	1	48
Japan	2	5
Netherlands	1	28
Singapore	1	2
UK	2	84
USA	4	52
Others	12	20

Sources: Reserve Bank of India, Annual Report, Report on Trend and Progress of Banking in India and statistical tables relating to banks in India, various issues.

products and better standards of service. The new Indian private-sector banks, however, pose a threat for foreign banks. As the larger domestic commercial banks also become more aggressive, foreign banks will increasingly try to leverage their international networks to stay competitive. At the same time, several foreign banks have rationalised their Indian operations (Economist Intelligence Unit, 2006). For instance, in 2005, Standard Chartered took over the Indian branches of Sumitomo Mitsui Banking Corporation and, in 2002, the retail assets of ANZ Grindlays. In 2003/04, Toronto-Dominion Bank, Oversea-Chinese Banking Corporation and Bank Muscat shut their branches in India. Following the worldwide merger of Crédit Lyonnais and Crédit Agricole Indosuez into Calyon Bank in May 2004, the two banks merged their Indian operations as well.

As for foreign ownership of Indian banks, the restriction is tighter: total foreign ownership in a private-sector bank cannot exceed 74 per cent of the paid-up capital,[13] while in state-owned banks the FDI limit remains 20 per cent. Moreover, mergers and acquisitions of Indian banks are subject to RBI approval and no individual foreign bank can own more than 5 per cent of a domestic bank without RBI approval. Furthermore, a 10 per cent cap on foreign investors voting rights exists at present.

Efforts have been initiated by the Government and the RBI to iron out various legal impediments inherent in the process of cross-border M&A. In particular, in the Union Budget Speech 2005–2006, it was announced that RBI had prepared a two-phase roadmap for removing significant barriers to entry of new foreign players:

- Since March 2005, foreign banks could either choose to operate through branches or set up a 100 per cent wholly owned subsidiary (WOS) or convert their existing branches to WOS status. The WOS will be treated on par with the existing branches of foreign banks for branch expansion. To allow Indian banks sufficient time to prepare for global competition, foreign banks M&A will be permitted only in private-sector banks identified for restructuring by the RBI.
- The second phase will start from April 2009. The removal of limitations on the operations of the WOSs and treating them on par with domestic banks will be designed and implemented after reviewing the experience with Phase I and consultations with all existing stakeholders. After a minimum period of operation, the WOSs of foreign banks will be allowed to list and dilute their stake so that at least 26 per cent of the paid-up capital of the WOS is held by resident Indians. After a review is made, foreign banks may be permitted, subject to regulatory approvals and such conditions as may be prescribed, to enter into M&A transactions with any private-sector bank in India subject to the overall investment limit of 74 per cent and the *one mode presence* limit.

So far, in several new private banks, the extent of foreign ownership is over 50 per cent; these banks account for roughly half of the total assets of domestic private banks. Even in several public-sector-owned banks, the extent of foreign ownership within the private holding is close to that of domestic private holding. Moreover, there is selected evidence of foreign banks owning significant shares of Indian private banks. For instance, Bank Muscat International (Oman) owns 18.64 per cent of Centurion Bank of Punjab, Rabobank International Holdings owns 20 per cent of Yes Bank, ING owns 44 per cent of ING Vsysa Bank, ABN AMRO Bank was holding 1.4 per cent of IndusInd Bank and foreign institutional investors hold just over 20 per cent of the shares of Kotak Mahindra Bank.

Notwithstanding such evidence, several issues are still hampering a broader consensus over larger foreign presence in the banking sector: (a) a concern about 'cherry-picking' practices of foreign banks, which could leave domestic banks saddled with less creditworthy customers; (b) the fact that the supervision of the more sophisticated activities of foreign banks entails a continuous challenge for regulators; (c) doubts on whether depositors in foreign banks would be entitled to receive the same degree of protection as depositors in domestic banks; (d) fears that the host country should extend the 'lender of last resort' umbrella to foreign banks; and (e) concerns about the still limited dimension and profitability of many Indian banks, which might make them exposed to hostile foreign takeovers. In fact, the profitability of the group composed by the State Bank of India and the other nationalised banks in 2006–2007, calculated as ROA (0.82 for State Bank of India group and 0.85 for the nationalised banks) is lower than the value of both foreign banks (1.65), but comparable to the other scheduled commercial banks (0.87), which account for around a fifth of total banking sector assets.

Financial deepening and financial inclusion

As the economy begins to grow rapidly and an increasing number of people migrate out of the poverty levels, the banking system will have to intermediate large amounts of funds than at present. The ratio of bank asset to GDP, loans and deposit to GDP and loans to deposits, although increasing in recent times, is still much lower than in other comparable bank-based economies (Table 3.9), which suggests significant scope for financial deepening. In such a changed scenario, banks would need to harness modern delivery mechanisms that economise on transactions costs and provide better access to the presently under-served customers. This will call for devising innovative channels for credit delivery coupled with risk-related pricing of products and services. The role of prudent risk management, in such a situation, can hardly be over-emphasised. Given the wide dispersion in risk appetite across banks, such risk management practices will need to be suitably integrated into the banks product profiles, business philosophy and customer orientation.

It is also increasingly recognised that large segments of the rural population face 'financial exclusion' and continue their traditional dependence on the informal sector. Cross-country data for 99 countries in 2003–2004 reported by Beck *et al.* (2007) indicates that, India ranked 24th in terms of geographic branch penetration (number of branches per 1000 sq. km) with a figure of 22.6 and 59th in terms of demographic penetration (number of branches per 100,000 people) with a figure of 6.3, whereas the highest for these indicators were 636.1 (for Singapore) and 95.9 (for Spain), respectively. The Government-appointed Committee on Financial Inclusion (Chairman: Dr C. Rangarajan) in its report in 2008 notes that, '45.9 million farmer households in the country out of a total of 89.3 million households do not access credit, either from

Table 3.9   Depth of the banking systems of various emerging markets, latest available data

	Loans + deposits/GDP (%)	Loans/deposits (%)
China	158	133
India	*103*	*67*
South Korea	108	97
Indonesia	37	59
Malaysia	228	110
Philippines	57	65
Thailand	139	76
Vietnam	84	91
Czech Republic	109	66
Hungary	109	127
Poland	77	83
Romania	60	94
Russia	58	107
Slovakia	105	72
Turkey	86	72
Ukraine	83	133
Weighted average	113	106

Sources: UniCredit New Europe Research Network, IMF World Economic Outlook, various national sources.

institutional or non-institutional sources'. Exclusion is found to be most acute in the Central, Eastern and North-Eastern regions of the country.

While resource limitations experienced by low-income households continue to constrain their access and use of financial products, the challenge remains for developing appropriate policies, procedures and products that can overcome this difficulty within the bounds of resource constraints. Some of the challenges that need to be effectively addressed include lack of adequate infrastructure in rural areas, relatively low volumes of transactions, comparatively higher transaction costs, and other factors such as the literacy levels of target customers. Apart from greater latitude in the range of identity documents that are acceptable to open an account, there is also a need for independent information and advisory service. Nurturing appropriate public–private partnerships and devising innovative ways of addressing the paucity of infrastructure lie at the core of the problem. Salient among these include use of computer systems which do not require uninterrupted electric power supply, networking using radio frequency and other non-conventional methods, centralisation of processing systems, provision of home-grown customised systems such as the low cost, multi-lingual ATM – all of which provide an impetus towards greater financial inclusion.

Another interesting facet of Indian banking in recent years has been the surge in retail lending, comprising nearly a fifth of banks' outstanding advances. Various factors have influenced banks' focus on retail lending. The major is that lower interest rates on housing and consumer durables financing due to competition and financial innovations related to credit/debit cards have enabled increased potential demand. Within retail lending, housing loans represent nearly half of the banking portfolio, while the reminder is mainly comprised of consumer durables. Although asset impairment on retail loans has remained low at less than 3 per cent of total loans, as a cautionary measure, the central bank has raised the risk weight on housing and retail loans in order to prevent the emergence of any unforeseen 'bubble' in this segment. A related area of concern in this respect relates to customer service. The focus of attention is on basic banking services provided to the common persons. A Banking Ombudsman facility has been established covering all States and Union Territories for redressal of grievances against deficient banking services.

In order to facilitate a deeper financial system and a wider inclusion, technology upgrading of the Indian banking system is crucial. In effect, technology has become the key to servicing all customer segments – offering convenience to the retail customer and operating efficiencies to corporates and government clients. Moreover, the increasing sophistication, flexibility and complexity of products and servicing offerings makes the effective use of technology critical for managing the risks associated with banking business. However, the 'technological penetration' in India has been quite modest. According to data reported in the *World Development Indicators* database, as of 2005, the number of computers per 1000 persons was about 16 in India compared to anywhere between 40–100 in most emerging markets and even higher developed economies (World Bank, 2007). Wide disparities exist even within the banking sector as far as technological capabilities are concerned: the percentage of 'computer literate' employees as ratio of total staff in 2000 was around 20 per cent in public sector banks compared with 100 per cent in new private and around 90 per cent in foreign banks (RBI, 2002). The challenge, therefore, remains three fold: acquiring the 'right' technology, deploying it optimally and remaining cost-effective whilst delivering sustainable returns to shareholders. In effect, 'managing' technology to achieve and maintain high service and efficiency standards so as to reap the maximum benefits remains a key challenge.

Conclusions

To sum up, the Indian financial system has undertaken several important steps on the road towards a modern and efficient financial system, which can be a positive contributor to its economic development. Many delinquent loans have been cleaned up and the stock market is entering hitherto unchartered territories. New efficient private banks and foreign banks are imparting significant dynamism to the financial marketplace. This is in line with the philosophy itself of the gradualist Indian financial reforms process. Nonetheless, many steps are to be done, yet. Among the many issues, development of a domestic market for corporate debt is crucial. Developing a debt market can in turn provide corporates with alternative sources of financing and complete the scope of the financial market with positive spillover on its resilience from financial crises and 'sudden stops' in financial flows from abroad. As well, bank ownership and control is relevant. Nationalised banks and the State Bank of India should strive to increase their profitability and soundness on a consistent basis, even through a further opening of their ownership to private and foreign investors. An easier access to foreign investors in Indian banks (already planned by the gradual phasing out of restrictions), and a further relaxation of pre-emption and priority lending could, finally, instill further competition in the market and be important tools for completing the modernisation of India financial sector.

Notes

1. Rajan (2008) argues that any sensible growth strategy for India would need to focus on its competencies. Unlike China, which has already built up an advantage in low value-added manufacturing, India would need to focus on its capabilities in skilled manufacturing, ranging from pharma to auto ancilliaries as also in services in areas ranging from IT and engineering services to healthcare.
2. The Reserve Bank of India is the central bank. It was established on 1 April 1935. Since nationalisations in 1949, the Reserve Bank is fully owned by the Government. Currently, its main functions are being the issuer of currency, the monetary authority; the regulator and supervisor of the financial system and the manager of foreign exchange reserves.
3. The Indian government nationalised 14 large private banks in 1969 with deposits of more than Rs500m and another 6 banks each having deposits of more than Rs2bn in 1980.
4. Scheduled banks are included in the Second Schedule of the Reserve Bank of India Act, 1934.
5. CRR and SLR requirements do not apply to inter-bank deposits.

6. Between 1938 and 1947, as many as 629 Indian joint stock banks, with paid-up capital of Rs2.2 crore were liquidated (RBI Statistical Tables, various years) and as many as 647 banks failed. Although the number of bank failures fell from thereafter 8 in 1959, bank failures continued to remain a major problem.
7. The Deposit Insurance Scheme (DIS) covers all classes of banks in India, including the cooperative banks. Deposit insurance is compulsory, although some states have yet to pass the relevant legislation extending the scheme to cooperative banks within their state, and, accordingly, some of these banks fall outside the parameters of the scheme. The cover per depositor per bank account is Rs100,000 (roughly six times per capita GDP), and covers about 75 per cent of total banking system deposits. The premium payable under the scheme by insured banks equals ten paise (one paisa is one-hundred of a Rupee). This, however, increased to 15 paise from fiscal 2006 onwards.
8. Under the extant statutes, government holding in public banks cannot decline below 51 per cent.
9. The major regulatory authorities are RBI, Securities and Exchange Board of India (the capital market regulator), the Insurance Regulatory and Development Authority (the insurance sector regulator) and the Pension Funds Regulatory and Development Authority (the pension funds regulator).
10. The RBI issued guidelines regarding the formation and functioning of private sector banks in January 1993.
11. Since 1993 the RBI has given out 12 licences to new domestic private banks. These banks are nine as of March 2006 because of mergers and amalgamations.
12. The derivative activities (comprising forward exchange contracts, guarantees, acceptances, endorsements) of foreign banks comprised 60 per cent of the total activities by commercial banks in 2005–2006.
13. Shares held by foreign institutional investors under portfolio-investment schemes through stock exchanges cannot exceed 49 per cent of the paid-up capital.

References

Ahluwalia, M.S. (1993) 'India's Economic Reforms', in R. Cassen and V. Joshi (eds.), *India: The Future of Economic Reform* (New Delhi: Oxford University Press).
Ahluwalia, M.S. (2002) 'Economic Reforms in India Since 1991: Has Gradualism Worked?', *Journal of Economic Perspectives* 16, 67–88.
Beck, T., Demirguc Kunt, A. and Soledad Martinez Peria, M. (2007) 'Reaching Out: Access to and Use of Banking Services Across Countries', *Journal of Financial Economics* 85, 234–66.
Banerjee, A., Cole, S. and Duflo, E. (2005) *Banking Reform in India. India Policy Forum*, (Brookings Institution: MIT, 2005).
Bosworth, B. and Collins, S.M. (2007) 'Accounting for Growth: Comparing China and India', NBER Working Paper 12943.
Burgess, R. and Pande, R. (2005) 'Do Rural Banks Matter?: Evidence From the Indian Social Banking Experiment', *American Economic Review* 95, 780–95.

Das, A. and Ghosh, S. (2006) 'Financial Deregulation and Efficiency: An Empirical Analysis of Indian Banks in the Post-reform Period', *Review of Financial Economics* 15, 193–221.

Desai, V.R.M. (1967) *Banking development in India* (Mumbai: Manaktalas 1967).

Diamond, D. and Dyvbig, P. (1983) 'Bank Runs, Deposit Insurance and Liquidity', *Journal of Political Economy* 91, 410–19.

Economist Intelligence Unit (2006) *India: Country Finance* (London: The Economist Intelligence Unit).

IMF, *Global Financial Stability Report* (IMF: Washington, DC, various issues).

Government of India (1991) 'Report of the Committee on the Financial System' (Chairman: Shri M. Narasimham) (New Delhi: Government of India).

Government of India (1998) 'Report of the Committee on Banking Sector Reforms' (Chairman: Shri M. Narasimham) (New Delhi: Government of India).

Government of India (2008) 'Report of the Committee on Financial Inclusion' (Chairman: Dr C. Rangarajan) (New Delhi: Government of India).

Mohan, R. (2005) 'Financial Sector Reforms in India: Policies and Performance analysis', *Economic and Political Weekly* XL, 1106–21.

Mohan, R. (2008) 'Global Financial Crisis and Key Risks: Impact on Asia and India'. Address delivered at the IMF–FSF Meeting, Washington, DC, available at www.rbi.org.in.

Prasad, A. and Ghosh, S. (2005) 'Competition in Indian Banking', IMF Working Paper 141.

Rajan, R.G. (2008) 'Financial Sector Reforms in India: Why? Why now? How?', Second Golden Jubilee Series Lecture (New Delhi: Institute of Economic Growth).

Reddy, Y. V. (2004) 'Monetary and Financial Sector Reforms in India: A Practitioner's Perspective', in Kaushik Basu (ed.), *India's Emerging Economy*, Cambridge, Mass.: MIT Press.

RBI (1954) *All-India Debt and Investment Survey* (Bombay: RBI).

RBI (1983) *The Reserve Bank of India: Functions and Working*, (Bombay: RBI).

RBI (2002) 'Expenditure Pattern and IT Initiatives of Banks'. *RBI Bulletin*.

RBI, *Annual Report* (various issues) (Mumbai: RBI).

RBI, *Report on Trend and Progress of Banking in India*, various issues (Mumbai: RBI).

RBI, *Statistical Tables Relating to Banks in India*, various issues, (Mumbai: RBI).

Rodrik, D. and Subramanian, A. (2005) 'From "Hindu Growth" to Productivity Surge: The Mystery of the Indian Growth Transition', *IMF Staff Papers*, 52, 193–228.

Standard & Poor's (2005) *Bank Industry Analysis: India* (Singapore: Standard & Poor's).

Visaria, S. (2006) 'Legal Reform and Loan Repayment: The Microeconomic Impact of Debt Recovery Tribunals in India'. Discussion Paper No.157, (University of Boston). Available at www.bu.edu/econ

World Bank (2008) 'Financial Structure Database', available at www. worldbank.org

World Bank (2008) 'World Development Indicators Database', accessed on 22 February.

Appendix

Table A1.1 Financial institutions – size, performance and international comparison

No.	Indicators	1990–91 (or earliest available)	2006–2007
I(A)	*Size* (nos)		
	No. of commercial banks	272 (a)	191 (b)
	No. of listed banks	Nil	36
	No. of bank offices in India	60570	73836
	Of which:		
	Rural and semi-urban branches	46115	47044
	Population per bank office (000s)	14	16
	Deposits (Rsbn)	2012	26083
	Per capita deposits (Rs)	2368	23382
	Credit (Rsbn)	1219	19289
	Per capita credit (Rs)	1434	17541
	Total commercial bank asset (Rsbn)	3275	34634
	Assets of listed banks (Rsbn)	–	29926
	Assets of listed banks/total bank asset (%)	–	86
I (B)	*Size* (ratios)		
	Bank concentration (assets of 3 largest banks/commercial bank assets)	0.36	0.31
	Bank asset/GDP (%)	58	93
	Bank deposits/GDP (%)	35	74
	Bank credit/GDP (%)	21	56
II	*Performance* (%)		
	Profitability (net profit/asset)	0.23	0.90
	Cost of Intermediation (net interest margin/asset)	3.31 (c)	2.69
	Administrative and staff costs (operating expense/asset)	2.60 (c)	1.91
	Soundness (capital adequacy ratio – CRAR)	10.4*	12.3
	Fragility (non-performing loan ratio – NPL)	23.2**	3.7** (2.5 – for Sch. comm. banks)
III	*International comparisons* (d)		
2006	ROA {min., max.}	79 countries	{0.2, 4.3}
2006	CRAR {min., max.}	75 countries	{7.1, 34.9}
2006	NPL {min., max.}	79 countries	{0.2, 24.7}
2006	Provisions/NPL {min., max.}	60 countries	{23.1, 229.1}

(continued)

Table A1.1   *(Continued)*

No.	Indicators	1990–91 *(or earliest available)*	2006–2007
2005	Net interest margin {min., max.}	94 countries	{0.61, 14.23}
2005	Bank concentration {min., max.}	95 countries	{0.30, 1.00}
2005	Bank deposits/GDP {min., max.}	96 countries	{0.6, 334}
2005	Bank credit/GDP {min., max.}	96 countries	{7.2, 202}

Notes: (a) including 196 regional rural banks (RRBs); (b) including 96 RRBs; (c) for 1991–92. * for 1996–97; ** public sector banks only in 1992–93; (d) includes Latin America, Emerging and Western Europe, Asia and Middle East and Central Asia.
Sources: RBI, IMF (*Global Financial Stability Report*) and World Bank (*Financial Structure Database*).

4
Indonesia

P. Bongini

Introduction

The product life-cycle theory, as developed in marketing studies, can be used as a useful tool for interpreting the development path followed by a banking system and its regulation. The theory predicts that products pass through distinct phases: first the product is introduced or launched into the market (introduction period); a period of growth follows, where sales and profits rise; eventually the market stabilises and the product becomes mature. A final phase of decline might then be experienced and the product is eventually withdrawn. By applying this scheme to banking systems and their regulators distinct stages of development can be drawn.

The initial phase is characterised by a limited financial depth of the economy and by a scarce level of international openness – in and out – of the banking system. This is mostly the result of a tight regulation aimed at limiting the entrepreneurial autonomy of banks, which are usually used as accounting vehicles in support of government policies. State-owned banks make the most of the banking system.

The second phase starts with a deregulation process aimed at boosting the banking system: greater autonomy in banking decision-making is favoured; constraints on capital movements are removed; business expansion is simplified; and the entry of foreign investors is encouraged thus opening the door to foreign competition.

In the third (and final)[1] stage the consolidation of the banking system takes place. The contribution of the banking system to the economy is high, both in terms of value added to GDP and in terms of number of employees; the degree of international openness – incoming and outgoing – is strong; finally financial deepening helps broaden the service coverage, the expansion of the volume and types of products as well as the allocation of scarce resources. From a regulatory perspective, (prudential) uniform rules of the game are set so that a level playing field is guaranteed to any player in the financial system (bank, non-bank intermediaries, capital market) and as such the soundness and efficiency of the whole financial system are achieved. This in turn is acknowledged as a necessary condition for the attainment of a harmonious economic growth.

The Indonesian banking system is no exception to the proposed scheme. However, commonly to other emerging countries, it experiences a crisis of systemic size that slows down the process towards the final maturity stage between the second and third phase.

In a nutshell, we can summarise the Indonesian banking history in the following four stages:

1. *The growth period* which begins in the mid-1960s, but truly takes off during the 1980s. The seeds of financial deepening are sown, although the banking system is dominated by banks, in particular state-owned banks which act as government agencies in the allocation of credit. Foreign banks are timidly allowed to enter the Indonesian banking market, although subject to many constraints. The years 1983–1991 witness a more intense deregulation phase. Regulatory reforms are initiated by the elimination of loan and deposit ceilings and they continue with the removal of constraints limiting domestic bank branching and the entry of foreign banks. Reforms are not only limited to the banking sector but also involved the capital market. The banking system grows at high speed, primarily thanks to an ascending role of private commercial banks, that dominated the banking sector with market shares exceeding 50 per cent in terms of total assets.
2. *The initial consolidation (1991–97)*, during which the regulatory and supervisory authorities seek to re-regulate (albeit with limited success) the financial system. As far as the banking system is concerned rules on capital adequacy (Basel I) are introduced;
3. *The crisis (1997–99)*, i.e. a phase when the 'twin crises' – banking and foreign exchange crises violently hit the economy and the Indonesian society as a whole. The effects of the crisis are devastating: in 1998 non performing loans account for 70 per cent of gross loans while the fiscal cost of the crisis is approximated to something exceeding 50 per cent of GDP.

4. *The restructuring (1999–present)*, where government and regulatory and supervisory authorities strive to create a sound, transparent and accountable banking system (and far more generally, a financial system) able to meet the challenges of increased globalisation. Achieving these conditions has long been recognised as an essential factor to deliver a sustainable economic growth and create an investment climate favorable to increase the country's attractiveness to foreign capitals.

The rest of the chapter is organised as follow. The following section describes the structure and the recent evolution of the Indonesian economy. Then the main steps of the bank restructuring plan undertaken in the aftermath of the 1997–98 systemic financial crisis are outlined. Next the structure of the Indonesian banking system is analysed and the effectiveness of the restructuring plan is assessed by looking at the post-crisis performance of the Indonesian banking system. Performance and lingering fragilities of the Indonesian banks are therefore put under a spotlight. The concluding section focuses on prospects for foreign banks in the Indonesian banking system.

The Indonesian economy: a five-step transformation

During the long Suharto presidency (1966–98), the Indonesian economy experienced a persistent and rapid growth, which enabled Indonesia to leave the ranks of 'low-income countries 'to become one of the 'newly industrialising economies (NIE)' and play a pivotal role in the so-called 'Asian Miracle' (World Bank, 1993). During the 1965–97 period, the economy grew at an average annual rate of 7 per cent and the Indonesian GDP jumped to 600 trillions rupiah (roughly US$ 69 billion) from the low level of 24 billion rupiah; per-capita income doubled; the poverty rate decreased to 16.7 per cent of the total population while life expectancy increased from 62 to 66 years and infant mortality halved.

Such a growth resulted from a process of transformation of the Indonesian economy and society, which can be summarised in five main stages.

The first stage (1965–73) is characterised by the suppression of hyper-inflation and the transition from a planned to a market-based economy, promoted by the liberalisation of trade and foreign investments.

The second stage (1974–81) coincides with increasing oil prices: as a result of windfall revenues from the oil boom, the Indonesian government started an ambitious import-substituting, state-led indus-trialisation. Such a project involved the establishment of various state-owned basic industries (steel, aluminium smelter, chemistry). The return of oil prices to their pre-boom level abruptly reduced Indonesia's oil tax revenues and the government was forced to adjust, if not cancel, its programme of large-scale industrialisation of the economy.

The third stage (1983–96) witnesses a gradual shift to export-promoting policies and a successful attempt to limit the fiscal depend-ence on oil tax revenues. Several reforms were introduced aimed at improving the investment climate for private investors, both domes-tic and foreign, and at encouraging export-oriented industrial projects. Prudent macroeconomic management, combined with an exchange rate policy aimed at keeping the real exchange rate competitive, proved suc-cessful in supporting the manufacturing sector, specifically the non-oil and gas sub-sectors, and its exports: during the period 1985–88 they grew, respectively, at an average annual rate of 13 per cent and 27 per cent, to further accelerate their growth over the period 1989–92 (Wie, 2006). A peculiarity of the Indonesian economy, relative to its regional competitors, was the type of export-oriented firms and to the nature of their manufactured exports. Exporting firms were mainly foreign-controlled or domestic SMEs, not large industrial conglomerates; Indone-sian exports were more oriented towards low skill labour-intensive productions, and less towards high value-added high-tech goods.

The fourth stage of transformation of the Indonesian economy relates to the 1997–98 period, when banking and currency problems exploded, leading to the twin crises (Kaminsky and Reinhart, 1999), more widely known as the 'Asian crisis'. In Indonesia the financial crisis became multidimensional, affecting not only the financial and real sectors but also having deep political and social consequences. The long Suharto era ended with the President's resignation driven by a political scandal involving some of his relatives; the serious economic recession of 1997–98 aroused widespread discontent that resulted in turmoil and rebellion among the general public. In fact, the financial crisis led to a brusque slowdown of economic growth, especially in the manufacturing sector (Table 4.1). Net Foreign Direct Investments (FDIs) contracted and became negative, while the inflation rate sky-rocketed to a two-digit level; last, but not least, the real exchange rate plunged (−300 per cent) over the same period.

Notwithstanding the intensity of the crisis, the first signals of recovery were swiftly visible: over the period 2000–2006, the economy has grown at an average annual rate of 5 per cent; inflation showed a remarkable

Table 4.1 The Indonesian economy: 1997–2006

	1997	1998	1999	2000	2001	2002	2003	2004	2005	2006
Indonesian GDP: annual rate of growth	4.7	−13.1	0.8	4.9	3.8	4.4	4.0	5.1	5.6	5.5
Indonesian Manufacturing sector: annual rate of growth	5.3	−15.0	3.9	6.0	3.1	3.5	7.2	7.4	4.6	4.6
Asian crisis countries: average rate of growth of GDP	4.0	6.3	6.1	6.6	2.0	5.3	5.0	6.0	4.7	5.3
Indonesian Net FDI (US$m)	4,667	−241	−1,866	−4,550	−2,978	145	−597	1,512	5,271	2,211
Net FDI (US$m) – other crisis countries	2,162	3,109	4,215	3,196	1,636	1,431	1,217	3,262	3,054	1,566
Inflation rate	6.2	58.5	20.3	9.3	12.5	10.0	5.1	6.1	10.9	12.7
Exchange rate (Rp/US$)	2,909	10,140	7,855	8,422	10,610	9,311	8,577	8,939	9.05	9,159
External debt/GDP	63	158	105.8	85.9	81.2	66.0	56.0	54.2	45.9	35.3

Source: Asian Development Bank and International Financial Statistics (IMF).

slowdown, returning to its pre-crisis levels; foreign debt, as a share of GDP, continued to decline and undershot pre-crisis levels. However, as Indonesia was the country most severely affected by the Asian financial crisis, also the recovery has been comparatively more sluggish, both in terms of GDP growth and of FDI inflows than elsewhere in the region. In particular, foreign investors showed a lack of interest in undertaking new investments in Indonesia: in 2004, net FDIs were half the figure registered in other Asian crisis-hit countries. In 2005, FDIs were recovering towards their pre-crisis level. Nonetheless, no sensible change in foreign investors' sentiment was in the pipeline: during 2006 FDIs, in fact, diminished.

As a matter of fact, the severe policy uncertainty and the enduring weakness of the exchange rate during the first few years of the current decade was holding back foreign investment. Scarce corporate governance and diffuse corruption in both national and local government are still considered critical obstacles by country analysts, managers of multinational corporations and international investors (CGI Report, 2003). Finally, the well-known fragilities of the export-oriented manufacturing sectors, among which stands up the shallow technological capability, are enduring. Still in 2003, the percentage of high-technology manufactured exports is as low as 14 per cent of total exports, with respect to an average of 30 per cent in other South-East Asian countries (Wie, 2006). To this point, Wie (2006) argues that Indonesia has an urgent need of an upgraded labour force: despite the progress in expanding education, the country still lags behind in educational progress compared to the other former crisis countries in terms of education inputs, participation in education and education outcomes.

Two positive issues are nowadays contrasting the above-mentioned list of open problems and are characterising the recent economic development of Indonesia.

First, since the crisis, Indonesia's growth has been by and large driven by consumption, both private and governmental. In other former crisis countries, reliance on exports or investments has been much stronger. A demand-led growth is positive in terms of long-term sustainability of the growth itself as the country can be less dependent on the economic developments of its major importers, the US *in primis*. So far, Indonesia has proved to have robust enough fundamentals to shield its domestic economy and financial markets from pressures emanating from increased global financial market volatility amid the 2007–2008 global financial turmoil.

Secondly, Indonesia is taking advantage of booming trade with China. Although export competition from China is rising, China is becoming an increasingly important export market for Indonesia. China is, indeed, emerging as a primary destination for Asian intermediates which are then assembled in China for world export or for domestic consumption (CGI Report p.3).

All in all the real sector is still beset by the aftermath of the financial crisis. However, notwithstanding the vulnerabilities – common to other emerging countries – the sustainability of the positive economic performance of the former Asian tiger does not seem in doubt, so far.

The 1997–99 Asian crisis: the onset and the way out

Indonesia was the country most severely hit by the Asian financial crisis, in terms of GDP decline, non-performing loan (NPL) volume and fiscal cost of crisis resolution (Table 4.2). The financial crisis soon turned into political and social crisis due to the deep and prolonged recession that followed the initial turmoil.

The main roots of the Asian crisis were corporate and financial weaknesses. On the financial side, bad lending practices were the norm, with evidence of connected lending and excessive concentration of loans to specific sectors.

Inadequate accounting and disclosure practices, expectations of implicit government guarantees, and the government's habit of promoting investment by forcing banks to extend loans to targeted sectors weakened banks' managerial autonomy, while prudential regulation and supervision was very weak. In particular, it failed to limit excessive foreign currency exposure or maturity mismatches.

Table 4.2 The dimension of the Asian crisis

	GDP (% change) 1997–98	NPL/loans (1998, %)	NPL/GDP (1998, %)	Fiscal cost of crisis resolution (as a % of GDP)
Indonesia	−13.7	70.0	53.0	51.0
Thailand	−10.0	50.0	70.0	32.8
South Korea	−5.8	35.0	35.0	26.5
Malaysia	−0.5	30.0	42.0	16.4
Philippines	−7.5	15.0	5.0	0.5

Source: Cooke and Foley (1999); Honohan and Kinglebiel (2000).

In such a situation, banks' extreme weakness paved the way for the crisis: when exchange rate devaluation and demand contraction hit companies' refund capacity, banks were abruptly faced with skyrocketing NPLs. At the end of 1998, NPLs (as a percentage of total loans) ranged between 48.6 per cent for Indonesia, 42.9 per cent for Thailand, 18.6 per cent for Malaysia, 12.4 per cent for the Philippines and 7.4 per cent for Korea. The bursting of the asset bubble made collateral insufficient to compensate the credit loss, aggravating the impact on banks' profitability. At the end of 1998, the average return on assets (ROA) was negative for Indonesia (−19.9 per cent), Korea (−3.2 per cent), and Thailand (−5.6 per cent). Deep liquidity problems and bank runs were quite frequent and, even worse, losses fully eroded the capital base for many banks.

Against such a backdrop, the first objective of the governments of the affected countries was to save their financial system through emergency measures. A huge liquidity support was extended to banks. Such flow of money had to be sterilised to avoid monetary overexpansion: in Indonesia the failure of the sterilisation triggered a Rupiah collapse.

After the emergency, a deep restructuring was needed. The strategy was aimed at preserving the functioning of the financial infrastructures, while minimising the public cost of the restructuring plan.

The first step was the closure of 16 insolvent financial institutions. Such a measure was aimed at restoring market confidence in the banking system. However, the shutting down of these small, deeply insolvent private banks was followed by bank runs, given the lack of clear guidelines on depositor compensation, opaque liquidation policies and political uncertainties (Batunanggar, 2002, p.9). Consequently, a number of banks run into liquidity problems and, from November 1997 to the end of 2000, the authorities undertook major rounds of intervention, including open bank assistance, recapitalisation and further bank closures. What initially seemed a crisis limited to only 16 small intermediaries turn out to be a systemic event, involving almost 40 per cent of the Indonesian banking system. Besides, a blanket guarantee was introduced to protect depositors and creditors and preserve trust in the financial system. Finally, the responsibility for the bank restructuring program was given to a newly created agency under the Ministry of Finance, the Indonesian Bank Restructuring Agency (IBRA) set up in 1998. Its mandate was to supervise and restructure the banking sector, fostering banks' closures, merger or take over and recapitalising troubled banks. IBRA was also given the tasks of restructuring the non performing assets of problem banks.

Summing up, the Indonesian bank restructuring programme implied:

a. the recapitalisation of 4 state banks and their merger into one bank (Mandiri);
b. the recapitalisation of 12 regional development banks and 10 private banks;
c. the closure of 64 private banks;
d. the receivership of 14 private banks, of which 9 were merged to 1;
e. the set up of a centralised state-owned asset management company (IBRA) in order to handle problem banks' non performing assets.

As a consequence of the financial crisis, the regulatory and supervising environment also experienced a deep transformation. The 1998 Banking Law required that the supervisory activity should be transferred to a financial supervisory agency by the end of 2002. Such Financial Supervisory Authority, modelled on the British FSA, should licence, regulate and supervise financial institutions and the capital market, as well as being responsible for individual bank resolution. Besides the creation of a single regulator, the law cast the foundations for the introduction of a limited deposit insurance scheme, to replace the blanket guarantee introduced at the outset of the crisis.

To date, only this second point has been accomplished and in September 2005 the Deposit Insurance Agency was established (LPS) to perform an explicit and limited deposit insurance scheme and to carry out the resolution of failing banks.[2]

On the other hand, the responsibility for financial supervision and financial stability is still split between four authorities: the Ministry of Finance; Bank of Indonesia, responsible for formulating and implementing the monetary policy, for regulating and ensuring a smooth payment system, and for regulating and supervising the national banking system; BAPEPAM, the Capital Market Supervisory Agency, and LPS, the Deposit Insurance Agency.

A bank-oriented financial system

The Indonesian financial system has traditionally been dominated by banks. Although their market share is lower than before the crisis, in 2005 Indonesian commercial banks still accounted for more than 90 per cent of the total assets of the credit system. When including both rural and Islamic banks along with commercial banks, the Indonesian banking system accounts for almost 95 per cent of total financial assets (Table 4.2). Such a prominent role of the banking system is further confirmed by comparing its contribution to GDP with that of the capital market: at the end of 2006, the ratio of total banking assets to GDP was 52 per cent, while, during the same period, market capitalisation and corporate bond outstanding accounted for, respectively, little more than 29 per cent and 2 per cent of GDP. In this respect, the Indonesian financial system can be considered underdeveloped relative to its regional competitors (Malaysia and Thailand), where market capitalisation and outstanding corporate bond exceeded 100 per cent.

In 2006, commercial bank lending, denominated in rupiah and in foreign currencies, equalled Rp 792.2 trillion, or 24 per cent of GDP, while the stock and bond markets' new issuances totalled Rp 384 trillion, or 11 per cent of GDP. However, bank debt does not play a major role in the financing of investment projects of Indonesian firms, at least during the period starting with the crisis's egress and up to 2005. Bank intermediation, defined as the ratio of bank loans to GDP, has decreased from a peak of 61 per cent in 1997 to 18 per cent in 2001, hence recovering to just 24 per cent of GDP in 2006: according to the IMF (2006) this is the lowest ratio in the whole emerging Asia. In fact, the primary source of financing for Indonesian firms is represented by self-finance, which in small and medium enterprises accounts for 65 per cent of total business finance (Bank of Indonesia, 2005).

As shown in Table 4.3, at the end of 2006 the Indonesian credit system comprised 130 commercial banks, almost 9,000 rural banks, 216 multi-finance companies and 128 sharia banks.

Commercial banks operate as universal banks, delivering both traditional banking and financial services (bank loans and deposits, factoring, credit cards) and trading services on a broker/dealer basis. Investment banking services are constrained to undertaking placement of funds among customers in the form of securities not listed in the Stock Exchange. Equity-participation in non-financial firms is forbidden, with the only exception of equity participation consequent to debt-restructuring programmes. Finally, insurance activity can only be performed by means of a subsidiary.

Rural banks are a composite group, comprising pawn shops, employee banks and paddy/village banks. These intermediaries share the small dimension, strong local roots and, from a regulatory viewpoint, the prohibition to accept demand deposits, to conduct business in foreign currencies apart from money change, and to take equity participation or perform insurance business.

Sharia banks or Islamic banks specialise in supplying banking services based on Sharia principles.[3] Sharia banks can either be Sharia Business

Table 4.3 The Indonesian financial system: 1997–2006

	July 1997	2000	2006	June 1997	2000	2006
	No. intermediaries			*No. branches*		
Commercial banks	238	151	130	7,860	6,524	9,110
State-owned banks	7	5	5	1,843	1,753	2,548
Private banks	160	81	71	5,095	3,835	5,154
Foreign banks (branches and subsidiaries)	44	39	28	100	110	191
Regional development banks	27	26	26	822	826	1,217
Rural banks	9,372	9,384	8,950*	9,421	9,447	10,098
Sharia banks	n.d.	n.d.	128	n.d.	146	531
Indonesian Banking system	9,610	9,535	9,208	17,281	16,117	19,739
Multi-finance firms	248	248	216**	–	–	–
Indonesian credit system	9,858	9,783	9,336	–	–	–
				Market share as % of total assets		
Commercial banks				99.35	97.43	91.46
State-owned banks				33.89	52.75	–
Private banks				52.83	35.82	–
Foreign banks (branches and subsidiaries)				9.81	12.47	–
Regional development banks				2.82	2.57	–
Rural banks				0.65	0.49	1.24
Sharia banks				n.d.	n.d.	1.44
Indonesian banking system				100.00	97.92	94.15
Multi-finance firms				n.d.	1.88	5.85
Indonesian credit system				100.00	100.00	100.00
				Market share as % of total loans		
State-owned banks				37.19	37.94	35.93
Private banks				52.19	30.64	42.55
Foreign banks (branches and subsidiaries)				9.42	27.66	14.41
Regional development banks				2.20	3.76	7.11
Indonesian commercial banks				100.00	100.00	100.00
				Bank service coverage		
No. of banks per 100,000 inhabitants				5.6	4.6	4.2
No. of branches per 100,000 inhabitants				10.0	7.7	8.6

Notes: *March 2006; **September 2006; ***December 2005
Source: Bank of Indonesia Annual Reports and web site statistics; Pangestu and Habir (2002).

Units of 'conventional' banks or hold a commercial or rural bank licence. As with many other Islamic countries, Indonesia promotes the development of Islamic banking; in particular, since 2002, the Bank of Indonesia has adopted a specific plan for the development of sharia banks, aimed at increasing the number of banks and the volume of bank activity based on sharia principles. At the end of 2006, there were three Sharia Commercial banks, 20 Sharia Business Units and 105 Sharia Rural banks, with a total of 531 branches covering 31 provinces (over a total of 33) and a market share of 1.4 per cent cent of total credit sector assets. The sharia network was complemented by the operation of 456 conventional bank branch offices providing sharia services. Financing micro-enterprises dominates the assets of sharia banks and this explains, besides the religious motifs, why the Bank of Indonesia is particularly keen in promoting the Islamic banking industry. In particular, Sharia banks have, in principles, a huge potential to support the micro, small and medium enterprises sector. In fact, as Islamic financing is guided by profit (loss) sharing principles, Sharia banks and their business customers share mutually supportive partnerships, which in turn should mitigate asymmetric information and credit rationing. Such greater transparency among interested parties should lead to fairer agreements between 'lenders' (owners) and entrepreneurs which could potentially alleviate the intensity of agency problems and reduce the problems of insufficient collateral.

Given the nature of their business, rural and sharia banks were less affected by the financial crisis and are therefore able to maintain higher loan to deposit ratios (82 per cent and 99 per cent[4] respectively) along with a lower credit risk for sharia banks (4.8 per cent in 2006) with respect to commercial banks (64.7 per cent and 7 per cent).

Within the commercial banks' group, banks can be further classified with respect to their ownership structure: at the end of 2006, there were 5 state-owned banks, 71 private banks, 28 foreign banks and 26 regional development banks.

Before the 1997 financial crisis, the ownership structure of private national banks was concentrated in the hands of large industrial businesses or wealthy families with powerful political protections, largely due to family ties. Private national banks were mainly captive banks, primarily lending to related parties. As a matter of fact, *connected lending* has been one of the major drivers of the Asian financial crisis.[5] Notwithstanding the 1992 Banking Law and its 1998 amendment, which imposed strict limits to loans to majority shareholders and related parties,[6] widespread contravention of such prudential legal lending limit was the norm among Indonesian banks. According to a recent study on corporate governance of Indonesian banks, prior to the 1997 financial crisis,

90 per cent of the Indonesian banking system breached the legal lending limit. In particular, three of the 16 banks ordered to be closed in November 1997 were reported to have lent to related parties far more than 100 per cent of their paid-up capital.[7]

After a widespread nationalisation, in 1999 as much as 95 per cent of the total liabilities of the the banking sector were under state-ownership. Afterwards, government ownership has been gradually reduced and in 2005 it stood at 38 per cent of total national banking assets. At the same time, increased foreign ownership has been favoured. The substantial entry of foreign banks in Indonesia is indeed a recent phenomenon: before the crisis, formal restrictions on the entry and operation of foreign banks limited their presence to joint ventures with domestic banking partners, with a maximum foreign ownership of 85 per cent. New branch opening was only permitted to foreign banks with a pre-existing presence in the country (Montgomery, 1997, 2003). After the collapse of the national banking system in 1997, the government raised the limit on foreign ownership in joint ventures from 85 per cent to 99 per cent. As a result of such regulatory change and to the consolidation process ignited by the post-crisis restructuring programme, in December 2005, twelve of Indonesia's private national banks were under foreign ownership control and foreigners owned more than 45 per cent of total national banking assets. In 1996, in a comparative perspective, their market share was lower than 10 per cent of national banking assets. At the same time, government ownership has dropped to less than 38 per cent, after a peak of 70 per cent in 1998.

The evolution of private commercial banks is clearly determined by the evolution of the regulatory environment and by the post-crisis bank restructuring programme. Private banks expanded rapidly during the early 1990s and reached a peak in 1996, with 239 banks and more than 7,000 branches, as a result of the 1988 deregulation package (PAKTO). However their number fell substantially (-55 per cent) at the onset of the 1997 financial crisis (see Table 4.2). Between 1997 and 2004, 64 banks were declared insolvent and closed, 4 (foreign) banks were voluntarily liquidated, 28 banks took part, on a voluntary or a forced basis, to M&A operations.

As a consequence of the consolidation process, the Indonesian banking system has experienced an upward concentration: in 1996, the five largest bank had a combined market share of less than 17 per cent of total banking assets; ten years later they account for 51 per cent of total banking assets. Similarly, the market share of the ten largest Indonesian banks has increased from 22 per cent to 64 per cent since 1996. As a matter of fact, the Indonesian banking system is quite clearly dominated by the largest fifteen banks which in 2005 held 73 per cent of all national banking assets.

After a sharp contraction during the crisis period, in recent years the branch network of Indonesian banks has been expanded, favoured by regulators. Indeed, in 2006 Bank of Indonesia set forth specific policies to underpin the banking structure. Among the others, two specific objectives were set: increasing the country's bank service coverage and promoting the consolidation process. In particular, a blueprint known as Indonesian Financial System Architecture (ASKI) was prepared which envisaged two or three major international banks; from three to five large domestic bank; a number of medium banks (retail, corporate and regional banks); finally a plethora of smaller banks, including rural and sharia banks.

Recent performance and lingering fragilities of Indonesian banks

Above, we have briefly outlined the Indonesian bank restructuring programme; it is now worth evaluating its effectiveness to the final goals of rehabilitating problem banks and strengthening the banking system in terms of adequate capital ratios, asset quality, profitability and efficiency.

First, to assess the effectiveness of the bank rehabilitation programme, the performance of the Indonesian banking system is compared to the average performance of the other four crisis-hit countries. The sample period spans from 2001 to 2005 (post-crisis period), while the chosen performance indicators are the followings: bank capital ratios (Capital Adequacy Ratio, CAR and Equity to Total Assets); profitability ratios (ROA; ROE; Net Interest Margin); asset quality ratios (NPL to Total Loans; Loan-Loss provisions to Gross Loans); credit intermediation ratios (Loans to Total Assets; Loans to Deposits). During the crisis, both the general public and investors did not always perceive the restructuring plan as a transparent programme able to solve significantly the problems of the banking system. However, ten years after the onset of the financial crisis, a positive judgment can be formulated on its results. As highlighted by the selected indicators (Figure 4.1), Indonesian banks compares favourably to the aforementioned peers. Indonesian banks have higher CARs, higher net interest margins and higher operational and capital profitability. While their cost structure is about average, Indonesian banks are less burdened by non-performing assets. In the more recent years, Indonesian banks have strongly increased their propensity to lend: between 2000 and 2004 their credit supply has

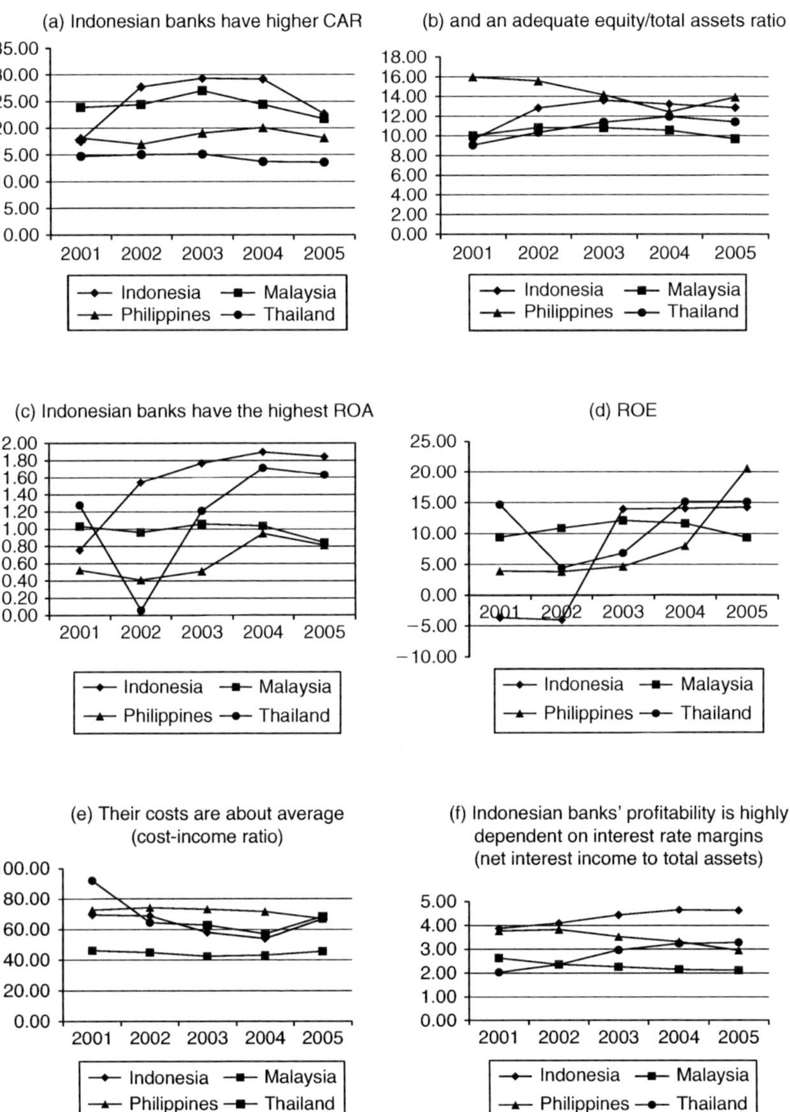

Figure 4.1 The recent performance of the crisis-hit South-East Asian banking system

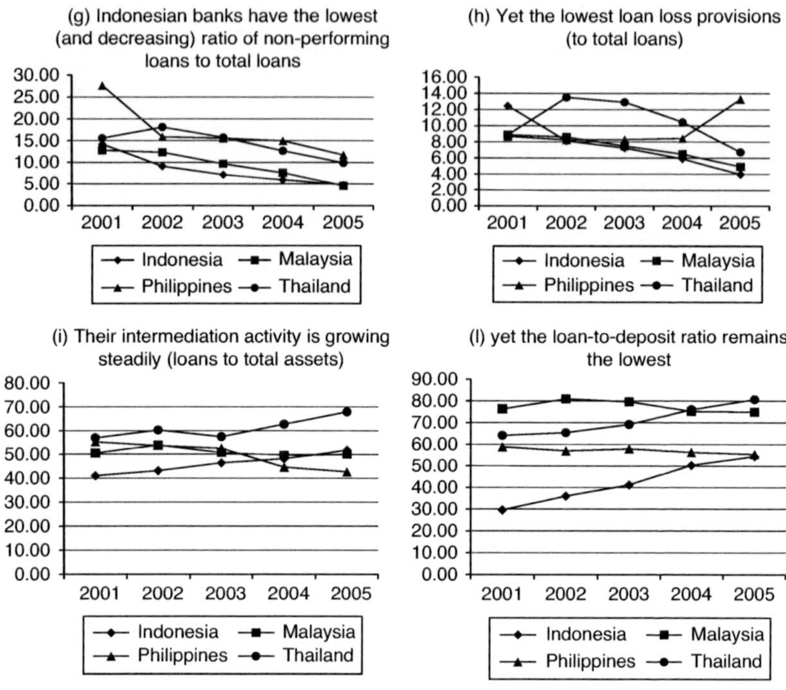

Figure 4.1 Continued

increased at a an annual average rate of 20 per cent, well above the rate registered by their regional competitors. However, Indonesian banks still present the lowest share of loans to deposits ratio, reflecting the relatively more severe impact of the crisis.

Next, the effectiveness of the plan is assessed by comparing the performance of a sample of Indonesian banks distinguishing between problem banks that underwent some restructuring (for instance, were taken over by IBRA, forced to merge, recapitalised) and banks which have weathered the crisis on their 'own two feet'. The first group comprises all State-Owned Banks (SOB) and few private banks. The second group includes the remaining Indonesian private banks and foreign banks. The latter are a sort of benchmark frontier against which it is possible to assess whether problem banks have, in recent years, rolled back on a virtuous growth path recovering adequate levels of profitability and efficiency. In other words, we try to assess whether the support offered to distressed banks has borne fruit (i.e., a managerial improvement) or it was a real 'waste of public money'.

Indeed, restructured banks have recovered in terms of profitability, efficiency and capital adequacy; however some gaps remain with reference to the volume of credit intermediation and the quality of loans. The latter, in particular, shows a sharp deterioration in recent years, when the closure of IBRA eliminated any external support in the restructuring and recovering of non performing loans.

Despite the mentioned factors of success, the Indonesian banking system faces lingering fragilities.

First, the NPL to loans ratio remains well above the threshold target of 5 per cent as indicated in the Bank of Indonesia's restructuring plan of 1998. At the same time the ratio seems to have left its decreasing trend: from a peak of 48.6 per cent in 1996, it declined to 5.8 per cent in 2004 and then increased back to 8.3 per cent in 2005. The causes of such an increase can be attributed to several factors. One reason lies in the unfavourable macroeconomic conditions, such as increased inflation and interest rates. A second explanation relates to the introduction, at the beginning of 2005, of new and more stringent rules for the classification of loans and the definition of non performing assets. Finally, one should not forget that after the crisis a majority of Indonesian banks have delegated the working-out of impaired loans to a centralised state agency – IBRA – to which the huge bad assets emerged during the crisis were transferred. With the liquidation of IBRA in 2004, banks are now required to internalise bad debt collection, an activity for which they might lack the expertise and the skills. As Figure 4.2 highlights, this change has produced a marked deterioration of the ratio for the cluster of restructured banks, especially state banks.

The second factor of weakness relates to the sources of bank profitability. The profitability of Indonesian banks lies in the high margins from traditional intermediation services, which may no longer be compatible with a more competitive environment especially in consumer lending, which has become strategic for most Indonesian banks. Indeed, Indonesian banks have shifted their business focus with respect to the pre-crisis period, when their lending activity was almost exclusively concentrated on large corporates. To date, on the contrary, a large part of their loan portfolio, equal to 30 per cent in 2005, comprises consumer lending. The preference for the retail segment can be explained by reference to both demand and supply factors. On the demand side, the high rate of growth of consumer credit is driven by the expansion of private consumption, the true engine of the recent economic growth. On the supply side, banks have an incentive to focus on consumer lending given its historically lower credit risk: in 2005 the NPL to loan ratio in consumer lending was

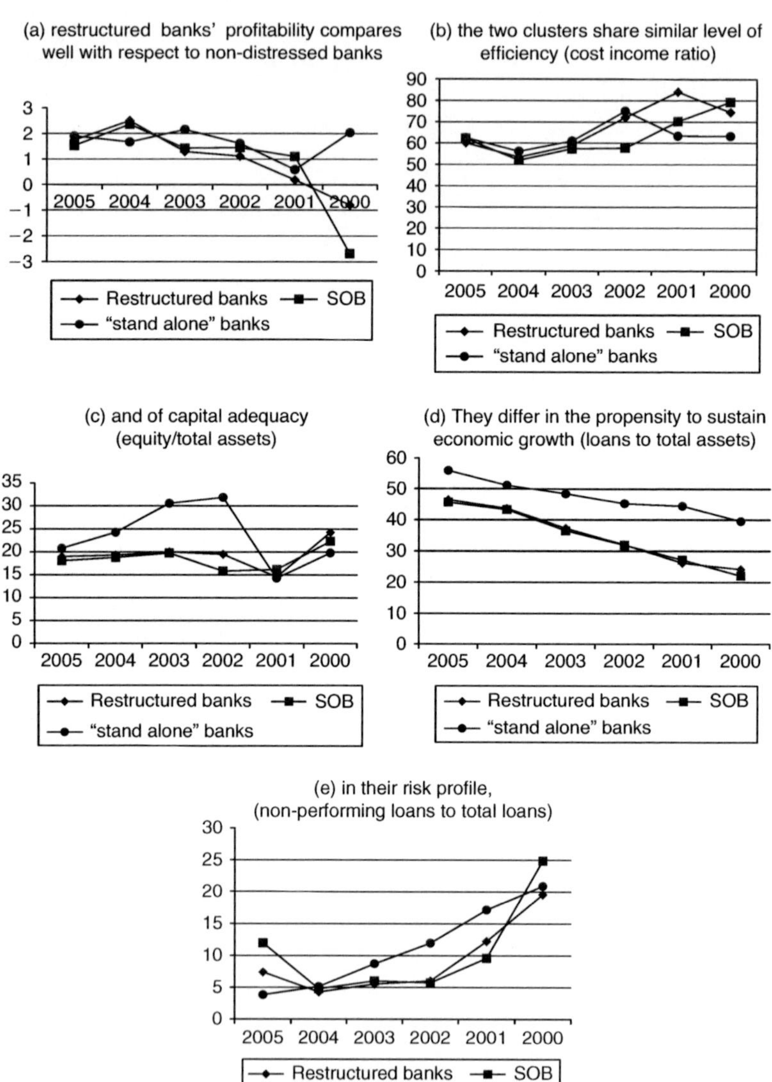

Figure 4.2   Indonesian Banks' performance: 2000–2005

below 2 per cent and compared to 5.13 per cent for working capital loans and to 7.85 per cent for investment loans.

It is exactly on such market segment that Indonesian banks experience a competitive pressure from foreign banks. In fact, if we exclude consumer lending, there are no other major areas of overlap between the activities of domestic and foreign banks, the latter being mainly focused on investment banking services. Despite a greater presence in domestic banks (also in the form of equity participation), foreign banks still play a limited role in lending to large corporation. After the crisis, for obvious reasons, foreign banks were very cautious in expanding their credit supply, which remains largely concentrated in the segment of consumer lending.

Third, although bank CARs appear broadly satisfactory and able to meet the international standards, these findings should be read with extreme caution in light of the low risk-weighted assets held by Indonesian banks. Following the restructuring of their problem loans, banks, especially state banks, held large part of their assets invested in government securities, which are typically assigned a zero weight in the definition of the Cook ratio. The slow but steady growth of the bank intermediation activity that Indonesia has been experiencing in recent years will require higher amounts of capital and could negatively impact banks' capital ratios.

Finally, signs of imbalances that can endanger the stability of the financial system stems from the segment of finance companies, rather than from the banking system. Indonesian finance companies are specialised in leasing, factoring, credit cards and consumer lending. Alike banks, since year 2000 finance companies have shifted their focus towards consumer lending, which now accounts for 65 per cent of their loan portfolio. However, unlike banks and thanks also to a less stringent regulation, finance companies seem to have adopted looser screening process, accepting to supply loans to more risky customers. It follows that in a context of increasing interest rates financial companies are more likely to be exposed to an increased credit risk.[8] Domino effect from the finance companies segment may endanger the banking sector: in fact the primary source of their funding stems from the banking sector (more than 50 per cent in 2006).

Foreign banks in Indonesia: role and perspectives

So far we have described the recent evolution of the structure and performance of the Indonesian banking system. The first conclusion that can be drawn is that Indonesia appears to have regained its economic, political and social stability put to severe test by the financial crisis. Notwithstanding some remaining macroeconomic uncertainties, the economy continues to grow although at moderate rates for an emerging economy (5–6 per cent yearly). The banking system, on its part, seems to have answered well to the restructuring plan, even if with lights and shadows, during the period 1999–2004. Indonesian banks' performances compares favourably relative to their regional competitors: a valuable result given the more sever impact of the crisis on Indonesia. Restructured banks' performance is now in line or even better than that of those Indonesian banks that weathered the crisis without any specific government aid. The bill of the restructuring plan, although high, can be paid without thinking that the banking rescue plan was a waste of taxpayers' money.

Since 2003, the Indonesian banking industry has been attracting foreign investments. Three are the main reason for such a renewed interest by foreign investors. First, Indonesia is a big market. Not only it is the largest economy in South-East Asia, but it also has a huge potential for retail, consumer and private banking services thanks to its demographic characteristics: 232 million of inhabitants with a per-capita income of US$1,300 and high share of young population (64 per cent are between 15–60 years old). Second, trade with India, China and the Middle East, alongside the historical commercial partner (Japan), is growing. It is not surprising that foreign investments mainly come from these countries. Last but not least, banking regulation has changed favouring foreign investors' entry: heavy restrictions to entry and operations previously imposed to foreign banks have been almost entirely removed; few constraints remain aimed at limiting the entry to major international financial institutions.

As for foreign bank penetration, a relevant discontinuity with respect to the past relates to the mode of entry, which has deeply changed mainly driven by a change in regulatory rules. In fact, while in the past the only options open to foreign financial institutions were represented by branch opening or joint ventures with local partners, today the preferred option is represented by the acquisition of majority stakes in small private banks local. Indeed the new capital adequacy rules adopted by the Bank of Indonesia in light of Basle II are requiring Indonesian banks, in a relatively short time frame, to increase their capital base in order to adequately take into account credit risk, market risks and operational risks. This has created a big market for acquisitions of small private banks – around Rs 100 billion, or 8.5 million euros of total assets – whose shareholders are not able to provide compliance to the new capital standards with their own resources.

To date, the most active foreign investors acquiring small local banks are from the Asian region (Singapore first, followed by Japan, India and

China). Undeniably, these countries are implementing a kind of 'follow-the-client' strategy: these are, in fact, the countries with which, in more recent years, Indonesia has greatly increased commercial trade. However, even if originating from the internationalisation of their domestic customer base, such banks are not limiting their activity to trade finance or to financing large corporates: the decision to acquire a local bank responds to a specific strategy aimed at exploiting the large potential for retail, consumer and private banking services.

In this context, European banks have the potential to access the Indonesian market with success: not only they have a consolidated retail experience in their country of origin, but also in emerging markets or in transition economies to which they have already embarked on a successful path of internationalisation (such as East Europe or South America). In truth, the interest of major European global players for Indonesia seems limited also because China is a formidable competitor, capable of attracting the attention of the international community and forcing its neighbours in a cone of shadow.

Notes

1. No evidence is given of a decline of a banking system in so far.
2. Up until 2004, such a task was accomplished by IBRA. With its liquidation in 2004, the resolution of problem banks with no systemic impact is undertaken by Bank of Indonesia, while problem banks with a systemic impact is to be resolved by the Ministry of Finance.
3. For further reading on Islamic banking see Iqbal and Molyneux (2005).
4. Financing-to-deposit ratio.
5. Bongini *et al.* (2001).
6. The rule called 'the legal lending limit' or 3L rule imposed that a bank could not lend over 10% of its issued capital to commissioners, directors, substantial shareholders and other related parties, or more than 30% of its issued capital to a group of related parties.
7. Tabalujan (2001).
8. The percentage of earning assets classified as doubtful loans or losses is in fact increasing (Bank of Indonesia, 2005).

References

Asian Development Bank, 'Key Indicators of Developing Asian and Pacific Countries', various years.
Bank of Indonesia, *Economic Report on 2005* (Jakarta: Bank of Indonesia, 2005).
Bank of Indonesia, *Economic Report on 2006* (Jakarta: Bank of Indonesia, 2006).

Bank of Indonesia, *Indonesian Banking Booklet* (Jakarta: Bank of Indonesia, various years).

Bank of Indonesia, *Financial Stability Review* (Jakarta: Bank of Indonesia, various years).

Batunanggar, S. (2002) 'Indonesia's Banking Crisis Resolution: Lessons and the Way Forward', Bank of Indonesia Working Paper.

Bongini, P. Claessens, S. and Ferri, G. (2001) 'The Political Economy of Distress in East Asian Financial Institutions', *The Journal of Financial Services Research* (IXX), pp. 5–25.

Cooke, D. and Foley, J. (1999) 'The Role of the Asset Management Entity. An East Asian Perspective', in *Rising to the Challenge in Asia: A Study of Financial Markets*, Vol 2 Special Issue, (Manila: Asian Development Bank).

Corsetti, G. Pesenti, P. and Roubini, N. (1999) 'The Asian Crisis: An Overview of the Empirical Evidence and Policy Debate', in P. R. Agenor, M. Miller, D. Vines and A. Weber (eds), *Financial Crises: Causes, Contagion and Consequences* (Cambridge: Cambridge University Press).

Furman, J. and Stiglitz, J.E. (1998) 'Economic Crises: Evidence and Insights from East Asia', Brookings Papers on Economic Activity.

Goldstein, M. (1998) 'The Asian Financial Crisis; Causes, Cures and Systemic Implications', Policy Analysis in International Economics, Institute for International Economics.

Honohan, P. and Kinglebiel, D. (2000) 'Controlling The Fiscal Cost of Banking Crises', World Bank Policy Research Paper no. 9.

IMF, *Indonesia: Selected Issues*, IMF Country Report no. 05/327, September (Washington, DC: IMF).

IMF, *Indonesia: Selected Issues*, IMF Country Report no. 06/318 in August (Washington, DC: IMF).

Iqbal, M. and Molyneux, P. (2005) *Thirty Years of Islamic Banking* (New York: Palgrave Macmillan).

Kaminsky, G. and Reinhart, C. (1999) 'The Twin Crises: Causes of Banking and Balance of Payment Problems', *American Economic Review*, Vol. 89, no. 3, pp. 473–500.

Lall, S. and Rao, K. (1995) 'Indonesia: Sustaining Manufactured Export Growth', report submitted to the National Planning Board (Bappenas), Main report, August.

Montgomery, J. (1997) 'The Indonesian Financial System: Its Contribution to Economic Performance and Key Policy Issues', IMF Working Paper 97/45.

Montgomery, H. (2003) 'The Role of Foreign Banks in Post-crisis Asia: The Importance of Method of Entry, Asian Development Bank Research paper no. 51.

Pangestu, M. and Habir, M. (2002) 'The Boom, Bust and Reconstructing of the Indonesian Banking System', IMF Working Paper 02/66.

Radelet, S. and Sachs, J. (1998) 'The Onset of the East Asian Financial Crisis', NBER Working Paper No. 6680.

Tabalujan, B.S. (2001) 'Corporate Governance of Indonesian Banks. The Legal and Business Context', *Australian Journal of Corporate Law 67* (2001).

Wie, T.K. (2006) 'Technology and Indonesia's Industrial Competitiveness', Asian Development Bank Institute Research Paper series No. 72.

World Bank, 'The East Asian Miracle. Economic Growth and Public Policy', World Bank Policy Research Report (1993).

5
Brazil

M. Lossani, L. Ruggerone and M. Zaninelli

Introduction

After the *lost decade* of the 1980s the Brazilian economy seemed to be trapped into a vicious circle, made of severe domestic macroeconomic imbalances and high-frequency external shocks. In 1994 the adoption of the Real Plan signed the end of a relatively long period of very high and unstable inflation due to undisciplined fiscal and monetary policies. At the beginning of the new millennium, Brazil is rightly considered an economic system very different from the one existing in the early 1980s. The reduction of several (external and domestic) sources of vulnerabilities has been associated with a substantial improvement of fiscal and monetary policy management and the resumption of economic growth.

In a similar vein, the Brazilian financial system underwent a deep and wide transformation. The process of macroeconomic stabilisation induced a major restructuring of the banking industry: in a short period of time the banking system shifted from a condition, where competition was scarce and state-owned commercial banks were the dominant players, to a situation where the role of private, universal banks (both domestic and foreign) is prominent and the majority of credit is allocated freely in an (almost) competitive market. Moreover, the improvement of the macroeconomic framework limited the frequency and the depth of recessions induced by banking crises – that were the main cause of a severe process of bank disintermediation[1] – giving a new boost to bank intermediation. At the same time, the new macroeconomic framework enabled Brazil to develop domestic securities markets and issue global bonds denominated in local currency, changing the debt structure originally biased towards foreign currency denominated debt. Although notably improved, the Brazilian banking system still presents some deficiencies as well as some anomalies. Adopting an international comparative perspective, it must be said that there is still a long way to go to reach the performances of the most dynamic and efficient banking systems located in East Asian emerging markets, where competition is tighter, the level of efficiency higher and bank lending activity more pronounced.

A long-term perspective on Brazilian development

Brazil experienced a sustained growth until 1964 when, for the first time in the post-war era, inflation hiked to a three digit level. In a few years the economy was stabilised and growth resumed. All in all, the 15 years between 1964 and 1980 can be considered as a period of strong development: average annual GDP growth was 7.8 per cent, with high investment activity sustaining the industrial sector expansion, which represented the engine of growth (+8.5 per cent yearly rate of growth).

In the early 1980s a debt crisis erupted as a consequence of an intensive use of (foreign) commercial bank loans to finance public investments and oil imports. The lost decade overlapped with the start of a new high inflation period and a sharp increase in the degree of macroeconomic volatility. Between 1980 and 1994 the inflation rate was always (with the only exception of 1986) higher than 100 per cent and reached 3.000 per cent per year on average in 1990. Five monetary reforms were not able to defeat inflation, also because the widespread system of indexation increased the capacity to accommodate the strong, ongoing increase of the price level. Private and public savings were extensively protected by means of this indexation system that – through the adoption of a crawling-peg regime (based on small devaluations on an irregular basis) – was able to insulate exporters from the negative consequences of inflationary shocks.

The burden of macroeconomic instability fell on investment in capital goods and infrastructure: during the period 1981–93 the investment rate was almost 5 per cent in real terms, lower than in 1964–80. Between 1981 and 1993 the real yearly average rate of growth was only 1.6 per cent, much lower than in the 15 previous years and even lower that the population growth (+1.9 per cent per year): consequently, the average per capita income declined by 0.3 per cent per year (Pinheiro *et al.*, 2004).

How Brazilian inflation was conquered: the Real Plan and the new institutional framework

A dramatic change took place in July 1994 with the adoption of the Real Plan, the introduction of a new currency (*Real*) and the permanent defeat of hyperinflation.

The Real Plan was a classical exchange-rate based stabilization programme. To anchor inflationary expectations a pegged exchange rate *vis-à-vis* the dollar was established. The monetary regime switch and significant neoliberal structural reforms delivered notable consequences in the short run. Along with a drastic reduction of inflation – that fell from almost 5,000 per cent in June 1994 to 33 per cent after and less than 10 per cent in December 1996 – there was a return to strong growth: between 1994 and 1997 GDP growth was on average equal to 4 per cent per year. In a short time the Brazilian economy moved from an inward-oriented, inflation and crisis-prone system – where the role of state planning was still large – to a situation where price stability and outward orientation set the ground for a larger role for the private sector.

However, after the stabilisation of inflation some serious imbalances were still at work. Fiscal policy was unable to produce a primary surplus, necessary to offset the increasing burden due to interest payments on public debt; monetary policy – targeted on an imperfectly credible pegged exchange rate – created a large real overvaluation, that magnified the import boom due to the trade liberalisation process undertaken after the establishment of Mercosur at the beginning of 1995.[2] The stock of public debt raised and the trade deficit widened until when – after the spread of the Asian and Russian crises – it became clear that a fiscal consolidation was not possible and the maintenance of the fixed exchange rate was no longer credible. The market reacted promptly: maturities fell (interest payment on domestic debt due just in the month of January 1999 were equal to 6 per cent of GDP), debt switched from fixed rate to floating (at the beginning of 1999 70 per cent of public debt was indexed to the overnight rate) and was partly dollarised (more than 20 per cent at the beginning of 1999). The dollar peg was abandoned in January 1999. However the ensuing currency crisis was – at least by Latin American standards – quite peculiar. In spite of the heavy fall of the Brazilian currency on the foreign exchange market, the Brazilian economy recorded a positive (although modest) GDP growth (1.0 per cent) in 1999.

After the currency crisis major institutional innovations – regarding fiscal and monetary policy management – were introduced. On the fiscal side, Brazil switched to less pro-cyclical fiscal policies, introduced fiscal responsibility laws and adopted better debt management practices: while the government inaugurated a long period of primary surpluses, the share of fixed rate government debt doubled in 5 years (increasing from 15 per cent to 30 per cent at the end of 2005) and the average maturity of public debt was considerably lengthened (as reflected by the first issuance of a 20-year fixed-rate global bond denominated in *Reais* that shifted the interest rate and exchange rate risk from the Brazilian government to investors). As far as monetary policy is considered, Brazil adopted an inflation targeting strategy (managed through the movement induced in the interest rate term structure by changes in the SELIC rate – the overnight rate for government bonds in the *Sistema Especial de Liquidacao e Custodia*) and joined a flexible exchange rate: the return to exchange rate flexibility was – among other factors – responsible for the improvement of the trade balance that switched to a surplus. All in all, the extent of macroeconomic vulnerabilities has been strongly reduced and the credibility of sovereign issuers improved substantially, as recently testified by Standard&Poor's decision to raise the country's long-term foreign currency debt rating to BBB– from BB+, that for the first time assigns to Brazil an investment grade credit rating.

Stability with slow growth: Brazil as a 'relatively slow grower' emerging economy

In spite of the dramatic transformations brought about by the Plano Real, the adoption of an inflation target, the establishment of a fiscal responsibility law and the reduction in the stock of public debt, Brazilian growth was still lagging behind other (Latin American and East Asian) emerging markets. The annual GDP growth rate between 1994 and 2000 was 3.1 per cent lower than Chile, equal to Mexico and the average Latin American region, but far distant from the performance recorded by Korea (5.3 per cent) and China (9.5 per cent). According to different analysts such underperformance was due to the incompleteness of reforms that should have been consolidated in order to reap the full gains of the great transformation of the Brazilian economy started in the second half of the 1990s.

However, since 2004 the situation seems quite different (Table 5.1). The average rate of growth has been 4.5 per cent per year, the fastest rate in the last 20 years. In 2007 the economy has grown at 5.4 per cent, as a result of strong household consumption and buoyant investment activity. The recent, sharp deceleration in US GDP growth will probably affect the Brazilian expansion only modestly, as a consequence of the continuing high prices and volumes of exports (mainly commodities such as iron ore and soybeans) able to sustain positively the trade balance and the current account. Inflation that was under control until 2007 (3.6 per cent) is now slightly above the Central Bank's target (4.8 per cent instead of 4.5 per cent), as a consequence of higher food and services prices, while fiscal policy has been able to deliver a string of primary surpluses and, for the fifth year in a row, a reduction in the stock of public debt, now

Table 5.1   Main economic indicators: 2000–2007

	2000	2001	2002	2003	2004	2005	2006	2007
GDP growth	4.3	1.3	2.7	1.2	5.7	3.1	3.7	5.4
CPI inflation	7.0	6.9	8.5	14.7	6.6	6.9	4.2	3.6
Budget balance (% of GDP)	−3.4	−3.3	−4.2	−4.6	−2.4	−3.0	−3.0	−2.1
Current account (% of GDP)	−3.8	−4.2	−1.5	0.8	1.8	1.6	1.3	0.3

Source: Economic Intelligence Unit (2008).

equal to 42.2 per cent of GDP (in 2002 it was still higher than 50 per cent). Last but not least, the positive growth performance together with the proper management of *Bolsa Familia*, a programme of cash transfer benefiting more than 11 million of poor families, has allowed more than 23 million citizens to move upward in the social ranking, abandoning a living condition close to poverty.[3] A notable result that – among others – has contributed positively to the development of a new flow of demand for credit by Brazilian households.

The Brazilian conundrum: why interest rates are so high?

Interest rates – albeit lower than the level prevailing in the first half of the 1990s are still much higher than in other emerging markets (the SELIC overnight rate was on average equal to 12 per cent during 2007, when consumer price inflation was lower than 5 per cent) along the whole spectrum of the yield curve. Why? It is important to notice that this problem is still unsolved, even after the adoption in 1999 of an inflation targeting regime and the abandonment of the peg to the dollar. The very high level of nominal and real interest rates determined – among others – a substantial reduction in public investment infrastructure, constraining the long-term potential growth rate. The mystery deepens once the public debt to GDP ratio – quite modest for any standard – and the primary balance – in surplus since 2002 – are taken into consideration. When the focus is shifted on external variables the puzzle still holds: real rates have been high also during the relatively long period of abundant world liquidity, prevailing until the summer of 2007.

Several, possible explanations have been provided. Favero and Giavazzi (2004) and Blanchard (2004) explain the high interest rate level with macroeconomic fundamentals, and particularly with the condition of 'fiscal dominance'. According to this view, the risk associated to the public finance situation is such that a tightened monetary policy (implemented by means of higher interest rates in order to target the announced inflation rate) would raise the probability of sovereign default,[4] causing a currency depreciation and an increase of imported inflation that in turn would trigger a further interest rate hike. An appealing explanation – showing that the high level of interest rates is motivated by a 'fiscal root' – which, however, is not fully consistent with the latest improvement characterising the Brazilian fiscal policy management of the last few years.

A similar explanation relates high interest rates to the imperfect anti-inflationary credibility suffered by the Central Bank: an element that seems to be not so relevant after that Banco Central do Brazil was granted more legal and operational independence from the government. Bacha *et al.* (2007) argue that – for a given level of systemic risk – high real interest rates are the price to pay to avoid dollarisation. However, this story is incomplete since real rates are still present after inflation targeting was adopted and the exchange rate allowed to float. Last but not least, another important element refers to the inefficient judicial system (Pinheiro and Cabral, 1999; Arida, Bacha and Lara-Resende, 2005): the missing credibility of financial contracts underwritten under the Brazilian jurisdiction could represent the cause of high interest rates and – to some extent – explain the use of world capital markets to raise funds. All in all, a convincing explanation of the determinants of high interest rates in Brazil is still missing. A vacuum that should be filled, given the relevance of high interest rates level for the magnitude of bank spreads.

The Brazilian banking system at the turn of the century

The Brazilian banking system evolved dramatically in the last 20 years (Takami and Tabak, 2007). At the end of the 1980s the banking system was dominated by state-owned commercial banks: 'directed credit' played a major role while competition was scarce. The presence of foreign banks was quite limited, after the peak reached in the early 1980s when foreign bank loans were about 40 per cent of domestic bank loans. In this context, profits were mainly generated by revenues associated to inflation: a large part of banks' profits was in fact due to the so called 'float', i.e. gains obtained investing non-interest bearing liabilities (such as demand deposits) in inflation-protected government securities.[5] The number of banks operating all over the country was continuously increasing; the opening of new banks and branches was functional to collect seignorage revenues, through an increasing issue of demand deposits. In this period, the expansion of state-owned banks (SOBs) was so strong that most of these state banks started being considered 'too big too fail'.[6] The reason why these banks grew so much is very simple. In a first stage they acted as development agencies and later on as financial agents ready to finance on demand the (inefficient) State Owned Enterprises (SOEs).[7] As the degree of inefficiency of SOEs increased, the health of the SOBs balance sheets deteriorated, generating negative consequences for the condition of public finance both at a state and at a federal level. Hence the capture of these state banks by their respective state governments generated not only a situation of inefficiency and fragility inside the banking industry, but also negative implications for the increasing budget deficit of the federal government.

From real plan towards the 'new millennium' banking system

The switch towards a market structure where private and foreign-owned banks increased their market shares is one of the several consequences of the economic revolution that affected deeply macroeconomic institutions, the regulatory framework and the trade and financial relations with the rest of the world. This regime switch was not painless, particularly for the banking system that – thanks to the large share of profits coming from inflation revenues, leading to a condition of overbranching – had never tried to minimise costs, improve the quality of services and introduce sound risk assessment techniques.

The increase in reserve requirements, implemented by the Central Bank of Brazil to support a restrictive monetary policy, was the major cause of massive reduction in the inflationary revenues of deposit banks: according to Nakane and Weintraub (2005), their share in the seignorage revenues declined from 3.4 per cent of GDP (equivalent to almost 40 per cent of banks' revenues from financial intermediation) in the 1990–93 period, to zero in 1995. At the beginning of the disinflation period Brazilian banks, instead of implementing a cost reduction restructuring process, reacted to the lower inflation tax transfers by increasing their lending activities and taking advantage from the contemporaneous consumption boom. In the first eight months after the launch of the stabilisation plan, total loans increased by 43.7 per cent. Unfortunately, in the second quarter of 1995 the Mexican crisis erupted, triggering a major increase in interest rates and a dramatic downturn in economic activity: in a short time (between the end of 1994 and the end of 1995) credit default rate rose from 4.4 per cent to 16.7 per cent, while non-performing loans (NPLs) increased substantially, also as a consequence of the lack of techniques and instruments useful to properly assess credit

Table 5.2 Share of bank system balance sheet items by ownership: 1994–2002

Year	Assets			Deposits			Loans		
	Private domestic	*Foreign*	*Public*	*Private domestic*	*Foreign*	*Public*	*Private domestic*	*Foreign*	*Public*
1994	41.3	7.2	51.5	39.4	4.6	56	35.5	5.2	59.3
1998	35.5	18.5	46.1	33.3	15.2	51.5	31.3	15.0	53.7
2002	37.3	27.7	35.0	37.1	20.1	42.7	40.5	30.5	29.1

Source: Nakane and Weintraub (2005).

risk. Only the most competitive and efficient banks were able to survive at the end of a period that saw many financial institutions (mainly state-owned banks) going bankrupt or facing heavy restructuring.

Restructuring the banking industry: PROER, PROES and PROEF

In order to contain the massive (financial and social) costs due to the widespread banking crisis, the PROER (Programme of Incentives for the Restructuring and Strengthening of the National Financial System) was launched in 1995. In this way M&A operations inside the banking system were conducted under the ruling of the Central Bank and could take advantage from credit and fiscal benefits provided to the institutions interested in buying private distressed banks: after 10 years the number of private Brazilian banks decreased substantially. In the same period, while the share of private (domestic and foreign) banks increased, the weight and the number of state-owned banks was dramatically reduced: in less than 10 years the number of these banks was more than halved, even if their share in the national banking industry evaluated in terms of assets, deposits and bank loans was still quite relevant (see Table 5.2). The establishment in July 2001 of the PROEF (Programme for Strengthening of the Federal Financial Institutions) was crucial to sustain the restructuring programme of banks owned by the Federal Government, while the institution of PROES (Programme of Incentives for the Reduction of the State Role in the Banking activity) in August 1996 played an important role in the restructuring of banks owned by Brazilian states. The increasing participation of foreign banks – both where foreign banks were already minority shareholders and through the entry of new banks inside the Brazilian system – was sustained by a huge flow of FDI, similarly to what happened in other Latin American countries and more generally in many others emerging market economies. The expectation of a renewed phase of macroeconomic and banking stability was the trigger for an increasing foreign interest in Brazilian banking and financial system: the share of total banks assets controlled by foreign-owned banks soared from 8 per cent in the early 1990s to almost 28 per cent at the end of 2002.[8] The net effect of the increased foreign participation was positive: the technology transfer applied by foreign banks both to products and processes delivered a higher efficiency within the banking industry and relevant positive spillovers on other sectors/industries; moreover, the larger presence of foreign banks strongly reduced the incidence of connected lending.

After restructuring: competition and concentration

At the beginning of the new millennium the share of public banks has been reduced, while the role of private, universal banks (both domestic and foreign) has notably increased. Most credit is now allocated freely in an (almost) competitive market. The current structure of the Brazilian financial system reflects the deep restructuring process that Brazilian banks went through since the mid-1990s, soon after the *Plano real* of 1994. As reported by the Brazilian Central Bank (as of February 2007), in the Brazilian financial system there are 2446 financial institutions – a slight decrease if compared to the beginning of the decade – of which 1,456 are credit unions[9] and 602 are banks: among the latter 156 are commercial and universal (multiple) banks, a number 25 per cent lower than that existing before the implementation of the Plano Real. Overall, there are more than 18,000 branches distributed all-over the wide Brazilian territory.

Such a high number of institutions should not induce the reader to draw the wrong conclusion: the Brazilian banking system is in fact concentrated. It is worth stressing that 11,484 of the 18,095 branches that make up the entire banking network belong to the first 4 banks, and 16,190 belong to the first 10. The same conclusion holds when the asset size, the amount of deposits and loans are taken into consideration. The first 10 largest banks of the country, account for 80 per cent of total assets, 85 per cent of total deposits and 84 per cent of total loans (World Bank, 2006a). Commercial banks still hold the lion's share in the provision of credit; as of 2004, 61 per cent of aggregate credit was in fact supplied by commercial banks, while the remaining 39 per cent was provided by other banks and non-bank financial institutions (BIS, 2006).

From a geographical point of view, the Brazilian banking sector does not appear to be evenly and homogenously distributed (see Figure 5.1). The South-East region,[10] by far the wealthiest in the country, hosts 1,412

Table 5.3 Structure of the Brazilian financial system: 2007

Type	Abbrev.	2001 Dec.	2002 Dec.	2003 Dec.	2004 Dec.	2005 Dec.	2006 Dec.	2007 Jan.	2007 Feb.
Multiple bank	BM	153	143	141	139	138	137	136	135
Commercial bank*	BC	28	23	23	24	22	21	21	21
Development bank	BD	4	4	4	4	4	4	4	4
Savings bank	CE	1	1	1	1	1	1	1	1
Investment bank	BI	20	23	21	21	20	18	17	17
Consumer finance company	SCFI	42	46	47	46	50	51	50	51
Security brokerage company	SCTVM	177	161	147	139	133	116	114	115
Exchange brokerage company	SCC	43	42	43	47	45	48	49	48
Security distribution company	SDTVM	159	151	146	138	134	133	134	133
Leasing company	SAM	72	65	58	51	45	41	41	41
Real estate credit company** and savings and loan association	SCI & APE	18	18	18	18	18	18	18	18
Mortgage company	CH	7	6	6	6	6	6	6	6
Development agency	AG FOM	9	10	11	12	12	12	12	12
Subtotal 1		733	693	666	646	628	606	603	602
Credit union	COOP	1,379	1,430	1,454	1,436	1,439	1,452	1,453	1,456
Micro-financing institution	SCM	23	37	49	51	55	56	56	55
Subtotal 2		2,135	2,160	2,169	2,133	2,122	2,114	2,112	2,113
Consortium manager	CONS	399	376	365	364	342	333	334	333
Total		2,534	2,536	2,534	2,497	2,464	2,447	2,446	2,446

Notes: * It includes foreign banks' full branches; ** It includes 15 societies of home loans that cannot catch resources together to the public.
Source: Unicad.

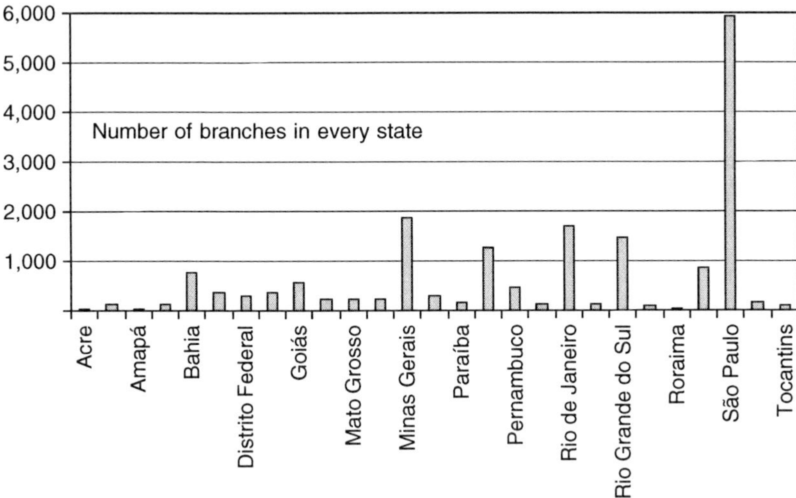

Source: Unicad.

Figure 5.1   Geographical distribution of bank branches

financial institutions, while the North is home only to 93. This means, for instance, that there are 5,928 branches in San Paolo, while only 19 in Roraima: a clear proof of the positive correlation, at a regional level, between the level of economic activity and the development of the banking industry.

The Brazilian system at the beginning of the new millennium: an emerging system with some 'anomalies'

In ten years time, the Brazilian banking system was almost literally turned upside down. The positive trend of the last decade does not necessarily imply that the revolution in the Brazilian banking and financial industry has been fully accomplished. Several weaknesses still remain and new important challenges have to be coped with, in the near future. When assessed along the three canonical dimensions (size, efficiency and stability) of a financial market, the Brazilian banking system shows a mixed evidence (World Bank, 2006b). In particular the Brazilian banking system is still affected by 'anomalies' such as:

1. low degree of credit intermediation;
2. high (lending-deposit rates) spread;

3. low degree of dollarisation; not to mention
4. (almost) total absence of long-term loans supplied to the private sector. In fact, firms usually either borrow long term, getting credit from official agencies, or use internal funds, due to retained earnings, to finance their long term projects.[11]

While feature 4. – consistent with the so called *original sin hypothesis* proposed by Eichengreen *et al.* (2004) – is common to most emerging market economies, the first three characteristics can be labeled as pure Brazilian anomalies. A good reason to provide a careful examination of the reasons behind them.

The degree of credit intermediation: low by international standards, high by regional standards

The historical underdevelopment of the bond and stock markets in Latin American countries contributed to the establishment of banks' dominant position in the southern cone, as well as in Brazil. At the beginning of the 1990s, when the financial liberalisation process triggered several innovations (such as deregulation, greater openness to foreign banks, reduction in the degree of government intervention inside the banking industry, development of domestic bond markets) this situation seemed to be ready for a change. Even though the bond markets have significantly increased its volumes,[12] a condition of bank dominance both inside the Latin American region and – to some extent – in Brazil still prevails (see Table 5.4).

The bank-based nature of the Brazilian financial market requires a more careful analysis. By international standards, the Brazilian banking sector remains shallow (BIS, 2006): domestic credit to GDP ratios are much lower than in the industrialised countries and in several emerging countries (such as East Asia), showing a low depth of bank intermediation, probably due to the poor level of information on potential borrowers and the scarce degree of enforceability of creditors' rights. By regional standards, Brazil represents an exception in the Latin American scenario. In fact, in Brazil the degree of credit penetration is second only to Chile and moved from 56 per cent to 62 per cent of GDP (between 1999 and 2005). Such a trend has been, on average, stronger than the one experienced by other Latin American countries (including Chile that in the same period followed a downward trend), thanks to supportive macro and sectoral elements such as growth resumption, favourable global monetary conditions and the restructuring process undertaken by the banking industry itself.

Table 5.4 Sources of finance in emerging and industrialised markets (share of GDP)

Country/ region	Domestic bank credit		Domestic debt securities outstanding		Stock market capitalisation	
	1999	*2005*	*1999*	*2005*	*1999*	*2005*
Brazil	56	62	55	74	42	61
Mexico	35	28	12	30	32	34
Argentina	31	38	15	14	30	36
Latin America	42	45	31	46	36	49
China	130	169	22	33	33	39
India	51	65	23	41	42	68
Central Europe	40	42	26	46	22	34
USA	80	92	150	163	150	112
Euro Area	122	154	n.a.	n.a.	74	59
Japan	161	150	134	200	104	94

Source: BIS (2006).

Lending to the private sector (both to households and firms) has been the true engine of credit growth in the last few years, sustained by the very gradual reduction of interest rates.[13] Through a continuous and constant growth of loans to small and medium-sized companies and to retail consumers, mostly in the form of payroll-deducted credits, bank credit to the private sector reached 34 per cent of GDP at the end of 2007. The credit expansion went along with the introduction of several new products aimed at mostly covering the demand of retail clients. As a matter of fact, in the second half of 2000, retail customers have moved away from less sophisticated forms of credit and started a new relationship with the domestic banking sector. More recently, the most common form of retail credit has been the issuing of credit cards (now accounting for 7 per cent of total bank lending), while less common has been the direct access to bank loans or account overdrafts. The credit picture looks even more rosy if we consider that, through 2006, the credit expansion has focused mainly in the 5,000–100,000 *reais* bracket, significantly higher than in the previous years. In the same period, a significant increase in loan maturities (both to consumers and to firms) has occurred. The quality of the credit portfolio has improved and the level of provisions for non performing loans has been decreased accordingly.

It must be noted that looking at the origination of the credit expansion, foreign owned banks appear to have been the most active players.

In the second half of 2005, the credit activity of these financial institutions grew by more than 16 per cent, reaching a market share higher than 22 per cent. Looking forward, this trend might significantly be strengthened, as foreign, banks are endowed with more sophisticated credit risk methodologies and can exploit rich liquidity channels from the parent companies abroad.

As it is often the case in emerging markets and in countries where macroeconomic stabilisation has been recently implemented, deposits are the main source of funding,[14] representing almost 50 per cent of the liabilities of the banking system and almost 35 per cent of GDP. It is worth noting that deposits collected by foreign private banks have recently grown very intensively (+15 per cent since the second half of 2005). *Repo transactions* are becoming another popular source of financing among Brazilian banks. In 2005 and 2006, growth in funding through *repo transactions* was 26.5 per cent and 38 per cent, respectively.

High (lending-deposit rates) spread

In spite of the several changes and innovations, the spread between lending and deposit rate – albeit reduced – remains extremely high, signalling a very low degree of efficiency of financial intermediation and possibly being the consequence of the high concentration and ensuing market power enjoyed by Brazilian banks. While the average spread in Latin America is around 10 per cent, the Brazilian spread is higher than 33 per cent – resulting from a lending rate above 43 per cent and a deposit rate equal to 10.6 per cent – and is by far the highest in the region and one of the highest in the world[15] (see Table 5.5). The very high level of Brazilian intermediation spreads implies a very high and volatile lending rate, leading to a reduced investment activity and a bias towards short term investment projects. Wide spreads imply also a bias towards the use of informal markets, particularly in the case of small and medium enterprises. All in all, the social costs of wide spreads seems to be extremely relevant (World Bank, 2006a).

What does lie behind these phenomenon? Several explanations have been provided. The first one is simply related to the high (nominal and real) level of Brazilian interest rates. Since there is a systematic relationship between the operational interest rate (in the case of Brazil, the SELIC) and the width of lending-deposit spread,[16] the high level of the SELIC rate is the main responsible for the high intermediation spread.

The second explanation rests upon the existence of wide and long lasting inefficiencies inside the Brazilian banking industry, that has faced scarce incentives to reduce operational costs. As previously discussed,

Table 5.5 Lending rates, deposit rates and intermediation spread: 2003–2007

	2003	*2004*	*2005*	*2006*	*2007*^
Lending rate (avg. %)	67,1	54,9	55,4	50,8	43,7
Deposit rate (avg. %)	22,0	15,4	17,6	13,9	10,6
Intermediation spread	45,1	39,5	37,8	36,9	33,1

Source: Economist Intelligence Unit (2008); ^ estimates.

the poor incentives to reduce costs are the consequence of very high margins earned on holding government debt indexed to overnight rates, when inflation was stubbornly high. Even if the system was characterised by heavy indexation, the intermediation process was quite risky: hence banks applied very high spread in their lending rates, to compensate for these risks. It turned out that spreads remained high as well as costs: nowadays overhead costs borne by Brazilian banks are still 50 per cent higher than in Argentina and Russia (and almost four times higher than in an advanced country like Spain) (World Bank, 2006a).

A third avenue of research has emphasised the role of 'jurisdictional uncertainty' (Pinheiro and Cabral, 1999; Arida *et al.*, 2005). Inside an inefficient judicial system, given the absence of a 'secure environment' where banks' rights are enforced, both debtors' willingness to pay and banks' willingness to lend is reduced. Moreover debtors have several ways to postpone a court decision, contributing to a lengthening of the time needed to be paid back. In this milieu creditors (i.e. banks) take into account – when fixing their spreads – the high default rate and the low recovery rate and the long recovery time.

A fourth explanation (Belaisch, 2003) has instead underlined the market power enjoyed by Brazilian banks: when banks can act as local monopolist, their incentives to promote efficiency gains are weak and the interest rate spread is large.

The high level of the intermediation spread raises two different issues. The first one is related to the detrimental effect on lending volumes. It follows that a reduction in lending-deposit spread might be functional to the increase of lending activity and hence to a deepening of the banking market. This phenomenon has already been experienced in the last few years, as interest rates started following a slow, downward trend. The second one is instead focussed on the risk of a sudden rise in non-performing loans. Considering that the average lending rates for Brazilian consumers and firms are respectively equal to 45.8 per cent and 23.4 per cent (at the end of 2007), it is straightforward to understand that an abrupt stop (or even a simple slow down) in income growth may easily trigger an immediate increase in non-performing loans as a consequence of borrowers' inability to pay. After 2003, when Brazilian growth resumed, the share of non-performing loans on total loans decreased, moving from 4.5 per cent at the end of 2002 to 3.1 per cent at the end of 2007.

Low degree of dollarisation

Most Latin American countries (and other East Asian emerging markets) share a high degree of dollarisation of their banking systems, where more than 40 per cent of deposits are dollarised. In this regard, Brazil is a notable exception: the share of dollar-denominated domestic deposits is close to zero, while the share of off-shore dollar deposits with respect to total (on-shore and off-shore) deposits is only 10 per cent. Similarly, dollar denominated loans are quite low. Hence, the Brazilian banking system can be defined as 'underdollarised' or even 'totally de-dollarised': a condition – consistent with the absence of currency mismatches[17] and leading to the disappearance of the exchange rate risk from banks' balance sheets – obtained as a result of the prohibition on most holdings of foreign currency deposits.

Given the prominent role played by liability dollarisation in recent episodes of financial and banking crises affecting emerging market economies, a condition of de-dollarisation is obviously a positive anomaly, contributing to the maintenance of financial stability and explaining the extreme resilience shown by the Brazilian banking system during the times of crises.

Profitability is relatively high and on a rising trend

The Brazilian banking system turns out to be quite profitable. According to IMF (2008), in 2007 the rate of return on assets (ROA) was 2.7 per cent while the rate of return on equity (ROE) was 27.8 per cent. Two major elements explain these impressive results: the first is the recent strong growth of lending activity, mainly driven by the consumer finance segment, which contributed to a relevant increase in revenues and profits originated by the intermediation activity; the second one is the improving management of operating costs, still high by international standards but on a downward trend. Revenues and profits from banking services fees have been considerably lower, even if characterised by strong dynamics.

Assessing the stability of Brazilian banking system

The Latin American region has been traditionally prone to financial crises that sometimes took the shape of twin crises, resulting from the contemporaneous occurrence of banking and currency crises. Brazil is once again a notable exception, having suffered banking and currency crises without having gone through a twin crisis, whose costs are usually much higher than those associated to either a currency or a banking crisis alone.

Lessons from the past: banking and currency (but not twin) crises in the 1990s

In the last twenty years, Brazil was hit by banking crises in 1990 and between 1994 and 1996, when the introduction of the Real and the elimination of inflation deprived banks of a large share of their income, pushing them to pursue a lending boom that in a short time ended in a dramatic increase in non-performing loans. The fiscal and quasi-fiscal costs of banking crisis were close to 8–9 per cent of GDP: an amount of resources relatively low if compared to the costs (equal to 12 per cent of GDP) suffered by other emerging markets hit by similar banking crises (Goldfajn *et al.*, 2003).

The containment of crisis costs can be partially ascribed to the establishment of PROER, the programme of a financial assistance that made the crisis less costly than otherwise would have been. A further important element for the explanation of a banking crisis with relatively limited costs was the lack of liability dollarisation and the maintenance of domestic currency denominated deposits inside the banking system. The capacity of the Brazilian banking system to manage pro-actively during the inflationary period avoided a flight to the dollar, by means of the preservation of households' and firms' confidence in domestic financial assets. In this way, the banking system was able to preserve the value of deposits denominated in domestic currency even during the most turbulent years (when inflation was higher than 50 per cent per month), thanks to the complex system of indexation arrangement.[18] However, according to the conventional wisdom the major element contributing to the relative soundness of the Brazilian banking system was the timely adoption of Basle I requirements. In 1994 Brazil decided to adopt risk-based capital requirements consistent with the Basle agreement. In June 1997, while the crisis was developing in East Asia, Brazil raised its capital requirement from 8 per cent to 10 per cent, and later on to 11 per cent. Furthermore, during 1998 the Banco Central do Brazil enjoyed more powers to force financial institutions to adopt systems of financial controls, in accordance with Basle resolution. Hence when – during 1997 and 1998 – interest rate hikes were engineered to contain contagion effects coming from the Asian and the Russian crises, the Brazilian banking system was enough capitalised. When the monetary policy stance in Brazil became restrictive to fend off the speculative attack against the Real, the negative effects of this interest rate shock were quite limited[19] and could not be magnified by the perverse effect of exchange rate depreciation due to liability dollarisation, for the very simple reason that the Brazilian system was not dollarised.

When in January 1999 the time of the currency crisis arrived, Brazil was able to avoid a twin crises. Why? One possible explanation is related to the fiscal root nature (along the classical first generation currency crisis model of the latin-american tradition) of the currency crisis, that triggered massive daily capital outflows (about US$1 billion per day).[20] Moreover the large devaluation suffered by Brazilian real (whose exchange rate *vis-à-vis* the dollar increased from 1.2 in the early days of January to 2.2 at the end of March 1999) was promptly stabilised. After two months the exchange rate stopped falling and reduced its trading volatility on the forex market, while in the case of Far Eastern currencies exchange rate stabilisation took much longer (Gruben and Welch, 2001). Finally, it should not be downplayed (once again!) the relative soundness of the banking system, as a consequence of the adoption of Basle requirements. As Gruben and Welch (2001) show, in Brazil the degree of banking leverage measured by any standard (M2/forex reserves, bank credit/forex reserves, bank credit/capital) was very low, in contrast to what happened in East Asian countries. The joint consideration of these elements is helpful to understand the rapid output recovery: during 1999 the Brazilian economy recorded only a slowdown in real economic activity – and not an output contraction – with real GDP growing at just 1 per cent.

Strengthening financial stability: from Basle I to Basle II and beyond

A distinctive element characterising the banking systems of emerging countries is the level of bank capital that is normally much higher than that observed in financially developed systems. Most banking regulators seem not to fully trust the ability of their regulated banks to analyse, monitor and control risks and requires higher levels of regulatory capital than those required in more advanced countries.

Brazil is no exception: although the Basle Committee requires[21] a Capital Adequacy Ratio (CAR), of 8 per cent, the Brazilian authority imposes much more stringent constraints. The minimum CAR for banks is in fact

Table 5.6   Brazil: bank regulatory capital to risk-weighted assets

	2002	*2003*	*2004*	*2005*	*2006*	*2007*
CAR	16.6	18.8	18.6	17.9	18.9	18.4

Source: IMF (2008).

11 per cent, while that for credit unions and development agencies is 15 per cent and 30 per cent, respectively. Looking at the average CAR of Brazilian institutions it is easy to see that this is very high and increasing over time (Table 5.6), confirming the banking system's solvency.

Banco Central do Brasil (2007a) just presented the results of two stress tests assessing the impact on CAR stemming from an increase in the credit risk (two-notch downgrade of the entire client base) and from an adverse movement of the interest and the exchange rate.[22] The results of these stress tests, applied to December 2006 figures, are reassuring: under the credit risk stress scenario, despite the reduction of the average CAR to 16 per cent, no financial institution would be classified as technically insolvent, although 19 of them would become non-compliant and would therefore require some sort of capital injection. More serious would be the impact of adverse movements of interest and exchange rates. The average CAR would go down to 12.6 per cent, and would make 35 of the major Brazilian banks non-compliant, requiring a serious recapitalisation effort. The most serious impact would be on private, foreign owned banks that, presumably, are the most active in trading activities and therefore are highly exposed to market volatility. The combination of both negative events – market and credit – would slash the average CAR to 10.7 per cent, making noncompliant 53 of the main Brazilian banks.

The ownership structure of Brazilian banks previously described highlights another important characteristic of the Brazilian banking system that makes it different from most other emerging countries. Contrary to what happens in Central and Eastern Europe, where banking systems are almost fully dominated by multinational western banks, in Brazil the largest and most important banks are owned by domestic players – public and private – and hold a market share above 80 per cent. In a home-host regulatory perspective, this fact implies that the local regulator bears the largest responsibility in assessing and maintaining the stability of the domestic financial system and in proceeding with the validation of internal models through the Basle II roll-out plan. In this respect, it must be noted that, in the last few years, Brazilian banks, supported by the local regulator, have been making enormous progress in implementing procedures and methodologies for risk governance. This improvement has been coupled by a substantial effort from the Brazilian regulator that has implemented Basle I back in 1994 and has taken active part in the Basle Committe working groups for non-G-10 countries, contributing to the gathering of data and participating in the Quantitative Impact Study (QIS) in 2001 and in 2005. Furthermore, Brazil has been the first emerging country to publish the implementation agenda for Basle II in 2004, together with detailed guidelines and definitions necessary for validation and for the final adoption of Basle II in 2011, containing also various indications concerning Pillar II and Pillar III.

For a long time, all main Brazilian banks have adopted internal rating models for both the corporate and the retail segments, although some effort is still to be made to gather significant statistical data for the entire Brazilian banking system, in order to have statistically significant estimates of risk parameters. This is particulary true for banks, whose default episodes are, as it is well known, fairly rare. Such a scarcity problem is particularly significant for emerging countries, where the credit expansion has taken place in a period characterised by high liquidity and fast economic growth. In order to reduce the impact of this problem, it cannot be excluded that Brazilian regulators will ask for even longer time series (three years is the standard) aimed at capturing the peaks, and possibly also the troughs, of the economic cycle. Together with the concepts of 'default probability', 'expected loss' and 'unexpected loss', the Brazilian regulator has introduced already in the late 1990s, the concept of operational risk. For this reason it seems reasonable to expect that most Brazilian banks will be in the position to adopt the advanced model to estimate the capital absorption of operational risk. Only small, domestically owned banks will continue to use standard models.

Conclusions

The Brazilian banking system has recently undergone important structural changes. At the end of the 1980s the banking system was dominated by publicly owned commercial banks: 'directed credit' played a major role while competition was scarce. The presence of foreign banks was quite limited. At the beginning of the new millennium the share of public banks has been heavily reduced, while the role of private, universal banks (both domestic and foreign) has notably increased. Most credit is now allocated freely in an (almost) competitive market.

The current structure of the Brazilian financial system reflects the deep restructuring process that Brazilian banks have been going through since the mid-1990s, soon after the introduction of *Plano real* in 1994. The restructuring process induced by macroeconomic stabilisation and supported by government plans (such as PROER, PROES and PROEF) was not painless; however, the costs suffered have been relatively contained, at least by international standards.

In spite of progress recorded, the Brazilian banking system still presents some deficiencies as well as some anomalies. By international standards the banking market is quite shallow, while the intermediation spread is extremely high with notable negative consequences for the process of capital accumulation; moreover, differently from many other emerging economies, Brazilian banks are totally de-dollarised and hence not exposed to exchange rate risk.

Last but not least, it is worth noting that in the last 10 years Brazilian banks have had to follow stringent regulatory requirements leading to a very high level of capitalisation. The cost deriving from the very low level of leverage has probably been more than offset by the benefits deriving from the extreme resilience shown by Brazilian banks during episodes of exchange rate devaluations and macroeconomic instability. For this reason the role of the Brazilian regulator should not be downplayed – great attention to the assessment of risks and the maintenance of the stability has been combined with a good deal of transparency. The attitude of the regulator towards the implementation and roll-out of Basel II is a clear sign that, after the initial efforts undertaken to guarantee an adequate degree of financial stability, the Brazilian banking sector is moving along a stable dynamic path that will soon enhance the convergence of the domestic banking system to the best international practices.

Notes

1. Bank disintermediation was due to a reduction both in credit demand (borrowers already indebted were reluctant to increase their indebtness) and in credit supply (the deterioration of the macroeconomic environment contributed to increase the banks' degree of risk aversion and the dimension of credit rationing).
2. The Treaty, establishing the formation of a common market, was signed by Argentina, Brazil, Paraguay and Uruguay in March 1991: *de facto* the common market was born on the 31 December 1994 with the introduction of a common external tariff. Even if less than 20 per cent of Brazilian exports was traded within the common market, the participation to Mercosur gave an important boost to the liberalization program.

3. *Bolsa Famiglia* and *Bolsa Escola*, jointly with the policies of higher minimum wages and social security transfers, have contributed significantly not only to a reduction of poverty, that declined from 28.17 per cent of the population in 2003 to 22.77 per cent in 2005, but also to a less unequal income distribution, as well. The income share of the 50 per cent poorest population grew from 12.5 per cent in 2001 to 14.1 per cent in 2005, while that of the richest 10 per cent receded to 45.1 per cent from 47.2 per cent.
4. This result is due to the increase in government deficit, induced by a higher debt service, that the market would likely assess as unsustainable.
5. Another profitable activity undertaken by Brazilian banks was the collection of huge amount of resources due to the exaction of water and energy bills (from the population) that were transferred on government's accounts only with some delay, usually 5 days later: a time long enough to obtain relevant gains.
6. It is interesting to notice that state-owned banks were present in all but two states of the Brazilian federation.
7. The State Owned Banks were the main purchasers of public bonds issued by their main shareholders: the states themselves! Acting in this way SOBs played a crucial role in the accumulation of public debt at a state level.
8. The comparison with the situation of other emerging market economies makes the Brazilian performance less impressive, since in several emerging markets the foreign ownership is really in a dominant position. On this issue see the introduction by Chiarlone and Ferri in this volume.
9. Such a high number should not be misleading, as the weight of these institutions is very limited: they control only 1.2 per cent of the total assets held by the national financial system.
10. Espìrito Santo, Minas Gerais, Rio de Janeiro and, obviously, San Paolo belong to this region.
11. To the contrary firms' working capital has been usually financed by means of costly short-term loans (denominated in domestic currency).
12. Most of the bond market development in Latin America was due to the strong expansion of the market for government papers, rather than an increase of the market for private sector bonds. A further proof that corporate bond markets are still underdeveloped in Latin America is given by the structure of corporate debt: corporate resources are mainly coming from commercial credit and commercial bank credit.
13. Because of the recent history of high inflation, monetary authorities are, in fact, extremely cautious in driving rates down.
14. Also on the liabilities side, the concentration of the Brazilian banking system is quite high: the first 100 banks hold more than 93 per cent of the total deposits. Public banks hold more than 45 per cent of the entire mass of deposits, while domestic private and foreign banks hold, respectively, almost 35 per cent and slightly less than 20 per cent.
15. It is important to point out that for most countries lending rates are the average for prime borrowers. Since in Brazil this indicator is not published, an overestimation of the actual Brazilian spread is likely. However, independently from measurement problems, the Brazilian spreads is an outlier when compared to the level prevailing in other countries.

16. Obviously this relationship is affected by the level of costs, leverage and default risk as well. According to Cardoso (2002) taxation is another factor influencing the relation between basic rates and the spread.
17. The absence of currency mismatches holds also at a macro level: at the end of 2006, the ratio between foreign currency debt and the total amount of debt is in fact lower than the ratio between exports and GDP (BIS, 2006).
18. Moreover, almost paradoxically, the high inflation environment acted as a major push factor inducing the adoption of high tech processes needed to speed up the management of financial transactions. In a few years the system switched to a widespread use of automation in check clearing; in a similar way the forex market underwent a significant increase in the adoption of automation processes.
19. In addition, banks anticipating an increase in default probability due to higher interest rates decided to re-switch their activities away from private sector lending to high-yield government securities.
20. In the case of East Asian countries, the currency crisis was instead preceded by a banking crisis.
21. In this case we obviously refer to Basle I.
22. For more detailed quantitative aspects, please refer to *Financial Stability Report* (2007).

References

Adrogué, R., Cerisola M. and Gelos, G. (2006) 'Brazil's Long Term Growth Performance – Trying to Explain the Puzzle', IMF WP/06/282.
Afanasieff, T.S., Villa Lhacer, P.M. and Nakane, M.I. (2002) 'The Determinants of Bank Interest Spread in Brazil', Banco Central do Brasil, Working Paper series no. 46.
Arida, P., Bacha, E. and Lara-Resende, A. (2005) 'Credit, Interest and Jurisdictional Uncertainty: Conjectures for the Case of Brazil', in Goldfajn I. and Giavazzi F. (eds), *Inflation Targeting, Debt and the Brazilian Experience: 1999–2003* (Cambridge, Mass: The MIT Press).
Bacha, E., Holland, M. and Goncalves, F. (2007) 'Is Brazil Different?: Risk, Dollarization, And Interest In Emerging Markets', IMF W.P.07/294.
Banco Central do Brasil (2005) 'Inflation Report', December.
Banco Central do Brasil (2007a) 'Financial Stability Report', May.
Banco Central do Brasil (2007b) 'Minutes of the 130th Meeting of the Monetary Committee', Copom.
BIS (2006) 'The Banking System in Emerging Economies: How Much Progress Has Been Made?' BIS Paper No. 28.
BIS (2007) 'Evolving Banking System in Latin America and the Caribbean: Challenges and Implications for Monetary Policy and Financial Stability', BIS Paper No. 33.
BIS (2008) 'New Financing Trends in Latin America: A Bumpy Road Towards Stability', BIS Paper No. 36.
Belaisch, A. (2003) 'Do Brazilian Banks Compete?', IMF Working Paper No. 03/113.

Blanchard, O. (2004) 'Fiscal Dominance and Inflation Targeting: Lessons from Brazil', NBER Working Paper 10389, at http://www.nber.org/papers/w10389

Cardoso, E. (2002) *Implicit and Explicit Taxation of Financial Intermediaries in Brazil: The Effect of Reserve Requirements on Bank Spreads* (Washington, DC: Georgetown University).

Cardoso, E. and Helwege, A. (1999) 'Currency Crises in the 1990s: The Case of Brazil', mimeo.

Centro de Politicas Sociais (2006) 'Poverty, Inequality and Stability: The Second Real', mimeo, at http://www.fgv.br/cps/pesquisas/site_ret_eng/

De Carvalho Filho, I., and Chamon, M. (2006) 'The Myth of Post Reform Income Stagnation in Brazil', IMF WP/06/275.

De Paiva Abreu, M. and Werneck, R. (2005) 'The Brazilian Economy from Cardoso to Lula: an Interim View', Texto Para Discussao No. 504, Departamento de Economia, PUC-Rio de Janeiro.

Economist Intelligence Unit (2008) 'Brazil', Country Risk Service, March.

Eichengreen, B., Hausmann, R. and Panizza, U. (2004) 'The Mistery of Original Sin', in Eichengreen B. and Hausmann R. (eds), *Other People's Money: Debt Denomination and Financial Instability in Emerging Market Economics* (University of Chicago Press).

Favero, C. and Giavazzi, F. (2004) 'Inflation Targeting and Debt: Lesson from Brazil', NBER Working Paper 10390, at http://www.nber.org/papers/w10390

Fitch (2007) 'Federative Republic of Brazil', International Credit Analysis, February.

Goldfajn, I., Hennings, K. and Mori, H. (2003) 'Brazil's Financial System: Resilience to Shocks, No Currency Substitution, But Struggling to Promote Growth', Banco Central do Brasil, Working Paper series No. 75.

Goldman Sachs (2003) 'Dreaming with BRICs: The Path to 2050', Global Economics Paper No.99, at https://www.gs.com

Gruben, W. and Welch, J. (2001) 'Banking and Currency Crisis Recovery: Brazil's Turnaround of 1999', Federal Reserve Bank of Dallas, *Economic and Financial Review*.

IIF (2007a) 'Special Briefing – Brazil', 6 February.

IIF (2007b) 'Summary Appraisal – Brazil', 24 May.

IMF (2007) 'Regional Economic Outlook – Western Hemisphere', *World Economic and Financial Surveys*, April.

IMF (2008) 'Global Financial Stability Report', April.

Nakane, M. and Weintraub, D.B. (2005) 'Bank Privatization and Productivity: Evidence for Brazil', *Journal of Banking & Finance*.

Pinheiro, A. and Cabral, C. (1999) 'Credit Markets in Brazil: The Role of Judicial enforcement and Other Institutions', Inter-American Development Bank, Working Paper R-368.

Pinheiro, A., Gill, I., Serven, L. and Thomas, M. (2004) 'Brazilian Economic Growth, 1900–2000: Lessons and Policy Implications', Inter-American Development Bank, Economic and Social Study Series RE1-04-011.

Rudebusch, G.D. and Svensson, L. (1998) 'Policy Rule for Inflation Tageting', paper prepared for the NBER Conference on Monetary Policy Rules, 16–17 January.

Soares Sales, A. and Tannuri-Painto, M.E. (2007) 'Explaining Bank Failures in Brazil: Micro, Macro and Contagion Effects (1994–1998)' Banco Central do Brasil, Working Paper series No. 147.

Tabak, B.M., Solange, M.G., Lima, E.J.A. and Chang, E.J. (2007) 'The Stability–Concentration Relationship in the Brazilian Banking System' Banco Central do Brasil, Working Paper series No. 145.

Takami, M.Y. and Tabak, B.M. (2007), 'Evaluation of Default Risk for the Brazilian Banking Sector', Banco Central do Brasil, Working Paper Series No. 145.

Tombini, A.A. and Lago Alves, S.A. (2006) 'The Recent Brazilian Disinflation Process and Costs', Banco Central do Brasil, Working Paper Series No.109.

World Bank (2006a) 'Brazil: Interest Rates and Intermediation Spreads', Brazil Country Management Unit, Report No. 36628-BR.

World Bank (2006b) 'Financing Growth', at http://www.financial-indicators.org/resources/financing-growth.pdf

6
North Africa

A. Cicogna

The economies of North Africa in the framework of Euro-Mediterranean relations

In 2006, the overall GDP of North African countries – whose banking systems are the subject of this chapter[1] – was in the range of US\$350 billion, when measured at current exchange rates.

This figure represents less than 7 per cent of the total GDP of Spain, France, and Italy (and area we shall refer to as EU-MED3), which are the three largest economies of the Mediterranean, as well as the European nations entertaining the most intense social and economic relations with North African countries. Such a wide gap reflects the relative backwardness of North African economies' development, whose per capita GDP (measured at Purchasing Power Parity) does not reach 20 per cent of those three European countries' average.

This gap is, nonetheless, gradually closing, as North African economies have grown between 2001 and 2006, at an annual trend rate nearly 3 percentage points higher than the one recorded on average by the three European counterparts (Table 6.1).[2]

Differences of such magnitude are inherently typical to comparisons between developing and advanced economies and are, therefore, a common background to the analysis of all countries reviewed in this book. What makes the relations between the two shores of the Mediterranean somewhat 'special' – both from the perspective of business opportunities for market players, and from that of policy implications for the respective economic authorities – is the geographical, historical, social and cultural context within which they have developed, thus establishing manifold, deep interdependence links between those two economic areas.[3]

Table 6.1   Economies of North Africa Development Indicators

Country/area	GDP 2006 (current US$ bn.)	GDP per capita 2006 (% of EU-15 average*)	GDP growth 2001/2006 (constant prices**)
Morocco	65.4	17.8	5.1
Algeria	113.9	24.0	5.0
Tunisia	30.8	27.8	4.6
Libya	50.4	39.8	4.9
Egypt	107.4	15.1	4.0
North Africa	368.0	19.4	4.6
Spain	1231.7	86.4	3.3
France	2252.2	98.5	1.7
Italy	1852.6	96.1	0.7
EU – MED3	5336.5	94.4	1.7
EU-15	13675.6	100.0	1.8

Notes: * PPP values; ** annual trend rate; for regional areas, aggregations are based on PPP values.
Source: IMF (WEO database).

This interdependence is, today, well-illustrated by energy relations between the two shores: the EU-MED3 area absorbs about 45 per cent of total North African oil and natural gas exports, which satisfy more than 20 per cent of those three European countries' needs (Table 6.2). South European oil companies have an important role, in partnership with their North African counterparts, in the hydrocarbon extraction sectors of those nations, where European companies are often also involved in the realisation of the related downstream projects (pipelines, refineries, power stations).

EU-MED3 markets provide, however, a primary outlet also for non-oil exports of North African economies, 40 per cent of which are absorbed by those markets. Overall, oil and non-oil exports to that area account for 44 per cent of North African total exports, and for 17 per cent of the region's GDP. These figures – which, for exports to EU-15 countries, respectively rise to 63 per cent and 24 per cent – provide a vivid illustration of the importance of European demand, and of its growth, for North Africa's economic activity, and for its dynamics.

Conversely, North African markets' contribution to European exports is still limited: in 2005, the three largest Mediterranean European economies (which account for two-thirds of EU-15 total exports to the region) exported goods to North Africa for little more than 3 per cent of their global exports (Table 6.3).

Table 6.2 Trade relations with main Mediterranean European economies: exports*

| Importing Country/area | EU-MED3 | | | | EU-15 | | | | Spain | | | |
| | Total exports | | of which: hydrocarbons | | Total exports | | of which: hydrocarbons | | Total exports | | of which: hydrocarbons | |
Exporting Country/area ↓	% of exporter total	% of importer total	% of exporter total	% of importer total	% of exporter total	% of importer total	% of exporter total	% of importer total	% of exporter total	% of importer total	% of exporter total	% of importer total
Morocco	57.5	0.5	21.8	0.1	72.4	0.2	40.1	0.1	16.3	0.7	1.6	0.1
Algeria	36.5	1.3	38.6	9.6	53.9	0.6	53.8	5.3	10.4	1.5	11.2	11.3
Tunisia	59.4	0.5	86.6	0.4	80.1	0.2	95.9	0.2	5.6	0.2	16.1	0.6
Libya (1)	52.9	1.3	52.9	9.5	75.7	0.6	75.7	5.0	8.7	0.9	8.7	7.2
Egypt	24.8	0.3	25.4	1.2	42.3	0.2	36.9	0.6	8.7	0.4	5.9	2.1
North Africa	44.1	3.9	44.6	20.9	62.9	1.8	62.9	11.2	10.1	3.6	10.9	21.4

(Continued)

Table 6.2 (Continued)

Importing Country/area	France				Italy			
Exporting Country/area	Total exports		of which: hydrocarbons		Total exports		of which: hydrocarbons	
↓	% of exporter total	% of importer total	% of exporter total	% of importer total	% of exporter total	% of importer total	% of exporter total	% of importer total
Morocco	37.3	0.6	18.8	0.2	4.0	0.1	1.3	0.1
Algeria	10.0	0.9	11.3	6.8	16.2	1.8	16.2	11.3
Tunisia	31.9	0.6	26.7	0.4	21.8	0.6	43.8	0.4
Libya (1)	6.2	0.4	6.2	3.0	38.0	2.9	38.0	17.8
Egypt	5.5	0.1	2.8	0.6	10.6	0.4	16.7	1.2
North Africa	13.9	2.6	9.3	11.0	20.2	5.8	24.4	30.8

Notes: (#) 2005 data.
* 2004 data.
(1) Due to lack of relevant data, Libyan oil exports' market breakdown is assumed to be the same as Libyan total exports'.
Sources: IMF (DOTS), Eurostat (Comext database), UN (Comtrade database).

Table 6.3 Trade relations with main Mediterranean European economies: imports*

Importing Country/area →	Morocco		Algeria		Tunisia		Libya		Egypt		North Africa	
Exporting Country/area ↓	% of exporter total	% of importer total	% of exporter total	% of importer total	% of exporter total	% of importer total	% of exporter total	%of importer total	% of exporter total	% of importer total	% of exporter total	% of importer total
Spain	1.4	11.7	0.8	7.1	0.4	5.5	0.1	2.8	0.3	1.8	3.0	6.0
France	1.5	30.2	1.3	28.3	0.7	25.7	0.1	4.8	0.4	6.7	4.0	19.9
Italy	0.3	5.5	0.5	7.8	0.8	23.0	0.5	21.6	0.5	6.2	2.5	10.1
EU-MED3	1.1	47.4	0.9	43.2	0.7	54.2	0.2	29.2	0.4	14.7	3.3	36.0
EU-15	0.4	62.9	0.3	59.5	0.3	74.1	0.1	54.6	0.3	35.2	1.4	54.7

Note: (*) 2005 data.
Source: IMF (DOTS).

The contribution from North African demand to EU-MED3 exports is constrained by the still modest size of those markets, and by trade barriers that, though being progressively removed, still protect domestic products there. While European sales volumes in North Africa are limited by these factors, European firms (and, among them, Mediterranean ones) often hold prominent positions in these markets, relative to their international competitors: in 2005, EU-MED3 products accounted for 36 per cent of North Africa's total imports. This points clearly illustrates the strong interest of European industries in the further opening up of North African markets, and in the expansion of these economies.

Equally notable is the economic dimension of the intense people movements taking place – in both directions – between the two shores of the Mediterranean: from North to South, they mainly consist of tourist flows; in the opposite direction, they are chiefly migration flows.

For Morocco, Tunisia, and Egypt the tourism industry represents a major source of income, jobs, and currency inflows. The contribution by European visitors – and, especially, those from the three main Mediterranean EU members – is a sizeable one: in 2005, nearly 5 million tourists from EU-MED3 countries traveled to these three North African nations,[4] providing currency inflows which can be estimated in around US$4.6 billions.[5]

No less important – though on a different level – is North African migrants' participation in Europe's labour markets. Geographical proximity and post-colonial ties make these markets the main outlet for the large migration flows originating from the Maghreb:[6] in fact, around 70 per cent of Maghreb migrants are estimated to have settled in Europe, with four-fifths of them living in EU-MED3 countries.[7]

According to OECD (2006), in 2003 more than 900,000 North African workers – about 3 per cent of total labour force in their countries of origin[8] – were employed in the EU-MED3 area: France hosted 450,000 of them, accounting for around 31 per cent of foreign labourers employed in the country; 250,000 worked in Italy (17 per cent),[9] 200,000 in Spain (19 per cent).

Making up for the short supply of local labour – particularly for manual occupations – North African workers provide an important contribution to production in European economies. On the other hand, they help support income, consumption, and investments in their countries of origin with their remittances (Settimo, 2004) – which, except in Libya, represent a major source of currency inflows throughout the region: in 2004, remittances from North Africans working in the EU-MED3 area were estimated in excess of US$6 billion (Settimo, 2004).[10]

However, large income gaps between the two areas, and the lack of employment opportunities in the countries of origin (also due to their still rapid increase in population), feed a heavier migration pressure than European countries are ready to physiologically absorb; part of this pressure is thus finding an outlet in the illegal immigration phenomenon, whose high social and economic costs further reinforce European authorities' shared interest in promoting development on the southern shore of the Mediterranean.

Promotion of economic growth in North Africa has, in fact, long been a priority for European authorities, most notably for those of Mediterranean EU member states, which have pursued this objective through a number of bilateral and joint cooperation initiatives. Over the last decade, the key tool deployed in this endeavor has been the 'Euro-Mediterranean Partnership', launched in Barcelona in November 1995 at a summit of Heads of State and Government of the EU and of Nations of the Southern shore of the Mediterranean, the so-called 'Mediterranean Partners' (Bank of Italy, 2000).

The Barcelona summit's initiative had recognised the essential role of economic development and integration across the region, as a key tool for achieving its broader objectives of peace and shared prosperity for the whole Mediterranean basin.

In order to spur a more efficient resource allocation and, through this, the growth acceleration needed to trigger social and economic progress in the area, the project set the establishment of a Euro-Mediterranean free trade area as its key operational objective, to be achieved through the gradual removal of trade barriers between the European Union and her Mediterranean partners, as well as among the latter. The Barcelona summit had foreseen the completion of this process by 2010.

While access to EU markets for Mediterranean partners' products had long enjoyed preferential treatment (at least as far as manufactures were concerned), the establishment of the Euro-Med free trade area would require the removal of the high barriers (both of a tariff and non-tariff nature) that had so far sheltered local production from European (and, more generally, international) competition.

The expected increase in competitive pressures in Mediterranean partners' markets would stimulate a more efficient resource allocation and, as a consequence, raise the growth potential of those economies, speeding up their convergence towards European development standards. For these effects to fully deploy, however, adjustments were needed to the institutional set up of those economies, in order to encourage the entrepreneurial initiatives and private investments needed to restructure the production systems of the region. The EU would support these efforts through generous technical and financial assistance, and with a substantial increase in EIB credit operations in the region.

More than a decade after its beginning, the Euro-Med partnership experience lends itself to a multi-faceted assessment (Cicogna, 2004; FEMISE, 2005, Morrison, 2005). On the one hand, the significant contribution should be underlined that this initiative has made to the increasing trade opening of North African economies: although delays in the enactment of the 'Association Agreements', regulating the nature and the timing of the reciprocal trade concessions between the EU and the various Mediterranean partners, is bound to push beyond 2010 the completion of the Euro-Med free trade area, the Barcelona process has helped stimulate widespread tariff abatements in the region, and promoted the gradual removal of non-tariff barriers.

EU-MED3 firms have benefited from these developments: during 1995–2005, the growth pace of their exports to the region (6.9 per cent annually) was well above the rate recorded by their overall sales in developing countries (5.7 per cent).[11]

On the other hand, the achievements made in the institutional upgrading of the Mediterranean partners' economic systems to promote private investments appear to be more limited.

Difficulties experienced in the initial implementation of EU technical and financial assistance projects does, in part, explain such delays: these problems have been largely overcome, however, by the fine-tuning of Community instruments, as well as by giving further impulse to EIB activities in the region, now managed through a dedicated financial facility, the so-called 'FEMIP' (EIB, 2006).

Going forward, European efforts supporting economic development in North Africa will also benefit from the recent evolution of the Euro-Med partnership as a component of the broader 'neighbourhood policy', designed by the EU to foster relations with areas close to its new borders, widened by the recent enlargement of its membership (European Commission, 2003).

By moving the partnership's focus from trade liberalisation – which, though still in need of further action, will be supported by the gradual entry into force of the 'Association Agreements' – to convergence of partners' institutional settings, the neighbourhood policy will be able to contribute to a 'deepening' of integration between North African and European economies, thus favouring the full deployment of the Euro-Med free trade area's potential benefits.[12] In particular, the gradual alignment of North African economic authorities' administrative activity

Table 6.4   Economic and social indicators: 2006

Country/area	GDP (current US$bn)	Gross income per capita (current US$)	Population		Unemployment (% of labor force)
			No. (m)	Growth (%)	
Morocco	65.4	1900	30.5	1.2	9.7
Algeria	113.9	3030	33.3	1.5	12.3
Tunisia	30.8	2970	10.1	1.0	14.2
Libya	50.4	7380	6.0	1.9	n.a.
Egypt	107.4	1350	75.4	1.8	10.9
For comparison:					
Lower-middle income countries		2037		0.9	

Sources: World Bank (WDI database); IMF (*Country Reports*).

with European best practices can benefit from the extension to Mediterranean partners, foreseen under the new arrangements, of twinnings (successfully tested during the EU enlargement process) between individual public authorities (e.g. industry regulators) of those countries and the corresponding institutions of EU member states.

Structural profiles of the North African economies

The gross domestic product of North African economies ranged, in 2006, from Tunisia's US$31 billion to Algeria's US$114 billion (Table 6.4). With the exception of Libya – whose gross per capita product (US$7.380) places her within the upper-medium income bracket – all North African countries are classified as lower-medium income economies, according to the World Bank ranking: among them, Algeria and Tunisia have the highest per capita GDP ($3.000), followed, at a distance, by Morocco ($1.900) and Egypt ($1.350).

Quite significantly, the country ordering based on demographic dimensions is, for this region, close to a mirror image of the one just illustrated, based on per capita income levels: the largest population is, in fact, that of Egypt, with 75 million people in 2006, followed by Algeria's (33 million), Morocco's (31 million), Tunisia's (10 million), and Libya's (6 million).

This contrast can be viewed as a reminder of the fundamental policy problem confronting economic authorities in the region: meeting an intense – albeit gradually diminishing – demographic dynamics (population is growing at annual rates ranging from 1 per cent in Tunisia to 1.9

Table 6.5   GDP breakdown: demand (% of GDP)*

Country/area	Household consumption	Public consumption	Gross investments**	Exports (goods and services)	Imports (goods and services)
Morocco	59.9	21.0	23.7	33.3	38.4
Algeria	39.9	14.1	30.1	39.4	24.2
Tunisia	63.4	15.7	26.0	45.7	49.5
Egypt	72.1	12.7	17.7	23.5	26.0
For comparison:					
Lower-middle income countries	53.8	15.4	27.4	29.8	28.2

Notes: * 2001–2005 averages,
** Does not include change in inventories.
Sources: World Bank (WDI database), national statistics; constant price values.

per cent in Libya) with an adequate development (as much qualitative as quantitative) of production sectors and related job opportunities – whose insufficient supply is responsible for unemployment rates near or above 10 per cent throughout the area.

An analysis of GDP structure by demand components points, in fact, to the opportunity of targeting economic policies in the region towards the deepening of capital accumulation: with the exception of Algeria (where the strong increase in energy revenues has allowed, over the last few years, the financing of a vast program of public works), in 2001–2005 gross fixed investment in North African countries has, in fact, generally been lower, as a share of GDP, than the average level recorded by lower-middle income economies (Table 6.5).

With the exception of Libya, and in line with the typical structure of countries at a similar stage of development, the sectoral breakdown of North African economies displays a still significant role of agriculture, whose GDP share ranges from 10 per cent in Algeria, to 16 per cent in Morocco and Egypt, with Tunisia (12 per cent) in an intermediate position (Table 6.6).

The development of industrial activities, in their broad extension,[13] is comparatively low in Tunisia and Morocco (28 per cent and 31 per cent of GDP, respectively), at an intermediate level in Egypt (36 per cent of GDP), and highest in Algeria (56 per cent) and, above all, in Libya (67 per cent of GDP). In the two latter countries, however, industrial output is mainly generated by the oil and gas sectors.

Table 6.6   GDP breakdown: supply (% of GDP)*

Country/area	Agriculture	Industry	Of which: oil & gas	Of which: manufacturing	Services	Of which: public services	Of which: commerce
Morocco	15.5	30.5	2.5	16.7	54.0	15.8	11.9
Algeria	9.9	55.9	37.0	6.5	34.2	10.2	8.1
Tunisia	11.8	28.4	3.4	18.0	59.7	13.3	9.5
Libya	4.6	67.4	58.6	2.7	28.0	10.7	7.2
Egypt	15.7	35.7	14.9	17.4	48.6	10.0	11.0
For comparison:							
Lower-middle income countries	12.2	41.2		25.7	46.5		

Note: * 2001–2005 averages.
Sources: World Bank (WDI database), IMF (*Country Reports*), national statistics; current price values.

In fact, the vast North African hydrocarbon reserve endowment is unevenly distributed across the various countries, with the largest shares in Libya and Algeria, two among the world's main producers and exporters of oil and natural gas. The energy sector dominates the economy of both nations, accounting for 59 and 37 per cent of the respective GDP; in 2005, oil related incomes accounted for 85 per cent of total fiscal revenues in Libya, and for 71 per cent in Algeria. For both economies the oil and gas contribution to total exports exceeds 95 per cent. As with all of the countries in the region, the exploitation of the nation's hydrocarbon reserves is restricted to public sector entities, which typically associate international firms in exploration, extraction, and refinement activities. As a consequence, the oil industry dominance in Libya and Algeria also implies a dominant role of the public sector in those economies.

At the opposite extreme of the range is Morocco, whose geological explorations have not so far yielded the discovery of large hydrocarbon fields: the country is, therefore, a net importer of energy products, with a related balance of payments outlay in excess of 5 per cent of GDP.[14] Egypt and Tunisia are in an intermediate position. In Egypt, the oil sector's output – which contributes 15 per cent of the nation's GDP – more than covers domestic needs (including those stemming from the energy intensive steel and cement industries), and is thus also a significant source of currency revenues (particularly as a result of the recent increase in natural gas production and exports): in the financial year 2005/2006, revenues from hydrocarbon exports exceeded 4 per cent of GDP. As for Tunisia, oil

Table 6.7 Balance of payments: current account structure (% of GDP)*

	Morocco	Algeria	Tunisia	Libya	Egypt
Exports of goods	20.6	37.3	33.8	58.8	11.7
Exports of services	13.9	2.2	12.8	1.4	13.4
of which: Tourism	7.8	–	6.8	–	5.7
Imports of goods	31.8	19.7	43.1	28.5	21.3
Imports of services	6.9	4.5	7.0	5.9	6.1
Trade balance	−4.3	15.3	−3.5	25.8	−2.3
Net incomes	−1.7	−4.0	−4.3	−0.8	−0.2
Net transfers	9.8	2.2	4.7	−3.4	5.1
of which: Remittances	8.7	2.2	5.0	−2.2	4.0
Current account balance	3.8	13.5	−3.1	21.7	2.6

Note: * 2001–2005 averages
Sources: IMF (*Country Reports*), national statistics.

and gas reserves, though limited, make a measurable contribution to the covering of domestic needs, thus containing, in 2005, the hydrocarbon import bill within 1.5 per cent of GDP.

The oil sector dominance, in Libya and Algeria, is reflected in the limited weight of manufacturing in the industrial structure of these countries, with GDP shares of 3 per cent and 7 per cent, respectively. In Morocco, Tunisia, and Egypt, on the contrary, the size of manufacturing sectors ranges from 17 per cent to 18 per cent of GDP, in line with these economies' current stage of development.

In all these three countries, the size of the services sector is considerable: its share of GDP is, in fact, close to 50 per cent in Egypt and Morocco; it reaches 60 per cent in Tunisia. The public administration contributes to the services sector's overall output with GDP shares ranging from Egypt's 10 per cent to Morocco's 16 per cent. Trade activities account for 10 to 12 per cent of GDP.

The economic importance of tourism, within the tertiary sectors of Morocco, Tunisia, and Egypt, is mainly highlighted by balance of payments data: during 2001–2005, tourism's gross currency revenues reached 5 per cent of GDP in Egypt, 7 per cent in Tunisia, and 8 per cent in Morocco (Table 6.7). Their significant contribution helps contain these countries' trade balance structural deficit – which contrasts with the wide surplus currently displayed by Libya and Algeria, thanks to the favorable market environment for their hydrocarbon exports.

As already mentioned, all the countries in the region – except Libya – have an important source of foreign currency revenues in expatriates' remittances: their size as a share of GDP is 2 per cent for Algeria, rising to 4 per cent and 5 per cent for Egypt and Tunisia, respectively, and approaching 9 per cent in the case of Morocco.

As noted, in Algeria and Libya the product structure of exports is dominated by hydrocarbon goods.[15] Oil and gas exports also account for 40 per cent of Egyptian exports, whose second largest item is 'base' manufactured goods[16] (19 per cent), particularly textiles (31 per cent of this category) and steel (25 per cent). In the cases of Morocco and Tunisia, exports are mainly made of manufactured products,[17] which account for 36 per cent and 45 per cent, respectively, of the two countries' total exports: for both economies, apparel stands out as the main item, representing more than 80 per cent of total exports of manufactures (Figure 6.1).

Concerning imports, the main category is machinery and transport equipment[18] throughout the region, with shares of the total ranging from Egypt's 21 per cent to Libya's 48 per cent. Imports of base manufactures (whose shares range from 15 per cent of total imports in Egypt, to 25 per cent in Tunisia) and of food products (with shares exceeding 20 per cent of total imports both in Egypt and Algeria) are also considerable (Figure 6.2).

Recent macroeconomic developments in North Africa

Consolidating recent improvements, in 2006 North Africa's GDP increased by 5.9 per cent (Table 6.8).

The current favourable trend marks a reduction in the growth gap of North Africa *vis-à-vis* the group of Emerging and Developed Economies,[19] led by the fast growing Asian nations: in fact this gap, averaging 1.6 percentage points in 1986–95, fell to 1.1 points in 1996–2005.

A catching up of incomes levels with European standards is also under way: in 1996–2005, the ratio of the region's per capita income over the average EU-15 level did, in fact, increase by 1.1 percentage points. Current projections discount a further improvement of this indicator, which would bring it above 20 per cent in 2008, a level that has not been surpassed since the 1980s.[20]

These positive trends help sustain macroeconomic equilibria, thus preserving the adjustments achieved in the region through the stabilisation programmes, undertaken in the late 1980s and early 1990s with the support of the IFIs, when the deterioration of international economic

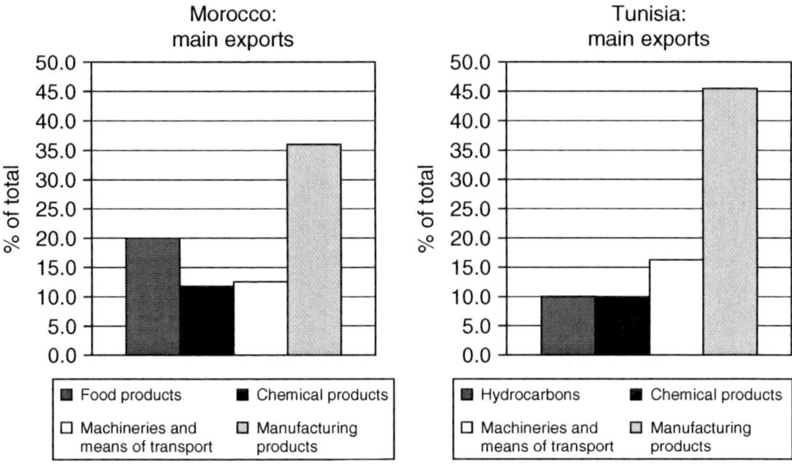

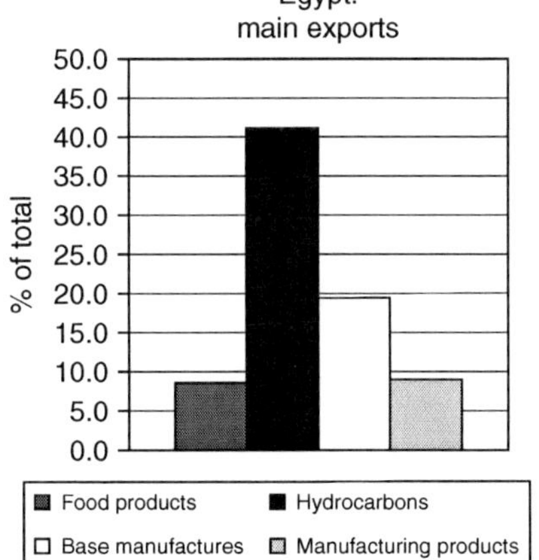

Note: * current prices: 2000–2004 averages.
Source: UN (Comtrade database).
Figure 6.1   Exports structure*

conditions had exposed the inherent fragility of the command economy development models then prevailing in the area.

Within an overall satisfactory framework (confirmed by IMF's recent assessments[21]), two potential sources of macroeconomic imbalance, however, warrant monitoring: on the one hand, inflation has recently been on the rise, fed by increases in international commodity prices, and by the buoyancy of domestic markets. On the other hand, the need

140

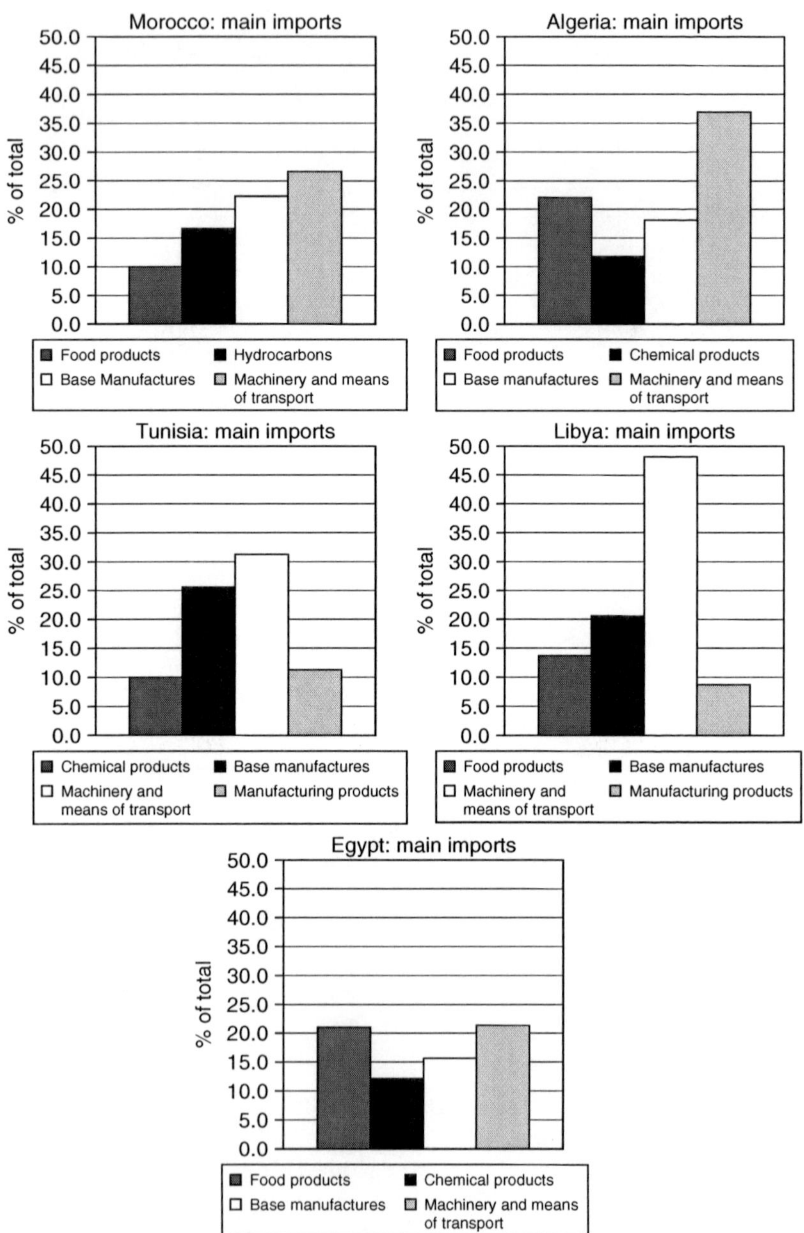

Note: * current prices: 2000–2004 averages.

Source: UN (Comtrade database).

Figure 6.2   Imports structure*

Table 6.8 Macroeconomic indicators: 2006

Country/ area	GDP annual growth (%)	Inflation annual rate (%)	BoP current balance (% of GDP)	Foreign debt.		Official reserves (months of imports)	Budget balance (% of GDP)	Public debt (% of GDP)
				Stock (% of GDP)	Service (% of Exports)			
Morocco	8.0	3.3	3.4	23.3	8.4	7.8	−2.1	58.2
Algeria	3.6	2.5	25.6	4.9	24.9	29.1	13.6	23.8
Tunisia	5.4	4.5	−2.3	59.1	19.0	5.1	−2.9	54.0
Libya	5.6	3.4	48.1	n.a.	–	31.5	39.1	–
Egypt	6.8	4.2	0.8	28.8	6.6	6.1	−9.2	79.8
North Africa	5.9	3.5	15.2					

Sources: IMF (WEO database, Country Reports), national statistics.

to support citizens' incomes and the low efficiency of public administrations are putting pressure on public finances in the region: with the notable exceptions of Algeria and Libya (whose state accounts are benefiting, in the current phase, of high energy revenues), public budget recorded, in 2006, deficits ranging from 2.1 per cent of GDP in Morocco to 9.2 per cent in Egypt.

Plans to rationalise public expenditures undertaken by authorities in these countries (with a view, in particular, to raising the efficiency of consumption subsidies), and the still manageable size of the region's public debts (ranging from Tunisia's 54 per cent of GDP to Egypt's 80 per cent) should help control public finance dynamics, in the medium term. However, the opportunity of maintaining favourable access conditions to international capital markets – which represent a significant source of debt financing, at least for Morocco and Tunisia[22] – should act as a reminder of the need for careful monitoring of these variables by the region's policymakers.

Three main factors influenced the recent behaviour of North African economies, and are likely to play an important role also for the area's medium term developments: oil market trends, competitive relations with Asian emerging economies (both in regional and international markets), progress in structural adjustment programmes under way in the area.

The first element clearly generates different challenges and/or opportunities for the various countries in a region which includes two of the world's main hydrocarbon exporters (Algeria and Libya); one economy – Egypt – displaying a milder, but still significant positive correlation with the oil market cycles, because of the country's oil and gas exports, as well as through its important financial links with Gulf economies (via workers' remittances and investment flows); and two net importers of oil (Tunisia and, above all, Morocco).

The sharp oil price increase during the current decade has strongly stimulated the Algerian and Libyan economies, causing, at the same time, the emergence of large budget surpluses and the accumulation of sizeable net foreign assets (including, in the case of Algeria, through the early repayment of international debt). Growing net energy revenues, increased workers' remittances from the Gulf, and large financial inflows from the same area have, in turn, significantly contributed to the recovery of the Egyptian economy from the difficult phase undergone at the beginning of the decade. For Tunisia, however, and especially for Morocco, the increase in energy import prices has translated into additional pressures for balance of payments and public finance (in connection with energy subsidies), slowing down domestic demand and damaging the cost competitiveness of national industries.

The increased competitive challenges that North Africa's manufacturing sectors are facing from Asian emerging economies have recently been highlighted by the difficulties that Tunisian and Moroccan textiles and apparel encountered in European markets, after the expiration of the multifibre agreement, in January 2005.

With the removal of the privileged market access, relative to Asian competitors, that such regime had granted them, Tunisian textiles and apparel exports to Europe decreased, in 2005, by 5.8 per cent, and Moroccan ones fell by 7.4 per cent. In the same year, European imports of those products from China grew by 41.5 per cent, whereas imports from India increased by 18 per cent (World Bank, 2006b).

Although production levels did partly recover, after the initial shock, both in Morocco and in Tunisia, this recent experience has underlined the need to speed up the modernisation of the area's manufacturing sectors.

On the other hand, Asian products' penetration into North Africa's own domestic markets has strengthened considerably over the last few years, heightening through this additional channel the competitive pressures exerted on the region's national industries: in 1995–2005, the Asian developing countries' share in North African imports increased, in fact, by nearly one-half, growing from 8 to 11.8 per cent[23] of the total.

Structural reforms in North African economies

These recent developments point to the importance of efforts aimed at increasing competitiveness of the region's industries.

A priority, in the current phase, should be the recovery in investment levels (particularly in the private sector), whose share of GDP, as noticed, is lagging behind international averages in most of the region's economies.

The recent low rates of capital accumulation are in sharp contrast with the large investment programmes in infrastructures and protected industries, used as the cornerstone of development strategies in the aftermath of newly conquered independence, as part of command-economy models prevailing in the region at that time. While these policies did initially favour a rapid increase in industrial production, they were soon to display the first signs of exhaustion of their potential, in connection with growing inefficiency in resource allocation processes.

Recent World Bank research points to the emergence, since the 1970s, of a clear contrast between the sharp increase in per capita investment levels (whose rate of growth doubled in Egypt, Algeria, and Morocco over the previous decade), and the widespread slowdown in total factor productivity dynamics, which declined by one-quarter in Egypt (falling from a 1.8 per cent annual growth in the 1960s to 1.3 per cent in the 1970s), even becoming negative in Algeria (−0.4 per cent, against +1.4 in the 1960s) and in Morocco (−0.4 per cent, against 4.6 per cent annual increase in the 1960s).[24]

The macroeconomic imbalances emerging in the following decade imposed a deep revision of development strategies in the region; with a sharp cut in public investments, brought about by financial consolidation programmes, authorities turned to the private sector as the key growth engine, in the framework of a policy of gradual liberalisation of economic activity.

Efficiency in resource allocation benefited from this: comparing the 1998–2003 period with the previous decade, a European Commission's research (2006) recently highlighted improvements in total factor productivity annual growth rates ranging from 0.6 percentage points in Tunisia and Egypt, to 0.7 points in Morocco, to 2.6 points in Algeria (where the previous period's deterioration in the indicator had been most pronounced). However, the still low levels of capital accumulation – relative to international standards – point to the partial results achieved so far by strategies aimed at rebalancing the sources of growth in favour of the private sector: these policies have not yet succeeded in mobilising enough investment resources to cope, on the one hand, with the rapid expansion in the labour force and, on the other hand, with the technological and managerial upgrading required to face an increased international competition.

While economic reforms in the region have, in fact, been quite effective in opening up local markets to international competition, achievements have so far been less satisfactory in the improvement of business climate conditions influencing investment decisions by the private sector.

International opening

The advancement in the area's integration within the growing flows of international commerce is well illustrated by the region's rising trade openness over the last 15 years: from 1990 to 2005, the increase in trade

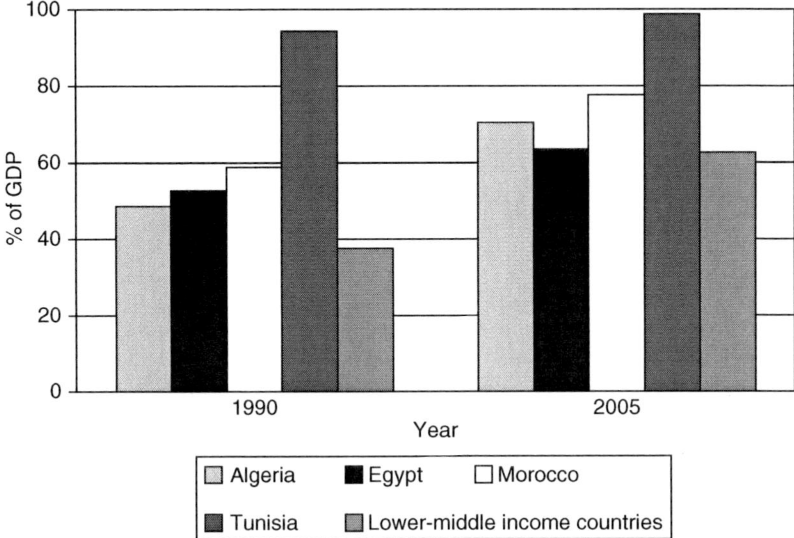

Note: Updated data for Libya are not available.
Source: World Bank (WDI).
Figure 6.3   Degree of openness (export + imports of goods and services)

in goods and services, as a share of GDP, ranged from 5 percentage points in Tunisia to 21 points in Algeria (Figure 6.3).

These dynamics are, of course, partly a result of the strong increase in Algeria's oil export value, with this country's degree of trade openness reaching 70 per cent, in 2005. Significant progress was, however, also shown by Egypt (from 53 per cent to 64 per cent) and, particularly, Morocco (from 59 per cent to 77 per cent), with both countries thus moving closer to Tunisia's already high degree of trade openness (99 per cent of GDP).

While noting the still high barriers (both tariff and non-tariff) limiting access to North-African markets, a recent World Bank study (2006c) highlighted the progress achieved, over the last few years, in the region's trade liberalisation, also thanks to the Euro-Mediterranean partnership's stimulating action. Especially notable, in this context, are the tariff reductions introduced by Egypt since 2004; together with other liberalisation measures adopted by Morocco, Tunisia, and Algeria, they contributed to putting the region at the top in a global ranking of advancements in trade reforms in 2000–2005, compiled by that study.

Institutional framework

More limited progress has been made, as noted, in bringing the region's institutional frameworks in line with conditions supportive of private sector growth.[25]

Nevertheless, authorities have recently been intensifying efforts in this direction, by introducing new tax legislation and administration procedures, by simplifying bureaucratic regulation for private businesses, and by privatising state companies. Notable in this context, is the new impulse economic reforms have been given in Egypt: from July 2004 to June 2006, in particular, 88 privatisation transactions were carried out, worth over US$3.5 billion;[26] business incentives have also been strengthened through a revision of income tax regulations. Structural reforms are also advancing in the Maghreb economies: recent examples are public administration reforms in Morocco, and the increased opening to foreign investments of Algeria's energy sector (World Bank, 2006c).

The foundations are thus being laid for the recovery in investment levels necessary, as mentioned, to turn the increased opening of the area's economies into a measurable improvement in their productivity standards and, as a consequence, into an opportunity for sustainable economic and social development of the region's population.

A fundamental role is assigned, in this process, to the region's banking systems, dealt with in the next paragraphs. The consolidation of their efficiency levels – within a framework of stability safeguard – can make an important contribution to the removal of financial obstacles which have often hindered modernisation and development initiatives of North Africa's production systems.

The banking systems of North Africa: quantitative indicators

Macroeconomic indicators commonly used to assess the evolution of financial systems point to a development level, for North African countries, consistent with the advancement stage of the respective economic systems, and with their phase of transition towards market-based institutional settings (Table 6.9).

With the exception of Libya – which has only recently embarked on a financial system modernisation programme – everywhere in the area the use of monetary instruments, as measured by the M2/GDP ratio, is above the level prevailing in middle income economies (around 50 per cent): this indicator, in fact, approaches 60 per cent in Algeria and Tunisia, and exceeds 90 per cent both in Egypt and in Morocco.

Table 6.9   Financial development indicators: 2001–2006 averages (%)

	Algeria	*Morocco*	*Tunisia*	*Libya*	*Egypt*
M2/GDP	56.0	96.1	58.1	36.6	93.2
Circulation/GDP	13.7	18.6	8.7	8.5	12.4
Circulation/M1	49.1	25.0	36.6	29.0	63.6
Bank assets/GDP	40.7	75.2	66.8	24.7	84.1
Bank credit to the private sector/GDP	11.1	57.7	61.1	13.2	53.0
Bank deposits/GDP	42.1	77.0	47.9	25.7	80.0
Stock market: capitalisation/GDP	–	39.3	10.6	–	46.3
Stock market: turnover	–	13.7	11.5	–	25.2

Sources: IMF (IFS), World Bank (FSDI).

Throughout the region, financial systems are still dominated by banking intermediation (Settimo, 2004, European Commission, 2004). Bond markets are still undersized, especially in their private component, although a few recent issues by Moroccan, Tunisian, and Egyptian companies bode well for these markets' future growth.[27] The development of equity markets is more significant, at least in Egypt and Morocco, where the recent stock price dynamism has brought market capitalisations in line with international averages for economies with similar income levels, while helping the underwriting of listed companies' new equity issues, and the market placement of privatised firms.[28] On the other hand, the size of Tunisia's equity market is still contained; in Algeria, a stock market was launched in 1999, but its development remains embryonic;[29] in Libya, the decision to establish a stock exchange was announced in 2006.[30]

Banks' domestic financial assets range, as a ratio of GDP, from Libya's 25 per cent to 84 per cent in Egypt, with Algeria (41 per cent), Tunisia (67 per cent), and Morocco (75 per cent) in intermediate positions. Cash is, however, still largely used: circulation outside the banking system is high throughout the region, both in relation to GDP (with ratios ranging from Tunisia's 9 per cent to Morocco's 19 per cent), and, significantly, as a share of M1 (values range, in this case, from 25 per cent, in Morocco, to 64 per cent, in Egypt),[31] thus confirming the ample margins for further development of banks' monetary function and, more generally, of retail banking services in the area.[32]

This does not prevent, however, bank deposits from reaching considerable proportions: their incidence over GDP exceeds, in fact, 40 per cent everywhere in the region except in Libya (26 per cent), with peaks of 77 per cent in Morocco and 80 per cent in Egypt.

Table 6.10   Banking systems of North Africa – branch networks: 2006

Country	No. banks	No. branches	No. branches per 100,000 inhabitants
Morocco	16	2,447	8.1
Algeria	24	1,278	3.8
Tunisia	20	987	9.8
Libya*	10	391	6.8
Egypt	41	3,000	4.1

Note: * 2005 data.
Sources: National Central Banks, IMF, World Bank.

Branch networks of North Africa's banking systems are fairly developed, in relation to these economies' advancement stage (Table 6.10): only Algeria and Egypt – the two most populated nations in the region – display, in fact, branch densities below lower-middle income economies' average levels (around 5 branches per 100,000 inhabitants).[33]

Similarly, bank credit extended to the private sector does not significantly deviate from levels prevailing in middle income economies (around 60 per cent of GDP):[34] this kind of financing, in fact, reaches 53 per cent of GDP in Egypt and 58 per cent in Morocco, increasing to 61 per cent in Tunisia. Notable exceptions, in this regard, are Libya (13 per cent of GDP), and, particularly, Algeria (11 per cent).[35]

A similar evaluation of North African financial systems' development is made in a recent study by Creane *et al.* (2007), focusing on a broad set of quantitative and qualitative variables: among these are indicators of banking sectors' structure, of non-banking intermediaries' development, of the systems' degree of international openness, and of their institutional contexts.

Based on these criteria, the study assigns a 'medium' overall development assessment to all North African banking systems, with the exceptions of Algeria and, particularly, Libya, whose banking systems are ranked among the 'less developed' ones. Throughout the region, the study finds that the quality of institutional environment (public administrations, judicial systems, protection of property rights, etc.) displays the less satisfactory levels among the various categories of assessment variables (Table 6.11).

Using a separate set of widely available quantitative indicators (including money stocks, banking assets, credit to the private sector), this study also defines another synthetic measurement of financial sector

Table 6.11 Banking systems of North Africa-development indicators*

Country	Banking sector	Non-banking intermediaries	Legislation and supervision	Monetary policy	Financial opening	Institutional environment	Overall index
Morocco	5.6	4.7	7.3	6.8	4.0	3.8	5.5
Algeria	2.5	3.0	3.5	4.4	4.0	2.3	3.2
Tunisia	7.7	4.7	5.3	4.5	5.0	5.0	5.6
Libya	1.3	0.7	2.0	0.5	0.0	1.0	1.0
Egypt	6.0	6.3	5.3	5.6	6.0	3.2	5.4

Note: * Scale: 0–2.5 = very low development; 2.6–4.9 = low development; 5.0–5.9 = medium development; 6.0–7.5 = high development; 7.6–10 = very high development.
Source: S. Creane *et al.*, 2007.

development, and uses it to assess the evolution of different regions' financial systems over the last few decades. While confirming a current level of financial development, in North Africa, higher than in most developing countries, the study notices the widening gap opening between this area and the newly-industrialized Asian economies: by pointing to a lower support by financial systems, such gap can help explain the difficulty experienced by North Africa in replicating, over the last decades, the fast growth processes enjoyed by Asian economies.[36]

The banking systems of North Africa: qualitative profiles

While the quantitative development of the region's banking systems is substantially in line with that of the respective economies, the assessment of their stability, efficiency, and effectiveness in supporting economic growth is less straightforward.

The qualitative evolution of the region's different banking systems reflects, first of all, their initial conditions when the respective national credit authorities, supported by the IFI's, launched their reform programmes, since the 1990s.

The pace of advancement of those interventions (including sector restructurings, updating in regulatory frameworks, enhancing and modernisation of supervisory systems) has, in turn, been influenced by the various intensity of broader economic reform efforts deployed by the region's governments, also reflecting the evolving domestic social and political equilibria, as well as the international scenario.

The interaction of these factors is reflected in the current situation, with banking system settings in the region's two oil economies – Libya

Table 6.12 Indicators of access to credit for the private sector

Country	Investments: bank financing (% of total)	Investments: internal financing (% of total)	Bank loans with collateral (% of total)	Bank loan collaterals: average amount (% of loan amount)
Morocco	19.6	63.4	98.9	226.2
Algeria	16.3	74.3	82.4	168.6
Egypt	6.9	86.2	89.4	123.6

Source: World Bank (Investment Climate Assessments, various years).

and Algeria – still distant from the requirements of a modern market economy. In both cases, however, authorities are currently committed to intensifying efforts in that direction.

Substantially more advanced – though not without some weak elements – is the convergence process of Moroccan, Tunisia, and Egyptian banking systems towards a configuration consistent with those economies' development strategies. Nevertheless, recent World Bank surveys point to the significant difficulties the region's firms meet in accessing credit. According to these surveys, the share of firm investment expenditures funded through bank loans is among the world lowest: in Algeria and Morocco such share does not, in fact, reach 20 per cent; in Egypt, it is even below 10 per cent (Table 6.12).

Problems of access to credit appear particularly important for small firms: the cited World Bank surveys put estimates of the share of Algeria's small enterprises with access to bank financing at 23 per cent, against 69 per cent for larger firms; in Egypt, those ratios are, respectively, 13 and 36 per cent (World Bank, 2006c).

A factor contributing to this phenomenon is likely to be the high incidence of collaterals, typical of banking activity in the countries under review (Table 6.12); though partly explained by pronounced information asymmetries often featuring bank lending relations in North African economies, these practices are likely to discriminate against investments of newly established enterprises, which normally lack large assets to be used as collateral.

Stability and efficiency

The more or less pronounced deficiencies of the various banking systems in North Africa do not entail significant systemic stability risks, according

Table 6.13 Banking systems of North Africa: financial soundness indicators: 2006 data (%)

Country	Solvency ratio	Non-performing loans/Total loans	ROA	ROE
Morocco	12.3	10.9	1.3	17.4
Algeria	14.9	34.2	0.6	13.9
Tunisia	11.8	19.2	0.2	9.1
Egypt	14.5	25.0	0.6	10.7

Note: No updated system-wide indicators are available on Libyan banks' financial soundness.
Sources: IMF (*Country Reports*), National Central Banks (*Annual Reports*).

to recent financial system assessment exercises (FSAP) conducted in the region by IMF and the World Bank.

This is not only because of system-wide capitalisation levels, which are – with solvency ratios ranging, in 2006, from 11.8 per cent in Tunisia to 14.9 per cent in Egypt – substantially in line with international standards, but also (and perhaps most importantly) thanks to the implicit government guarantee on individual intermediaries' solvency (particularly in the case of state owned banks, which, as we shall discuss later, are often the ones with the largest efficiency problems) prevailing in the area (Table 6.13).

This notwithstanding, the IMF's FSAP assessment conducted in 2003 in Algeria did point to the considerable fiscal costs of the repeated recapitalizations required by state banks, over the previous decade, to provision their loan losses: according to that assessment, the financial burden of these bail-outs is likely not to have been far from the cost of recent banking crises in Turkey or in Thailand (which can be estimated between 30 per cent and 40 per cent of the respective GDPs).[37]

A poor quality of loans is not, however, only a feature of Algerian banks. It is, on the contrary, the chief problem that credit authorities throughout the area have to face: while not reaching the levels of Algeria (34.2 per cent), the incidence of non performing loans (NPLs) over the total loan portfolio recorded in 2006 in Morocco (10.9 per cent) and, especially, in Tunisia (19.2 per cent) and Egypt (25.0 per cent) indicate that even in the region's three most advanced banking systems the containment and correct management of credit risks is currently the major challenge for banking intermediaries' capital strengthening and management efficiency.

It is, in fact, the high NPLs (and the pressure exerted by supervisory authorities to have them emerge) that are mainly responsible for the limited levels of profitability recorded by the area's banking systems over the last few years: also due to the significant burden of credit provisions, in 2006 ROA exceeded 0,6 per cent only in Morocco.

The high weight of non performing loans on North African banking assets is, to a considerable degree, a legacy of the past phases of central economic planning, when control over banking systems was firmly in the hands of the State, and credit allocation was determined by administrative choices. Sharing the common experience of economies sorting out of protracted phases of 'central planning', North African banks have inherited a sizeable portfolio of doubtful loans, extended to inefficient state-owned companies.

The problem mainly affects the state-owned component of the area's banking systems.[38] Such component has, anyway, still a significant, when not a prevalent role within those systems: against a world average, for economies with similar income levels, below 15 per cent, public sector banks control around 30 per cent of banking assets in Morocco and Tunisia, nearly 50 per cent in Egypt, and about 90 per cent in Algeria and Libya.

State-owned banks are affected by widespread shortcomings in credit and risk management systems. Their delay in bringing management models in line with the requirements of a market economy environment weakens their efficiency standards and, ultimately, their financial soundness. Those banks' asset quality and profitability are not, in fact, only negatively affected by loans forcedly extended to inefficient state-owned firms: the incidence of NPLs is, actually, often substantial also for credits extended to private concerns, and usually higher than the one recorded by private banks in the same market.

Recent reforms

It is not surprising, in the light of the previous paragraph's remarks, that the region's credit authorities have placed a special emphasis, within their recent reform initiatives, on the improvement of banks' credit and, particularly, risk management systems.

A special importance is given, in this context, to the adoption of organisation models which clearly define, on the one hand, the responsibility (and, consequently, the accountability) of banks' management bodies for credit decisions and, on the other hand, provide continuity and effectiveness to credit relations' monitoring.

At the same time, supervisory actions have been enhanced aimed at improving banks' asset quality measurement systems, and at gradually disposing of accumulated non performing loans. These initiatives' first results are encouraging. In Tunisia, non performing loans decreased, from 2003 to 2006, by nearly 5 percentage points as a share of total loans, while provisions' coverage of potential losses grew by more than 6 points, to 49.2 per cent; authorities have, most recently, imposed on all banks to achieve, through provisions, a loan loss coverage ratio of 70 per cent by 2009, subjecting dividend distributions to compliance with that regulation (IMF, 2006c; Banque Centrale de Tunisine, 2007).

In Morocco, the incidence of NPLs diminished, from 2003 and 2006, by more than 7 percentage points; the provisions' coverage ratio increased by more than 16 points (Bank al Maghrib, 2007).

In Egypt, authorities have been giving new impetus, since 2004, to the country's banking system reform and modernisation programme, including, in addition to the privatization of a significant share of the industry, to its consolidation,[39] and to the strengthening of prudential supervision,[40] the renewal of management and the organisation restructuring of public sector banks, also through the gradual liquidation of their sizeable portfolio of loans extended to troubled state companies.

Egyptian authorities have also made considerable efforts to favour the restructuring of NPLs extended by banks to private concerns: to this aim, a conciliation and arbitration body was established which allowed banks, in 2004–2006, to renegotiate (and to partly recover) more than half such loans, avoiding the recourse to long and uncertain court actions (Enders, 2007). This latter initiative is related to an issue of considerable importance for North African banking systems' current efficiency levels and, above all, for their prospective capacity to support private sector development in their respective economies.

The functional shortcomings of the region's banking systems are not, in fact, only due to their own structural and operational weaknesses. Environmental variables are also exerting an important influence, which can stem the banks' capacity to fully meet the real sector's credit demand, and thus adequately support its productive investments. We are referring, in particular, to the region's legal and judicial system shortcomings, which do not allow adequate support to contract execution and the full protection of creditor rights.

No less important are, in this context, the effects of the limited and scarcely reliable financial information available in the region to support private firms' loan applications – a problem further reinforced by the large weight of the informal sector in these economies.

The frequent request for large credit collaterals by banks is partly a consequence of this. In institutional settings where claiming such collateral is often a difficult endeavor (especially in the case of real estate property), it might be argued that their request by banks mainly serves the purpose of confirming the borrower's financial soundness, given the problems in carrying out a reliable assessment of the funded entrepreneurial activities' own economic potential (World Bank, 2006c).

A further effect of information asymmetries prevailing in North African banks' operating environment is their tendency to focus on a restricted number of large customers, with whom they entertain established financing relations. While these practices are motivated by the difficulty in adequately assessing the merit of credit of a broader potential customer base, they also expose banks to the equally important risk of a high portfolio concentration.

Interesting initiatives have been taken by the region's authorities also in this domain, to promote bank lending in favour of broader sections of the private sector, without compromising the principles of sound and safe conduct of banking activity (World Bank, 2006c).

In Tunisia, judicial procedures to claim collaterals in case of credit default have recently been streamlined. Moreover, the obligation to audit the accounts was introduced for some companies in 2005, and balance sheet regulations were strengthened. In Morocco, the Central Bank itself has promoted a standardisation of the minimum financial information required by banks to consider a loan application; credit registry is also being established (Bank al Maghrib, 2007).

Privatisations and the role of foreign banks

As noticed, the scarce efficiency of state controlled units is one of the key, though by no means the only, reason for North African banking systems' functional limitations. Taking stock of that element, recent development strategies devised by the region's credit authorities have, in fact, all included privatisation of at least part of the banking sector as one of their key priorities for action. Although, as already mentioned, the weight of the government sector component in the region is still high, compared to world average levels, privatisations made so far in Tunisia, in Morocco and, most recently, in Egypt have opened up considerable room for private players and, among them, for foreign banks. In fact, by actively participating, as purchasers, in those operations, international banks (mainly European ones), have substantially consolidated their market position in the region, in the last few years.

In Tunisia, about one-third of the banking system is currently controlled by foreign intermediaries.[41] In Morocco, more than 20 per cent of the system's total assets are foreign controlled.[42] In Egypt, privatisations have transferred, between 2004 and 2006, the control over around one quarter of the country's banking system from the government to the private sector sphere: the latter has now a clear prevalence of foreign ownership, with an important European component.[43]

Conclusions

The above reviewed reform and modernisation processes in North Africa's banking systems cannot, of course, be considered as completed. However, progress achieved so far and, above all, national authorities' commitment to further pursue their action, often with the IFI's support, are measurably contributing to overcoming functional and operational efficiency limitations of banking intermediation in the region.

Also in Algeria and Libya – the two least advanced countries in the region, as far as transition of banking systems to a market based set up – have, recently, been recorded signals of reform process acceleration. In Algeria, where the costly crisis, in 2003, of Khalifa Bank (then the largest private credit institution in the country) induced authorities to introduce tighter capital and governance requirements for banking operators, the supervisor (a body closely connected to the central bank) recently granted two new banking licences, one of which assigned to France's Calyon.[44] A further, important sign of relaunch of the banking modernization process in the country is the announcement of the privatisation of the publicly owned Credit Populaire d'Algerie: authorities aim at transferring its control to high standing international banks, with a view to stimulating the spreading of modern management models throughout the Algerian banking system (IMF, 2005b).

A similar orientation has recently been shown by Libyan authorities, by signalling their intention to facilitate the entry of international players into the Libyan banking market. Particularly worth noticing, in this framework, is the partial privatisation, in 2007, of Sahara Bank, the main commercial bank in the country: authorities transferred 19 per cent of the bank's capital to France's BNP-Paribas, also granting it an option to take over, in the medium term, the bank's control.[45] A similar initiative was later launched for the privatisation of Al Wahda Bank (the country's fifth largest bank), 19 per cent of whose capital was planned to be sold to an international strategic investor in 2008.

The inherent complexity of problems affecting banking systems in North Africa should not, however, be overlooked. Such problems involve, as noted, multiple areas and institutional subjects within the respective economic systems: the structural setting and the management effectiveness of the region's banking systems are, in particular, influenced by the scope and the characteristics of government intervention in the respective economies, both in the production sector (through state property of borrowing companies and/or of banks financing them), and in defining the institutional framework (legislation, administrative bodies, etc.) which banks operate in.

Medium term development prospects for the area's banking systems – and, in particular, for those which have most recently begun their reform processes – thus appear closely linked to the evolution of such factors. More precisely, the effectiveness of market forces and of the authorities' very reform initiatives aimed at spurring progress in the area's banking systems, will crucially depend on a consistent and well coordinated evolution of the variables mentioned above.

The recent history of Egypt's banking reforms provides a good illustration of the importance of this link: after stalling for a protracted period, the acceleration, since 2004, of the banking modernisation process in Egypt has coincided – being stimulated by and, in turn, stimulating it – with a not less energetic recovery in the broader transition process of the Egyptian economy to a market based system, promoted by the national authorities.

The relaunch of the government's privatisation programme has, in particular, provided the background for the sizeable reduction in the public sector role in banking, culminated, in the current phase, with the privatisation of Bank of Alexandria. The premises have thus been laid for an injection of managerial and competitive stimuli which, in the authorities' hopes, should favor a quicker completion of the entire system's modernisation process, in the service of the nation's economic progress.

As in Tunisia and Morocco before, also in Egypt the presence of international banks – and especially of European ones – has now taken on a considerable role: by acquiring a significant direct presence in these markets, European banks have accepted to meet a significant challenge, investing in the development potential of the region.

Looking ahead, the contribution of European banks can be especially valuable for the further strengthening of banking systems in the area, by acting as a transmission vehicle for the transfer of management and technological know-how across the Mediterranean. In this framework, particularly important will be their contribution to the development of credit activity in favour of small and medium firms, which represent the vast majority of North Africa's private sector. By supporting productive investments in the area, this development will also open up new business opportunities for European banks' own national client base, be it in the form of capital goods sales or of industrial partnerships, or in that of new entrepreneurial initiatives in the region.

Notes

1. From West to East, they are: the three Maghreb states of Morocco, Algeria, and Tunisia; Libya; and Egypt.
2. Provisional data point to a continuation after 2006 of North African economies' catching-up with the EU-MED3 area: for 2007–2008, the IMF estimates a trend growth differential of 4 percentage points in favour of the former group of countries (WEO database, October 2007).
3. For a historical introduction to Euro-Mediterranean relations, see (Braudel, 1987).
4. In particular, more than 85% of the 3.3m foreign visitors in Morocco came from Europe (60% from EU-MED3 countries); in Tunisia (6.4m visitors), the corresponding shares were 61% and 26%, respectively; in Egypt (8.6m visitors), 71% and 17% (source: national statistics).
5. This (conservative) estimate, based on balance of payments data from national sources, is obtained assuming, for Morocco and Egypt, currency inflows per EU-MED3 tourist equal to the average value. In Tunisia (the only North African country publishing detailed estimates of tourists' expenditures for the main countries of provenance), per capita expenditures of Italian and French tourists are, however, exceeding the average value by 34%.
6. The size of Egyptian migration to Europe is smaller, being limited to a few tens of thousands. The large community of Egyptian migrant workers (2.3m people, according to Egypt's national statistics) is, in fact, mainly employed in Arab Gulf countries and in North America. Libya is, on the other hand, a net importer of labour, mostly coming from Africa.
7. (OECD, 2004). As with any developing country, estimates of overall migration from North Africa are subject to wide margins of approximation. The referred to OECD work puts it at around 4m people, in 2000. In the same year, around 250,000 of them were in Italy, according to (Caritas, 2007); in 2005, their number had risen to 350,000, according to the same source.
8. Source: World Bank, *World Development Indicators.*
9. Including 37,000 Egyptian workers. Italy is one of the main destinations for the limited Egyptian migration to Europe (OECD, 2004).
10. In 2004, nearly two-thirds of Tunisian migrants' total remittances (US1.4bn) came from EU-MED3 area. For Morocco, the EU-MED3 share can be estimated at around 70% of the total amount (US$4.2bn, in 2004). Virtually all Algerian migrants' remittances (US$2.5bn, in 2004, according to estimates by World Bank, 2006a) are originating for the EU-MED3 (Settimo, 2004). In the case of Egypt, 2004 remittances from EU-MED3 countries reached US$130m, out of a total US$3.3bn (source: national statistics).
11. Source: IMF, *Direction of Trade Statistics* (data in current US$).

12. For an analysis of dynamic benefits of 'deep' economic integration in the Euro-Med framework, see (Hoekman and Konan, 1999).
13. Data used here (drawn from the World Bank's World Development Indicators) include manufacturing activities, utilities, mining, and constructions in the industrial sector.
14. Also in this country, however, the extractive industry provides an important economic contribution: Morocco is, in fact, one of the main world producers of phosphates, whose exports account for a sizeable share of the country's balance of payments revenues (3.5% GDP, in 2005).
15. Updated export structure statistics are not available, however, for the latter country.
16. Section 6 of the SITC classification.
17. Section 8 of the SITC classification.
18. Section 7 of the SITC classification.
19. As per the IMF's *World Economic Outlook* classification.
20. Source: IMF, WEO database (October 2007); data based on Purchasing Power Parity.
21. (IMF, 2006a).
22. Egypt's external debt is, on the contrary, mainly funded by official creditors, often on concessional terms.
23. Source: IMF, Direction of Trade Statistics.
24. Keller and Nabli (2002).
25. Recent business climate surveys in the region highlight, in particular, bureaucratic obstacles to starting a business, labor market rigidities, inadequate property registration systems, weak legal protection of contractual rights (World Bank, 2005).
26. Source: Egypt's Ministry of Finance.
27. Source: Bloomberg, quoted in (World Bank, 2006c).
28. In Egypt, the Capital Market Authority authorised new equity issues by listed companies, in the financial year 2005/2006, worth about US$8bn.; during the same period, privatisations (partly carried out through placements in the stock exchange) yielded budget revenues worth about US$2.5bn. (sources: Central Bank of Egypt, Ministry of Finance). In Morocco (where about 10.4% of Maroc Telecom was offered by the State on the Casablanca Stock Exchange, at the end of 2004, meeting considerable interest by investors, and yielding about US$700m. to the Treasury), ten IPO's were launched in 2006 by private companies, raising about US$500m. in the market (source: Economist Intelligence Unit).
29. In 2006, only three companies were listed on Algier's stock exchange.
30. Source: Economist Intelligence Unit.
31. By way of comparison, circulation in the eurozone amounts to approximately 5% of GDP and 15% of M1.
32. In Egypt, only 10% of population has a bank account.
33. Source: World Bank, World Development Indicators.
34. Ibid.
35. In line with recent international trends, also in North Africa household loans are accounting for increasing shares of bank credit portfolios: this phenomenon is particularly remarkable in Morocco, where the brisk expansion in mortgages drove the growth in that share by over 6 percentage points, from

2000 to 2005, to reach 33.4% (Bank El Maghrib, 2006). In Tunisia, household loans increased, between 2002 and 2005, from 12.9% to 17.3% of total loans (Banque Centrale de Tunisie, 2006); in Egypt, their share rose from 12.2% in 2003, to 16.4% in 2006 (Central Bank of Egypt, 2007).

36. For a comparative analysis of the growth performances, from the 1960s to the 1980s, of Middle East and North Africa and emerging Asian economies, see Page (1998).

37. (IMF, 2004).

38. In Egypt, authorities indicated NPLs accumulated by the four largest public sector banks to be worth 26bn Egyptian pounds, corresponding to 5% of GDP in 2004/2005, and to 20% of those banks' total loan portfolio (Bank of Alexandria's share was reimbursed in cash – through a government financial institution – before the bank's privatization) (Central Bank of Egypt, 2007). In Algeria, after the recapitalisations of the last few years, the government recently stated the intention of taking charge of insolvent state companies' debt obligations towards public sector banks, for an amount corresponding to 4% of GDP (IMF, 2007).

39. The increase of the minimum capital requirement for banks from 100m to 500m Egyptian pounds (around 70m Euro) has triggered a series of mergers and acquisitions, as well as the market exit of a few marginal participants: between 2004 and 2006, the number of operating banks has, thus, decreased from 57 to 41 units. Authorities indicated a preference for a further reduction of the country's banking population to 37 units (Central Bank of Egypt, 2007).

40. Within the framework of the Euro-Med partnership, the Eurosystem completed in November 2007 a two-year programme of technical assistance on banking supervision with the Central Bank of Egypt.

41. The foreign presence in Tunisian banking was significantly strengthened with the privatisations of Union Internationale de Banques – whose control was acquired in 2002 by Société Générale of France – and, in 2005, of Banque du Sud, sold to a consortium including Banco Santander of Spain and Attijariwata Bank of Morocco (Banque Centrale de Tunisie, 2006).

42. (Bank Al Maghrib, 2006). The main banking institution in the country, Attijariwata Bank (product of the merger between Banque Commercial de Maroc and Wafa Bank), has Spain's Banco Santander as its second largest shareholder (with over 14.7% of the capital), and a number of other European banks, including Italy's Unicredit among its shareholders. Credit Commercial du Maroc, the third largest bank in the country, is controlled by the French group Credit Agricole. Both BNP-Paribas and Société Générale also have controlling stakes in Moroccan banks.

43. Besides the sale to S. Paolo-IMI (now Intesa Sanpaolo) of a controlling stake in Bank of Alexandria (the fourth largest bank in the country), Egypt's recent privatizations included the public sector's shares in the equity of 'joint-venture' banks, established in partnership between public and private sector shareholders: in particular, operations involving European banks included the sale of Misr International Bank to France's Société Générale (which incorporated it into its Egyptian subsidiary National Société Générale); Calyon did, in turn, acquire the control of Egyptian American Bank; Piraeus Bank of Greece took over Egyptian Commercial Bank. Procedures to privatise Banque du Caire, the country's third largest bank, were initiated in 2007.

44. Source: Economist Intelligence Unit.
45. Source: Economist Intelligence Unit.

References

Bank of Italy (2000) 'Le economie del Mediterraneo' (Roma).

Bank Al Maghrib (2006) 'Rapport Annuel sur le controle, l'activité et les résultats des établissements de crédit – Exercice 2005' (Rabat).

Bank Al Maghrib (2007) Rapport Annuel sur le controle, l'activité et les résultats des établissements de crédit – Exercice 2006 (Rabat).

Banque Centrale de Tunisie (2006) *Rapport Annuel relatif a l'année 2005* (Tunis).

Banque Centrale de Tunisie (2007) *Rapport Annuel relatif a l'année 2006* (Tunis).

Caritas (2007). Dossier Statistico Immigrazione – Migrantes (Rome).

Central Bank of Egypt (2007) *Annual Report 2005/2006* (Cairo).

A. Cicogna (2004) 'Crescita e riforme nelle economie del Mediterraneo: il contributo e le prospettive del partenariato euro-mediterraneo', in F. Zallio (ed.), *L'Europa e il Mediterraneo – Partner o vicini scomodi?* (Milano: Egea).

Creane, S. *et al.* (2007) 'Measuring Financial Development in the Middle East and North Africa: A New Database', in IMF Staff Papers, Vol. 53, No. 3.

EIB, FEMIP (2006) *Facility for Euro-Mediterranean Investment and Partnership – Annual Report 2005* (Luxembourg).

K. Enders (2007) 'Egypt – Searching for Binding Constraints on Growth', IMF Working Paper 07/57 (Washington, DC).

European Commission (2003) 'Wider Europe – Neighbourhood: A New Framework for Relations with Our Eastern and Southern Neighbours', COM (2003) 104 (Bruxelles).

European Commission (2004) 'Economic Review of EU Mediterranean Partners', Occasional Paper No. 6, Directorate-General for Economic and Financial Affairs (Bruxelles).

European Commission (2006) 'European Neighbourhood Policy: Economic Review of ENP Countries', Occasional Paper No. 25, Directorate-General for Economic and Financial Affairs (Bruxelles).

FEMISE (2005) 'The Euro-Mediterranean Partnership, 10 Years after Barcelona: Achievements and Perspectives' (Marseilles).

Hoekman, B. and Konan, D. (1999) 'Deep Integration, Non-Discrimination and Euro-Mediterranean Free Trade', Discussion Paper No. 2095 (London: CEPR).

Keller, J. and Nabli, M. (2002) 'The Macroeconomics of Labor Market Outcomes in Mena over the 1990s', unpublished paper (Washington, DC: World Bank).

IMF (2004) *Algeria: Financial System Stability Assessment* (Washington, DC).

IMF (2006a) *Regional Economic Outlook – Middle East and Central Asia* (Washington, DC).

IMF (2006b) *Morocco: 2006 Article IV Consultation – Staff Report* (Washington, DC).

IMF (2006c) *Tunisia: Financial System Stability Assessment Update* (Washington, DC).

IMF (2007), *Algeria: 2006 Article IV Consultation – Staff Report* (Washington, DC).

Morrison, J. (2005) *Le partenariat euroméditerranéen* (Grenoble: Presses Universitaires de Grenoble).

OECD (2004) *Working Abroad – The Benefits Flowing from Nationals Working in Other Economies* (Paris: OECD General Secretariat).

OECD (2006) *International Migration Data 2006* (Paris: OECD).

Page, J. (1998) 'From Boom to Bust – and Back?: The Crisis of Growth in the Middle East and North Africa', in N. Shafik (ed.), *Prospects for Middle Eastern and North African Economies* (London: Macmillan Press).

Settimo, R. (2003) 'Banking and Financial Sectors in Mediterranean Countries: an Overview', unpublished paper (Roma: Banca d'Italia).

Settimo, R. (2004) 'The Role of Workers' Remittances in Mediterranean Countries', unpublished paper (Roma: Banca d'Italia).

World Bank (2005) *Doing Business in 2005* (Washington, DC).

World Bank (2006a) *Global Economic Prospects 2006* (Washington, DC).

World Bank (2006b) *Morocco, Tunisia, Egypt and Jordan after the End of the Multi-Fiber Agreement*, Report No. 3576 MNA (Washington, DC).

World Bank (2006c) *2006 Economic Developments and Prospects – Middle East and North Africa Region* (Washington, DC).

World Bank (2006d) *Fostering Higher Growth and Employment in the Kingdom of Morocco* (Washington, DC).

7
Russia

A. Marra

Introduction

The Russian banking system is the result of the difficult and somehow still uncompleted transition of the country from a planned to a market economy, started in the late 1980s with M.Gorbachev's reforms.

The lack of an adequate legal framework to regulate activities and protect depositors together with ineffective supervision hampered the confidence in the banking system of an impoverished population. On the other hand, banks have constantly played a very limited role in supporting the real sector. The fast recovery following the August 1998 default did not significantly increase the relevance of the banking system as witnessed by low levels of financial intermediation. From 2002 the Russian authorities have committed themselves to improving the legal and regulatory framework and tightening banking supervision. These steps were crucial to restore public confidence. In the meantime a favourable economic cycle has raised the living standards of the population and helped the financial recovery of enterprises therefore increasing the demand for banking services. In the last few years the banking system has been one of the fastest growing and most profitable sectors in the economy. It remains, however, still inadequate to fully comply with the needs of the country and still far from Western standards. This explains the growing interest of foreign groups in this market.

The Russian Federation is still relatively protectionist compared to other Eastern European countries (including the former USSR member States). Instead of allowing foreign groups to gain control of their domestic banking system in order to fill the huge gap with Western systems, Russia has been slow and cautious in reducing entry barriers. Strongly opposing a 'colonisation' of its system, the authorities have been pursuing the further development and strengthening of the system according to their own strategy clearly expressed in two documents jointly drafted by the Bank of Russia and the Ministry of Finance in 2001 and in 2005. The authorities are getting increasingly aware about the potential benefits of a major involvement of foreign investors in view also of forthcoming accession to World Trade Organisation (Putin, 2006). They are, however, still cautious in removing entry barriers. The strategy highlights the role of State-controlled intermediaries: few global players (so called 'national champions') able to compete, within a limited period of time, with much stronger foreign banking groups.

The Russian economy: from default to recovery

In Russia transition from a planned to a market economy took the form of a 'shock therapy'. For the majority of the population, the political and economic reforms started with 'perestroika' resulted in widespread unemployment and general impoverishment. At the same time, the privatisations of the 1990s led to a concentration of a significant part of State assets in the hands of a relatively small group of people (the 'oligarchs'). This paved the way to the establishment of the Financial–Industrial Groups (FIG), which control a large share of the economy including many large-medium banks. Political and economic instability led to August 17 1998 default of the Government on its domestic debt. From 1999, however, Russia experienced a somehow unexpected fast economic recovery (see Table 7.1). Between 1999 and 2007 the gross domestic product grew at an average annual rate of more than 6 per cent; international reserves rank third after China and Japan and the financial position is solid. In 2008 Russia has entered the tenth consecutive year of growth and the overall prospects are positive, apart for inflation. Main driver of present growth is high energy and natural resources price (World Bank, 2005; Ahrend, 2006). 'Russian appetite' spread among Western investors while major domestic companies are increasingly listing abroad or have access to foreign borrowing.

International organisations keep warning about potential weaknesses of an economy still largely depending on oil prices: long-term sustainability of actual growth might be hampered by the slow pace of structural reforms and the relatively ineffective efforts to diversify the economy. Besides that, the 'Yukos *affaire*', which started in July 2003 and ended up with the State gaining control of the major private oil company, has literally frozen the business climate for more than two years and ushered in a new era: the Government is determined to play an active

Table 7.1 Selected macroeconomic indicators: 1999–2007 (US$bn)

	1999	2000	2001	2002	2003	2004	2005	2006	2007	
Nominal GDP	166	251	300	342	451	604	752	1,010	1,346	
Current account surplus	28	61	48	46	60	86	120	139	118	(1)
Oil Urals p.b. (US$ end period)	17.3	26.9	23.1	23.5	27.3	35.6	54.4	55.8	92.6	
External debt of RF	178	161	149	152	186	215	259	310	463.5	
Public sector external debt*	n.a.	n.a.	n.a.	n.a.	n.a.	n.a.	151	134	190.9	
– general Government	133	117	104	97	98	97	71	45	37.4	
– Banks	n.a.	n.a.	n.a.	n.a.	n.a.	n.a.	19	41	65.5	
– Other sectors	n.a.	n.a.	n.a.	n.a.	n.a.	n.a.	49	45	78.9	
Net capital export/import by private sector	−20.8	−24.8	−15.0	−8.1	−1.9	−8.9	0.1	42.0	82.3	
Oil Stabilisation Fund	–	–	–	–	–	18.8	43.0	89.1	156.8	
Net international reserves	12.5	28.0	36.6	47.8	76.9	124.5	182.2	303.7	476.4	
(y-on-y)										
Real GDP growth (%)	3.2	8.3	5.0	4.3	7.3	7.2	6.4	6.7	8.1	
– Industrial production	8.1	9.0	4.9	3.7	7.0	7.3	4.0	3.9	6.3	
– Fixed capital investments	1.0	17.7	8.7	2.6	12.5	10.9	10.5	13.7	21.1	
– Retail trade (private consumption)	−7.7	8.9	10.8	9.2	8.0	12.5	12.0	13.9	15.2	
Refinancing rate	55	25	25	21	16	13	12	11	10	
Exchange rate Ruble/US$ (end period)	27.0	28.2	30.1	31.8	29.4	27.8	28.8	26.3	24.5	
Exchange rate Ruble/€ (end period)	27.2	26.1	26.5	33.1	36.8	37.8	34.2	34.7	35.9	
Stock market index (RTS)	153	−4.5	79.2	39.8	57.9	6.9	83.3	70.8	19.6	
Unemployment rate (ILO definition)	11.7	9.7	8.7	8.8	8.9	8.5	7.7	6.9	6.1	
CPI inflation (end period)	36.5	20.2	18.6	15.1	12.0	11.7	10.9	9.0	11.9	

Notes: *liabilities of Government, banks and enterprises subject to State control (>50% +1 voting share).
Source: RosStat (GosKomStat), CBR (Central Bank of Russia), Russian Trading System (RTS), Troika Dialog.

role in strategic sectors of Russian economy (including banking) through State-controlled enterprises. Differently from what IMF, OECD, EBRD have suggested, the Government plans to transform them into 'national champions' competing with major foreign companies.

Transition to market economy has still to be fully completed and we will make use of the expression *à la russe* (Russian style) meaning a kind of approach where often too many compromises have been reached, where reforms or new regulations have been approved but never efficiently implemented; therefore resulting in a sort of legal and economic 'patchwork', leading to a co-existence of old and new, of Western liberalism and Soviet or Tsarist *dirigisme*. Russia is in many ways 'lost in transition' and despite the impressive performances of recent years is still to be considered an emerging economy (Ahrend and Tompson, 2005).

From Perestroika to the new millennium: banking reforms *à la Russe*

From Gorbachev's banking reforms to August 1998 default

It is widely agreed that before the economic reforms (*perestroika*) started in 1987 by M. Gorbachev in the former Soviet Union, Russia had no real banking system: until then State Bank of USSR (GosBank) granted 95 per cent of all loans to domestic enterprises. The two-tier structure was practically unknown. The reform intended to transform GosBank in a pure central bank and establish a limited amount of State-owned specialised commercial banks with no more access to public financial support. According to the plans, in the medium term a significant number of new banks either with private or public-private ownership would have been established (Aganbegjan *et al.*, 1988; Boffito, 1994; Caselli and Koutznetzov, 2005).

As of 1 January 1988, five State-owned intermediaries started to operate as separate entities from GosBank: PromStroyBank (Industry and Construction Bank), AgroPromBank (Agricultural and Industrial Bank), ZhilSotsBank (Housing and Social Bank), VneshEconomBank (Bank for Foreign Economic Relations, the former VneshTorgBank-VTB) and SberBank (Savings Bank).[1] Loss-making enterprises, however, still had full access to State support and the reform failed to ensure more efficient credit allocation. The first banks with private capital were established: in October 1989 GosBank issued the first licence to International Moscow Bank (IMB);[2] hundreds of very small intermediaries were established by local enterprises for tax reasons or to ease access to credit.[3] Not infrequently banks were involved in illegal activities and money laundering (Corda-Stanley and Synnott, 1996; Tompson, 2004). Specialised State-controlled banks were gradually split into smaller entities with public or private ownership. In the meantime two crucial laws were adopted in December 1990: the Law on the State Bank of USSR and the Law on Banks and Banking Activity.[4]

From the very start Russian banks experienced the difficulties of a country facing a deep economic recession: political and social instability, poor legal framework, hyperinflation, currency devaluation. Support to the real sector was modest. Banks financing domestic enterprises (especially State-owned) were faced with a growing share of non performing loans. However, during the 1990s a large number of banks took advantage of financial instability and made huge profits from trading (with currencies, State securities, derivatives, etc.). In an economy afflicted by overall illiquidity, some intermediaries took full control of relevant State assets extending loans to the almost bankrupt Government or taking part in the privatisation deals. Banks with access to liquidity were the key to real wealth. Most of present major Financial Industrial Groups (FIG) controlling the larger private banks were established in the 1990s.

Liquidity crisis of August 1995 and 1998 caused hundreds of intermediaries to exit the market. Hundreds thousands of depositors lost their savings as a result of the scarce protection provided for by an inadequate framework and ineffective banking supervision. No deposit insurance system was in place at the time. To avoid large scale confidence crisis among the population and widespread social consequences, on September 1998 the Government ordered the transfer of deposits held in major bankrupt intermediaries to State-owned Sberbank. However, by that time, people had lost trust in the system and it took years to restore their faith (Tompson, 2000; Chapman, 2001).

From financial recovery to development through the cleansing up of the system

Political stability, sound fiscal policies, economic growth as a result of fast rising oil price help explain the dramatic improvement in the financial condition of banks and enterprises between 1999 and 2001. From extreme illiquidity the economy experienced a somehow excess of liquidity thus resulting in a re-monetisation of the real sector. By the end of 2001, the banking sector fully recovered from the crisis. Although crucial for the smooth functioning of the payment system, the banking sector became almost of no relevance in supporting the economic growth. Government and non-financial enterprises were in no need for liquidity. Overall the banking sector was healthy but of no support to the real sector as showed by the extremely low level of intermediation (Barnard and Thomsen, 2002; Tompson, 2002): 32.3 per cent the ratio between total assets and GDP as of January 2001, and 11.5 per cent the share of loans to households and non-financial enterprises to GDP.

The loss of confidence of an impoverished population in the system was confirmed by the modest share of household deposits (6 per cent) to GDP since the Russians preferred to keep their savings 'under the mattress'. Restoring confidence in banks was a priority. Banking reform had become an urgent need after years during which very little had been done. In December 2001 the Bank of Russia and the Government approved a joint strategy for the development of the banking system. Crucial legislative acts were finally approved: (i) the laws establishing a deposit insurance system,[5] thus breaking up the monopoly of State-controlled banks on household savings; (ii) the law introducing the *International Financial Reporting Standard* (IFRS); and (iii) the law establishing the so-called archives on credit histories.[6]

To enter DIS-*Deposit Insurance Scheme* banks had to pass a severe screening. The comprehensive process that led to the establishment of a deposit insurance is, however, a typical *à la russe* solution. Aimed at cleansing up the sector from banks which were weak or involved in money-laundering business, the screening process it allowed nevertheless many intermediaries lacking the requisites to be admitted in the DIS. It may be still considered a milestone in restoring public confidence and promoting competition between public and private intermediaries. At present DIS covers only household deposits up to 700,000 rubles (20,000 euros) from initially 100,000 rubles. On January 2008, 909 out of 1,136 credit institutions (1,092 banks and 44 non-bank credit institutions) are part of the deposit insurance system (with a share of more than 99 per cent of household deposits).

Following the first rounds of reforms, in April 2005 the Government approved a new strategy for developing the banking system up to 2008. The appropriate system for Russia is identified in a combination of big banks (with a network all over the country and in CIS); small–medium regional banks and specialised intermediaries (in consumer lending, residential mortgages, loans to SMEs). The followings are the targets to be achieved by end-2008: total assets/GDP equal to 56–60 per cent; capital (own funds)/GDP equal to 7–8 per cent; and loans to non-financial enterprises/GDP equal to 26–28 per cent.[7] Four areas of business should drive growth: residential mortgages, loans to SMEs, consumer lending and microfinance due also to their social relevance in promoting the economy in underdeveloped Russian regions.

Foreign investments are deemed crucial for the development of the banking system and should be promoted, removing obstacles to the acquisitions of shares in the capital of domestic intermediaries. With reference to State-controlled banks, the Government has planned to reduce its share in the system. It will nevertheless continue to hold control on Sberbank, VneshTorgBank (VTB) and so-called 'strategic' banks, defined as those pivotal for economic policies.

In May 2006 it was approved the law fixing in 5 million euros the minimal capital requirements for new established banks starting 1 January 2007.[8] The purpose was to align the Russian legislation with Western standards and to increase the capitalisation of the banking system. This target was missed thus resulting in a typical *à la Russe* solution: the capital requirement applies only to newly licensed banks. All other intermediaries are not subject to the law and may conduct business regardless of the amount of capital.[9] This compromise was strongly supported by domestic banks; it takes into account the needs of large shares of the population having scarce access to banking services, fearing the winding-out of hundreds of small and minor banks, the only ones providing services in the most secluded areas of the immense Russian territory.

In December 2006 the law on banks' ownership was amended.[10] It finally removed the obstacles hindering foreign acquisitions of Russian banks (so-called 'blessed-share system') and established a unified regime for both domestic and foreign investors. The recent amendments witness the awareness of the authorities about the need to up-grade the system making easier for foreigners to access the banking system. It shows as well how that the Government intends to make use of foreign capital and experience to promote the strengthening of the system although according to its own strategy. A plan that, as the 2005 joint-strategy clearly points out, will grant the State a strong influence in the banking system.

A better legal and operational framework, a stronger commitment by the authorities in improving the system, a higher credibility of the Central Bank of Russia, the gradual introduction of Basle regulations and the favourable economic cycle on the first place all contributed to the impressive growth of banking assets in recent years.

Structure and development of the Russian banking system

According to the Russian legislation, credit institutions may operate as banks or non-bank credit institutions.[11] Banks are not allowed to take households deposits in the first two years of business. Credit institutions may take the form of joint-stock companies – either 'close-end' JSC,

Table 7.2   No. of operating credit institutions

	1.01.01	1.01.02	1.01.03	1.01.04	1.01.05	1.01.06	1.01.07	1.01.08
Credit institutions (CI) licensed	1,311	1,319	1,329	1,329	1,299	1,253	1,189	1,136
To conduct banking operations								
– banks	1,274	1,276	1,282	1,277	1,249	1,205	1,143	1,092
– non-bank credit institutions	37	43	47	52	50	48	46	44
CI with foreign stakes	130	126	125	128	131	136	153	202
– with a >50% foreign stake	33	35	37	41	42	52	65	86

Source: Central Bank of the Russian Federation (CBR).

'Z.A.O.' in Russian or 'open-end' JSC, OAO in Russian –[12] or limited liability company (OOO).

The sharp increase in assets has proceeded together with a significant reduction in the number of credit organisations (due to revocation of licences, liquidation of weaker intermediaries and, to a lesser extent, mergers and acquisitions, see Table 7.2). Foreign-controlled credit institutions in the same period have more than doubled (see Table 7.9).

In 2007, banks decreased by a further 50 units to 1,092 while the figure for credit institutions with a foreign stake shows an increase of almost 50 units to 202 (of which 86 are foreign-controlled entities).

Table 7.3 shows the uneven distribution of credit institutions in the Russian territory: banks are mostly concentrated in the Moscow Region and the Central Federal District, in the North-Western part, where the old capital St. Petersburg is located, in the richer areas along the Volga River and the South. Moscow is by far the real economic and financial centre and has strengthened its position in the latest years: 49 per cent of banks at the end of 2007 are based in the capital (44 per cent at the beginning of 2001). This contraction had severe consequences on the scarcely populated (although rich in natural resources) regions in Siberia and Russian Far East where the banking presence was already low.

The reduction has been mostly counterbalanced by a strong growth in the banking network. The improvement of living conditions beyond the capital and St. Petersburg has pushed major Moscow-based banks to expand their business in the regions (see Tables 7.4 and 7.5). Started in 2004–2005 this shift gained momentum from early 2006. A lack of comprehensive statistical data by the Central Bank of Russia on branching might lead, however, to a misperception of the trend in progress.

Table 7.3 No. and distribution of operating credit institutions within the seven Federal Districts of the Russian Federation

	1.01.01	1.01.02	1.01.03	1.01.04	1.01.05	1.01.06	1.01.07	1.01.08
1. Central Federal District	693	714	738	752	742	714	673	632
– of which Moscow	578	620	645	661	656	631	593	555
2. North-West FD	93	91	88	86	87	84	80	81
– of which St. Petersburg	42	42	42	43	44	42	42	41
3. South FD	148	143	142	137	130	128	124	118
4. Privolzhsky (along Volga river) FD	159	157	156	154	151	146	139	134
5. Urals FD	82	82	77	76	71	67	65	63
6. Siberia FD	90	86	82	80	75	71	68	68
7. Far East FD	46	46	46	44	43	43	40	40
Total CI in the Russian Federation	1,311	1,319	1,329	1,329	1,299	1,253	1,189	1,136
– of which banks	1,274	1,276	1,282	1,277	1,249	1,205	1,143	1,092
– of which non-bank C.I.	37	43	47	52	50	48	46	44

Source: CBR.

Table 7.4 No. of branches of credit institutions in the seven Federal Districts

	1.01.02	1.01.03	1.01.04	1.01.05	1.01.06	1.01.07	1.01.08
No. of branches (including Head Office)	4,752	4,655	4,548	4,537	4,548	4,470	4,591
– no. of branches	3,433	3,326	3,219	3,238	3,295	3,281	3,455
1. Central Federal District	1,482	1,475	1,461	1,464	1,442	1,405	1,390
– of which Moscow	959	966	971	953	774	735	711
2. North-West FD	487	470	459	451	460	473	512
– of which St. Petersburg	153	154	160	166	172	183	202
3. South FD	630	622	603	598	599	592	603
4. Privolzhsky (along Volga river) FD	874	838	785	799	817	835	880
5. Urals FD	511	496	493	465	448	430	460
6. Siberia FD	513	499	497	508	523	486	504
7. Far East FD	255	255	250	252	259	249	242
No. of branches (including Head Office)	4,752	4,655	4,548	4,537	4,548	4,470	4,591
– of which Sberbank	1,234	1,163	1,046	1,012	1,010	860	837
– branches of 100% foreign-owned banks	32	40	47	49	70	142	232

Source: CBR.

Table 7.5 Operating points of credit institutions

	1.02.2006	1.07.2006	1.01.2007	1.01.2008
Total number of credit institutions (C.I.)	1,247	1,229	1,189	1,136
– of which banks	1,199	1,174	1,143	1,092
(A) Total number of branches	3,294	3,243	3,281	3,455
– of which Sberbank	1,004	923	859	809
– branches of 100% foreign-owned banks	29	79	90	169
(B) Total number of branches (including Head Office)	4,541	4,472	4,470	4,591
– of which Sberbank	1,005	924	860	810
(C) Total number of additional offices of CIs	n.a.	12,737	15,007	18,979
– of which Sberbank	n.a.	6,166	7,282	8,623
(D) Total number of cash points of CIs		17,067	15,885	14,689
– of which Sberbank		13,218	11,983	10,839
(E) Total number of credit and cash offices of CIs		786	996	1,543
– of which Sberbank		1	–	–
(F) Total number of operations offices (of branches)	–	–	–	497
– of which Sberbank	–	–	–	–
(G) Total number of cash points (of branches)	–	–	–	51
– of which Sberbank	–	–	–	50
Total (B + C + D + E + F + G)	4,559	35,080	36,376	40,317
– of which Sberbank	1,024	20,328	20,144	20,291

Source: CBR.

According to Russian legislation credit institutions may operate through a diversified network: fully operating branches, additional offices, cash points, credit and cash offices, and operations offices of branches. Until end of 2006 CBR statistics were limited to operating branches. This explains why Table 7.4 shows an apparently different picture – a reduction in the number of branches between 2001 and 2007.

Tabke 7.5, however, shows a rather different picture: all operating credit institutions are increasing their network according to the different typologies allowed by CBR and not only through full operating branches. State-controlled Sberbank, the first Russian bank, is converting fully operating branches into additional offices and this helps explain the apparent contraction of its network seen in Table 7.4. Foreign-owned banks are increasing their presence at a very fast pace, opening a few full operating branches in a region and then a number of additional offices and/or credit and cash offices, with more limited business but also less administrative burdens.

This shift to the regions has also been driven by the strong competition in the 'historical' capitals, Moscow and St. Petersburg. Two factors should however be highlighted: on the one hand, Sberbank is distorting competition, especially in the regions where small local (and often privately owned) credit institutions are unable to compete with the State-controlled 'giant'; on the other hand, a huge share of the Russian territory is still left out of any serious prospects of economic development and is therefore heavily under-banked.[13]

Recent evolutions and perspectives: between dirigisme and opening the market

Between 2001 and 2006 banking assets grew at an average annual rate of 35 per cent, loans extended to non-financial institutions and households at 46 per cent, household deposits at 44 per cent, capital (own funds) at 35 per cent (see Table 7.6). According to CBR statistics, the increase has been driven by the increasing demand for banking services from households and SMEs as a consequence of the favourable economic cycle (Banking Supervision Report 2000–2006; 2007). This trend was confirmed for 2007. According to data released by the CBR banking assets have grown by 44.1 per cent, loans to households and non-financial enterprises by 53 per cent. Loans to households marked a slowdown (+57 per cent compared to +75 per cent in 2006) due to less aggressive

Table 7.6 Dynamic of the banking system: 2001–2007 (bn euro)

	1.01.02	1.01.03	1.01.04	1.01.05	1.01.06	1.01.07	1.01.08
Total banking assets	119.2	125.3	152.2	188.8	285.1	404.8	563.8
growth rate (% y-on-y)	33.7	31.2	35.1	27.4	36.6	44.1	44.1
Own funds (capital)	17.1	17.6	22.1	25.0	36.3	48.8	74.4
growth rate (% y-on-y)	58.5	28.1	40.2	16.2	31.2	36.3	57.8
Loans to households and non-financial enterprises	49.9	54.3	73.0	102.8	159.5	231.5	342.3
growth rate (% y-on-y)	56.2	35.7	49.5	44.8	40.3	47.3	53
Household deposits	25.6	31.1	41.2	52.3	80.5	109.3	143.1
growth rate (% y-on-y)	52.1	51.9	47.4	30.3	39.3	37.7	35.4
Exchange rate Ruble/€ end of period	26.5	33.1	36.8	37.8	34.2	34.7	35.9

Source: CBR.

practices in consumer lending but also tighter regulatory requirements on disclosure of information on effective interest rate in the still poorly regulated consumer lending. Banking capital (own funds) increased by almost 58 per cent as a result of the Initial Public Offering of VneshTorg-Bank, the second bank by assets and the issue of additional shares by Sberbank. Household deposits grew at a rate of more than 35 per cent.

In the same period banks have changed their balance sheet structure. Focused on more profitable credit allocation, the share of loans to private individuals (mostly consumer lending) on total assets grew five-fold to 16 per cent; the share of loans to non-financial enterprises grew to 42 per cent. Credit to real sector has reached 43 per cent of global loans as a result of increasing support to SMEs.[14] The share of household deposits increased from 22 per cent to 28 per cent. The share of ruble-dominated deposits on total household deposits increased to 83 per cent as a result of the ruble's appreciation against the US dollar and public confidence in the domestic currency. Resources raised by resident and non-resident organisations, however, remain the main source of funding (with a share of 33 per cent) especially for large private and foreign-owned banks, which take advantage of customer confidence and can provide a wider range of services. Funds raised from non-resident banks or on international markets showed a strong growth due to borrowing by State-controlled and large private banks with higher credit ratings. Banks, however, still face a liquidity risk due the 'natural' mismatching between assets and liabilities as a consequence of the existing contradictions in the present legislation.[15]

Banking has become one of the most dynamic and profitable area of business in the Russian economy. Profits have grown at an average annual rate of 40 per cent. Major banks are highly profitable due to the huge spread between funding and lending rates. Consumer lending is by far the most profitable area of business.[16] In 2007 banks registered an increase in profits of 36.7 per cent which marked a slowdown compared to previous years (+42 per cent in 2006 and +47 per cent in 2005). The return on assets (ROA) also decreased to 3 per cent in 2006 while the return on equity (ROE) showed a slowdown to 22.3 per cent from 26.3 per cent in 2006. Due the easier access to cheap funding, according to CBR, foreign and State-owned credit institutions were the most profitable, followed by competitive large-private banks controlled by FIGs.

Despite the impressive growth rates, financial intermediation in Russia continues to be limited to a modest 60 per cent GDP of gross domestic product (see Table 7.7), far below Western countries but also other emerging economies.

Table 7.7 Main indicators of the Russian banking sector (%)

	1.01.02	1.01.03	1.01.04	1.01.05	1.01.06	1.01.07	1.01.08
Banking sector assets as % of GDP	35.3	38.3	42.3	41.9	45.1	52.3	61.4
Banking sector own funds (capital) as % of GDP	5.1	5.4	6.2	5.6	5.7	6.3	8.1
Loans and other funds to non-financial institutions and households as % of GDP	14.8	16.6	20.3	22.8	25.2	30.0	37.3
Household deposits as % of GDP	7.6	9.5	11.5	11.6	12.7	14.1	15.6
Banking sector own funds (capital) as % of total assets	14.4	14.0	14.5	13.3	12.7	12.1	13.2
Loans and other funds to non-financial institutions and households as % of total assets	41.9	43.3	47.9	54.5	55.9	57.2	60.7
Household deposits as % of total assets	21.5	24.8	27.1	27.7	28.3	25.4	25.4

Source: CBR.

The Russian banking system remains highly concentrated and fragmented: few major banks controlled by the State or FIGs (Trust Investment Bank, 2005; S&P, 2006) a limited number of medium-big banks (among which those controlled by foreign capital) and hundreds of small and minimal banks. Out of 1,165 credit institutions (1,120 banks and 45 non-bank credit institutions) as of 1 July 2007, the first five banks account for 45 per cent of total assets, 44 per cent of loans to non-financial sector and 59 per cent of household deposits (see Table 7.8). The first twenty banks – seven under State control, five controlled by FIGs and the three major foreign-owned banks –[17] account for more than 64 per cent of total assets, 65 per cent of loans to non-financial sector and more than 72 per cent of household deposits. Almost a thousand small intermediaries have a share of less than 9 per cent of total banking assets, 8 per cent of loans to non-financial sector and 7.7 per cent of household deposits.

State-controlled banks and the impact on competition

In Russia the State influence on the banking system, as in other economic sectors, is relatively high. According to CBR statistics, as of January 2008, twenty-four credit institutions are under State control (thirty-one

Table 7.8 Selected indicators of CIs' performance grouped by assets (in descending order) as of 1 July 2007 (%)

	1–5	*6–20*	*21–50*	*51–200*	*201–1000*	*1001–1165*
Number of full operating branches	30.3	14.2	13.6	19.8	19.8	2.2
Credits extended, of which:	43.6	21.1	12.4	15.1	7.8	0.1
– corporate loans	45.6	19.6	12.5	14.8	7.5	0.0
– personal loans	38.5	25.7	12.2	15.5	8.0	0.1
Personal deposits	59.4	12.9	7.9	12.1	7.7	0.0
Own funds (capital)	46.0	16.9	10.5	15.1	11.2	0.2
Total assets	44.7	19.9	12.1	15.1	8.1	0.1

Source: CBR.

as of 1 Jaunary 2007). Seven out of the first fifteen banks are under State control, among them the first four by assets: SberBank, VneshTorgBank (VTB), GazPromBank and Bank of Moscow. According to CBR statistics, in 2007 state-controlled banks strengthened their position with a share of 39.2 per cent (from 37.8 per cent in 2006). Some analysts, however, share the view that the influence of the State in the banking system accounts for 50 per cent of total assets.

A strategic role is played by the major credit institution, Sberbank – with branches all over the Russian territory – in a country where 42 per cent of citizens still have no access to banking services. In the regions, however, Sberbank is hindering the development of private small intermediaries. The bank is a *de facto* market maker for interest rates on both deposits and loans. Unlimited access to cheap funding – and State guarantee on household deposits (till end of 2006) when no deposit insurance system was in place – does not allow credit institutions to compete on equal terms with the exception of banks controlled by foreign groups or FIGs.

Despite opposite advice from international organisations, the Government has been pursuing a significant strengthening of major State-controlled banks: SberBank, GazPromBank, VneshTorgBank, the future 'national champions'. VTB has started an acquisition campaign in Russia and abroad, including CIS countries,[18] relying on State support.[19] The Government is also increasing its influence on the economy through specialised intermediaries.[20]

The authorities underline that the State influence is lower than in other emerging economies like China, Brazil and India. It is of clear evidence, however, that the present situation is hindering competition: this will eventually increase but only as a consequence of competitiveness of major private banks.

Foreign-controlled banks: a trend on the rise but not risk-free

Investors interested in entering the Russian banking system complain about the obstacles they had to face, first of all, protectionism. Foreign groups are not allowed to open branches in Russia. They may conduct banking operations only through a subsidiary. This rule is not subject to any significant change in connection to the forthcoming access of Russia to the WTO.[21]

The establishment by major foreign groups has been steady anyway due to the huge potential in the Russian economy. Between 2000 and 2007 foreign-controlled banks have grown more than two-fold through newly established intermediaries (often the same banks who had deserted Russia in 1998) or acquisitions of operating credit institutions (see Table 7.9).

Table 7.9   Number of CIs with foreign stakes

	1.01.01	1.01.02	1.01.03	1.01.04	1.01.05	1.01.06	1.01.07	1.01.08
Credit institutions (C.I.) licensed	1,311	1,319	1,329	1,329	1,299	1,253	1,189	1,136
To conduct banking operations								
– non-bank credit institutions	37	43	47	52	50	48	46	44
C. I. with foreign stakes	130	126	125	128	131	136	153	202
with a >50% stake	33	35	37	41	42	52	65	86
– 100% foreign-owned	22	23	27	32	33	41	52	63
– >50% but <100% foreign stake	11	12	10	9	9	11	13	23

Source: CBR.

As with domestic banks, foreign credit institutions are focusing their attention on the Russian regions and to retail customers. In the past years they have registered the fastest growth compared to domestic banks (see Table 7.10) due to an impressive increase in their branch network but also to the *de facto* unlimited access to funding.

After a slowdown in 2006, in 2007 foreign-controlled banks showed higher growth rates of profit than the banking sector average. ROA is

Table 7.10 Growth rates (%) of foreign-controlled banks (bn euros)

	1.01.04	1.01.05	1.01.06	1.01.07
Total banking assets	152.2	188.8	285.1	404.8
growth rate of foreign-controlled banks (% y-on-y)	23.3	32.0	48.6	109.9
total growth rate (% y-on-y)	35.1	27.4	36.6	44.1
Total own funds (capital)	22.1	25	36.3	48.8
growth rate of foreign-controlled banks (% y-on-y)	31.7	37.0	55.4	87.0
total growth rate (% y-on-y)	40.2	16.2	31.2	36.3
Total loans to households and non-financial enterprises	73	102.8	159.5	231.5
growth rate of foreign-controlled banks (% y-on-y)	27.3	47.2	68.8	97.5
total growth rate (% y-on-y)	49.5	44.8	40.3	47.3
Household deposits	41.2	52.3	80.5	109.3
growth rate of foreign-controlled banks (% y-on-y)	45.8	71.4	58.3	147.4
total growth rate (% y-on-y)	47.4	30.3	39.3	37.7

Source: CBR.

Table 7.11 Main performances of foreign-controlled credit institutions as share on total banking system indicators (%)

	1.01.01	1.01.02	1.01.03	1.01.04	1.01.05	1.01.06	1.01.07	1.01.08
Assets	9.5	8.8	8.1	7.4	7.6	8.3	12.1	17.2
Own funds (capital)	9.4	7.7	7.1	6.6	7.8	9.3	12.7	15.7
Loans to non-financial organisations	7.1	7.2	7.1	6.1	6.2	7.4	10.0	15.6
Household deposits	1.7	2.3	2.3	2.3	3.0	3.4	6.2	8.9
Funds from enterprises and organisations	14.0	11.7	10.4	9.3	9.4	9.6	13.3	17.7

Source: CBR.

around 3.2 per cent (3 per cent in 2006) while ROE has increased to 25 per cent (from 23.5 per cent in 2006).[22] The share of banks controlled by foreign capital is at 17.2 per cent of total assets as of 1 January 2008 as showed in Table 7.11.

Foreign investors are also increasingly buying minority stakes in domestic intermediaries. Local banks welcome foreign partners as 'strategic investors' providing experience and resources to support development strategies. On their side, foreign banks are interested in medium-sized or even large (by local standards) domestic banks with a well-established network.

What are the main risks foreign investors should be aware of? First, asset quality and credit risk should be investigated, as a result of connected lending and more recently, of the dramatic increase of consumer credit.[23] Special attention should be paid when buying stakes in banks under the control of FIGs.[24] Last, but not least, the reliability of accounting data is under doubt due also to the persisting difference in accounting standards even after the adoption of IFRS in 2004.[25]

Conclusions

The difficult and still on-going transition of Russia from a planned to a market economy had a deep impact on the development of its banking system. In the past years the financial sector has experienced dramatic growth favoured also by a severe improvement of regulatory framework. The Russian banking system, however, is still lagging behind Western standards due also to a somehow formal, superficial implementation of international consolidated rules.

Foreign investors share the view that the system is still protectionist. According to the Government, local banks are still inexperienced and lack adequate resources (financial, technological, managerial, etc.) making them unable to compete on fair terms with major foreign financial groups. These limitations therefore are needed to allow domestic intermediaries to partially fill the huge gap with Western banks. They are intended to avoid Russian financial system being 'colonised' as the recent experience of Eastern European Countries and the Baltic State has showed.

However protectionist the system might be the present framework has not discouraged foreign groups from settling in the country, opening up subsidiaries (or representative offices) or buying majority or minority stakes in domestic banks.

Russia presents foreign investors with wide business opportunities. The huge economic potential and an underdeveloped highly profitable financial sector constitute a powerful attraction. Foreign investors are, therefore, increasingly moving back.

The authorities look at foreign investors with renewed interest: a stronger foreign presence might even be promoted. The importance of fully understanding the legal and operational framework and the 'new rules of the game' should not be underestimated. The authorities might well be aiming at a zero-cost upgrade and strengthening of the banking system by shifting the burden and costs of modernisation to foreign groups. It will be crucial for investors to be able to cautiously select from among hundreds of potential targets in a context that is not risk-free.

Notes

1. Established in 1841, Sberegatelny Bank (or Sberbank), the Savings Bank, is one of the oldest credit institutions in Russia. Traditionally Sberbank has always served as the bank for households and the only intermediary entitled to deposit-taking from private individuals. Until 1987 banking reform, Sberbank collected 100 per cent of household deposits.
2. IMB was established by a pool of banks: three Russian banks, VneshEconom-Bank (with a share of 20 per cent), Sberbank (10 per cent), Promstroybank (10 per cent) and five foreign banks: Banca Commerciale Italiana, Bayerische Vereinsbank AG, Creditanstalt-Bankverein, Credit Lyonnais and Kansallis-Osaki-Pankki, each with a share of 12 per cent. At present IMB belongs to Unicredit Banking Group.
3. There were 1,500 in 1991, over 2,000 in 1993 and around 2,600 before the liquidity crisis of August 1995.
4. Law 395-I of 2 December 1990 (at present Federal Law-FL 86 of 10 July 2002) and FL 17 of 3 February 1996.
5. Federal Laws 177, 178, 179, 180, 181 and 182 of 23 December 2003. The Deposit Insurance Agency (DIA) holds responsibility for the DIS.
6. Federal Law 218 of 30 December 2004. Another major step has been the approval of the Federal Law 115 of 7 August 2001, and the establishment of a *Financial Intelligence Unit*, the Federal Agency for Financial Monitoring.
7. The ratios at the time the documents was drafted (end 2004) were: assets/GDP: 42.5 per cent; capital (own funds)/GDP: 5.6 per cent; loans to non-financial enterprises/GDP: 19.5 per cent.
8. FL 60 of 3 May 2006 amending art. 11 of FL 17/1996 and artt. 62 and 63 of FL 86/2002.
9. The only requirement is that the level of capital may not be lower than the amount as of 1 January 2007.
10. Artt. 11 and 18 of FL 17/1996 and art. 61 of FL 86/2002.
11. Non-bank credit institutions are mostly specialised in clearing or cash services (i.e. Western Union).
12. 'Closed-end JSC' may not exceed 50 shareholders (art. 7 of Federal Law 208 of 26 December 1995).
13. As pointed out by President Putin, in a meeting with major banks in November 2006, 60 out of 142 million inhabitants still do not have access to banking services; only $1/4$ of population has a bank account and only 10 per cent makes use of a credit card.
14. Major Russian enterprises are increasingly borrowing or listing their shares abroad. This trend has witnessed a sharp increase since Russia was promoted to investment grade by major rating agencies.
15. According to art. 837, 2 of Russian Civil Code, depositors may claim back their savings anytime regardless of contractual agreement with the bank.

16. Association of Regional Banks (2006).
17. IMB (Unicredit Bank), Raiffeisenbank Austria and Citibank.
18. In 2005 the Government gave VTB control of the foreign network of former USSR URSS-Gosbank: Ost-West Handelsbank (Germany), East-West United Bank (Luxembourg), Donau-Bank (Austria), BCEN-Eurobank (France) and Moskow Narodny Bank (United Kingdom). With reference to CIS countries, VTB controls two banks in Ukraine (VTB Bank and Mriya Bank). In 2005 VTB has taken over the third Georgian bank by assets.
19. During liquidity crisis of July 2004, VTB took over Guta Bank. Re-branded VTB-24, the bank ranks 11th by assets and is focused on households and SME. In 2005 VTB has taken control with more than 75 per cent share of Promstroibank (14th by assets and re-branded VTB-North West).
20. An example is Rosselkhosbank (Russian Agricultural Bank), ranking 9th by assets, and Russian Development Bank, a newly established intermediary as the result of a merger among three State-owned banks: Vnesheconombank (VEB), Rossisky Bank Razvitia (Russian Development Bank) and Roseximbank (Russian Bank for Import and Export).
21. Banking legislation theoretically allows the establishment of foreign branches (art. 2 of FL n. 17/1996: 'Banking system of the Russian Federation shall include the Bank of Russia, credit organizations, and also branches and representative offices of foreign banks'). Regulations to implement the law were however never adopted.
22. The Central Bank of the Russian Federation (2006), 'Banking Supervision Report 2005'.
23. S&P (2005). Despite advances, Russian banks' creditworthiness is constrained by a weak legal and supervisory environment, non-transparent ownership, and high concentration in lending, funding and revenues. We still consider the Russian banking sector to be one of the world's riskiest from a credit perspective. S&P's Bank Industry Country Risk Assessment (BICRA) classifies Russia in the ninth risk out of 10, ranging from the strongest banking system (group 1) to the weakest (group 10). S&P (2006).
24. 'The FIG structure poses several risks. The usually web of cross shareholdings among financial and industrial firms that make up FIG is difficult for regulators to monitor, and the nature of ownership relationships can be murky. The absence of transparency is challenging for investors seeking to take an equity stake or a credit position with respect to FIG-owned bank. It is telling that no private-sector bank is actively traded in Russia when, in contrast, financial institutions usually represent a significant portion of the market capitalization of emerging market stock exchanges'. (S&P 2006).
25. Tompson (2004) and S&P (2006).

References

Aganbegjan, A.G., Ciocca, P.L., Sylos Labini, P. and Zacharov, V.S. (1988) *Perestroika e ristrutturazione produttiva* (Il Mulino).

Ahrend, R. (2006) 'Russia's Post-crisis Growth: Its Sources and Prospects for Continuation', *Europe–Asia Studies*.

Ahrend, R. and Tompson, W. (2005) 'Fifteen Years of Economic Reform in Russia: What has been achieved? What remains to be done?' *Economic Department Working Papers* No. 430, (OECD).

Alexander, W.E., Hoelscher, D.S. and Fuchs, M. (2000) 'Banking System Restructuring in Russia', IMF, Conference on Post-Election Strategy (Moscow, 5–7 April).

Association of Russian Regional Banks (2006) 'Mortgage Development in Russia in the Context of International Experience', IV International Banking Forum, Russian Banks – XXI Century (Sochi, 7–10 September).

Barisitz, S. (2004) 'Distorted Incentives Fading? 'The Evolution of the Russian Banking Sector since Perestroika, in Focus on European Economic Integration', (Österreichische Nationalbank Eurosystem).

Barnard, G. and Thomsen, P.M. (2002) 'Financial Sector Reform in Russia: Recent Experience, Priorities, and Impact on Economic Growth and Stability', IMF, Conference on Russian Banking Sector (London, 3–4 December).

Boffito, C. (1994) 'Il sistema bancario russo' (Banca Commerciale Italiana, Ufficio Studi).

Caselli, G.P. and Koutznetzov, D. (2005) La riforma del sistema bancario russo dal piano al mercato: un cammino lungo venti anni, No. 10 (Bancaria).

Chapman, S.A. (2001) 'La crisi finanziaria e il sistema bancario russo. Un'analisi critica della ristrutturazione', No. 3 (Economia, Società e Istituzioni).

Corda-Stanley, S. and Synnott, D. (1996) *Banking in Russia* (FT Financial Publishing).

European Central Bank (2005) 'Challenges for Banking Sector Stability in Russia and the Euro Area', ECB background paper to the Joint High-Level Eurosystem – Bank of Russia Seminar, St. Petersburg 12–14 October).

Gavrilenkov, E. (1997) 'Banking, Privatization and Economic Growth in Russia', in P.J.J. Welfens and H.C.Wolf (eds), *Banking, International Capital Flows and Growth in Europe* (Springer).

Georgieva, K. (2006) *BRIC Countries in Comparative Perspective* (World Bank).

Kozlov, A. (2005) 'Banking Supervision Principles and Framework in Russia', in M. Olsen (ed.) *Banking Supervision: European Experience and Russian Practice* (EU–Russia Cooperation Programme, Central Bank Training III).

Ledeneva, A.V. (2002) 'Underground Banking in Russia', *Journal of Money Laundering Control*, Vol. Five, No. 4.

Litwack, J.M. (1994) 'Corporate Governance, Banks, and Fiscal Reform in Russia', Corporate Governance in Transitional Economies, Insider Control and Role of Banks, Economic Development Institute of The World Bank, 99–213.

Putin, V. (2006) 'Opening Address at the State Council Presidium Session', 14 November, President of Russia Official Web Portal.

Standard & Poor's (2005) 'Transparency And Disclosure By Russian Banks: Disclosure Practices Of Russian Banks Currently Dismal' (S&P).

Standard & Poor's (2006) *'Bank Industry Risk Analysis: Russian Federation'*, (S&P).

Stern, N. and Hicks, J. (1996) 'The Transition in Eastern Europe and the Former Soviet Union: Some Strategic Lessons from the Experience of 25 Countries over Six Years', European Bank for Reconstruction and Development, (EBRD).

Stieglitz, J.E. (2002) *La globalizzazione e i suoi oppositori* (Einaudi).

The Central Bank of the Russian Federation (2000–2007) 'Banking Supervision Report'.

The Central Bank of the Russian Federation (2000–2007) *'Bulletin of Banking Statistics'*.

Tompson, W. (2004) 'Banking Reform in Russia: Problems and Prospects', Economic Department Working Papers No. 410, (OECD).

Tompson, W. (2002) 'The Present and Future of Banking Reform', in D. Lane (ed.), *Russian Banking: Evolution, Problems and Prospects* (London, E.Elgar), 56–78.

Tompson, W. (2000) 'Nothing Learned, Nothing Forgotten: Restructuring Without Reform in Russia's Banking Sector', *Shaping the Economic Space in Russia*, (Ashgate), 65–101.

Trust Investment Bank (2005) 'Fixed Income Research. Russian Banks: Safe Enough for Your Money?

World Bank (2005). 'From Transition to Development. A Country Economic Memorandum for the Russian Federation'.

Zhuravskaya, E. (1995) 'The First Stage of Banking Reform in Russia is Completed: What Lies Ahead?', in J. Rostowsky (ed.), *Banking Reform in Central and the Former Soviet Union* (Budapest: CEU Press).

8
Turkey[1]

A. Cimenoglu, M. Ferrazzi and D. Revoltella

Introduction

Following the economic crisis of 2001, the Turkish economy and its financial sector undertook a profound transformation. This transformation, together with the strategic geo-political role of the country and the large size of the local market, makes Turkey a particularly interesting case among emerging markets.

Moreover, the process of European Union convergence, with the beginning of accession negotiations in October 2005, laces the country in a particular, and to some extent privileged, situation despite the current ambiguity in the EU over Turkey's future membership prospects:[2] beyond the traditional external anchor common to other emerging markets, represented by the IMF, Turkey could count on the big support deriving from EU convergence to start a massive programme of reforms that concerned the economic, political and administrative spheres (Emre Alper and Önis, 2003).

The unprecedented six consecutive years of economic growth, in a context of a very favourable environment for many emerging markets – supportive global growth, booming trade flows, abundant liquidity – increased the interest towards a country with a huge potential, in particular, if one considers its demographic characteristics: 70 million people with a young population and a very educated middle class. The renewed stability of the Turkish financial system has been one of the main pillars of the recovery that followed the 2001 financial crisis. The recovery was supported by a rigorous fiscal policy and helped by the decision to let the domestic currency floating.[3]

These favourable conditions, coupled with a more encouraging attitude towards foreign investments, have lured financial international players, who entered the local market through the networks of local banks. HSBC, BNP Paribas, Unicredit, Citibank, Fortis, ING, General Electric Consumer Finance, Dexia, the National Bank of Greece, to name a few, have now a relevant presence in Turkey. The entry of foreign institutions has been substantial in the last three years and is likely to continue as long as the privatisation process progresses, given that some major banks are still state-owned. In the meantime, banking volumes – loans and deposits – are rapidly increasing, particularly on the loans' side, supporting the financial sector to generate profits after a period spent in deep water. However, recent problems in global financial markets are expected to take their roil on banking volume growth in Turkey starting from the last quarter of 2008.

Turkey, after a rather difficult political transition in 2007, with Parliamentary and Presidential elections, is now looking ahead waiting for the continuation of the process of EU accession, while in need to work on reforms to further align the country to EU standards.

Recent trends in the Turkish economy

In the last years the Turkish economy has been able to grow on a sustained path. From 2002 to 2007 real growth has recorded annual peaks close to 9.5 per cent, and the Turkish economy is now more than double the size it was at the end of 2001. Hence, the period of high uncertainty and sluggish performances characterising the 1980s and the 1990s has been left behind.

Indeed, ups and downs have characterised the recent Turkish history, with economic slumps above 5 per cent in 1994, 1999 and 2001 (Özatay and Sak, 2003). During the last crisis the Turkish GDP contracted by 5.7 per cent, and inflation[4] reached almost 70 per cent. At that time the budget balance and the public debt reached, respectively, impressive shares of 12 per cent and 79 per cent of GDP. In few months, between February and October 2001, the Turkish lira depreciated by 130 per cent.

From 2001, in a short period of time, the Turkish economy has been able to transform itself, especially through a consistent stabilisation plan based on reconverting agents' expectations (Domaç, 2003) by dealing with the problems of the public finances and by strengthening the financial system. This policy has been effective and years of chronic inflation faded away. Inflation fell below 10 per cent in 2004. Two measures has been the core of such structural change. First, the redefinition of the Central Bank operational rules: from May 2001 a new law stated independence of the Central Bank, with price stability as its main monetary policy target. This measure has supported the Central Bank in reducing

Table 8.1 Macroeconomic scenario in Turkey: a comparison with the recent past

	Average 1998–2001	Average 2002–2006	2007[5]
GDP growth (in real terms, %)	−0.4	7.2	4.6
Inflation (December, %)	61.5	15.0	8.4
Interest rates	81.6	23.8	15.8
Public Debt/GDP (%)	70.7	60.1	41.6
Budget Balance/GDP (%)	−11.3	−5.4	−2.2
FDI/GDP (%)	0.9	1.5	3.4

Source: Central Bank, UniCredit New Europe Research Network.

drastically the inertial component of inflation. Secondly, the three years agreement (2002–2004) with the IMF provided fresh funds and reduced the credibility gap. This allowed the Central Bank to cut interest rates several times. Moreover, from 1 January 2005 the Turkish lira has been rescaled through a technical operation (six zeros has been dropped), providing an additional signal of the commitment by the authorities to contain inflation. Public finances has been also restored during the last years: the primary surplus remained around 6 per cent of GDP since 2002, the budget balance is today below 2 per cent and public debt, over 100 per cent just few years ago, is well below the 60 per cent required by the Maastricht criteria (see Table 8.1).

However, in spite of the positive economic performance during 2002–2007, vulnerabilities – common to other emerging markets – still persist: public debt is still a heavy burden, especially if considering the heavy cost of servicing it, given the high interest rates, and the disinflation process is still far to be completed. So far Turkey remains a relatively risky country. It is among the few countries in Central Eastern Europe with a rating below the investment grade – a cut-off level between risky and non-risky countries.[6] The Turkish economy is still very sensitive to international market mood, as evidenced, for instance, during the 'mini-crisis' in Spring 2006 and the US subprime mortgage concerns in 2007 and again during the 2008 financial crisis. In 2006, between May and June, a massive international sell-off in the international markets, on top of some local events (the impasse in the appointing of the new Central Bank governor, to name one), resulted in a depreciation of 30 per cent of the local currency against the euro. Monetary authorities had to raise the policy interest rate to contain inflation. As a consequence, economic growth slowed down during the second half of 2006 and during 2007, highlighting the vulnerability of Turkey to 'exogenous' shocks, and the transmission from financial variables to real variables (Brooks, 2007). In

2007 the episodes of volatility related to the US subprime mortgage crisis were affecting Turkey more than other countries in the Central Eastern European region.

Although the Turkish economy was already relatively open to foreign investments in the past – never being a soviet-style planned economy – the role of Foreign Direct Investments (FDIs) in the country has never been as relevant as in recent years. FDI inflows experienced a rapid surge in 2005 and 2006, especially in services, mainly finance and telecommunications (Ferrazzi and Yucel, 2007). During the period 2005–2007, Turkey attracted three times the amount of foreign investments received in the previous twenty years. This vast flow of capital, contributing to the financing of the mounting current account deficit, as imports are by far bigger than exports, was the by-product of an acceleration in the privatisation process.

Along with a stable economic environment, political stability represented another prominent achievement.[7] Since November 2002, the AKP (Justice and Development Party, a conservative party) has been able to rely on a solid two-thirds parliamentary majority[8] and, although the initial scepticism of the international community, it undertook a vast process of reforms with the final aim to join the EU. The goal of joining the EU has helped to glue together an array of political forces, including kemalists, Islamists, nationalists and liberals (World Economic Forum, 2006; Cizre and Çinar, 2007; Robins, 2007). The convergence to the EU played a beneficial role for Turkey and on 3 October 2005 negotiations were officially opened. In the Parliamentary elections of July 2007, the AKP was even more successful, collecting about 47 per cent of the votes, and consolidating its power in the Parliament. The AKP party, after a very eventful period, was also able to elect the president (namely Abdullah Gul, former foreign minister) in September 2007: the Prime Minister and the President are now both from the AKP. The EU convergence process will last years (at least ten) as it is encountering some hurdles[9] but the outcome is all but assured. Even if it is far from being completed, the EU convergence process is boosting foreign investments and reducing the country risk[10] (hence, with a favourable impact on interest rates).

The overall economic growth is sustaining both the service and the industrial sector, for an economy that seems to be dualistic: the service sector is well developed but the agricultural and the manufacturing ones (including the important roles of textile and apparel) are still very relevant. Some big Turkish conglomerates, mainly family-owned, coexist with a huge number of micro-enterprises. The first three large financial–industrial conglomerates – Koç, Sabancı and Doğuş – practically pervade

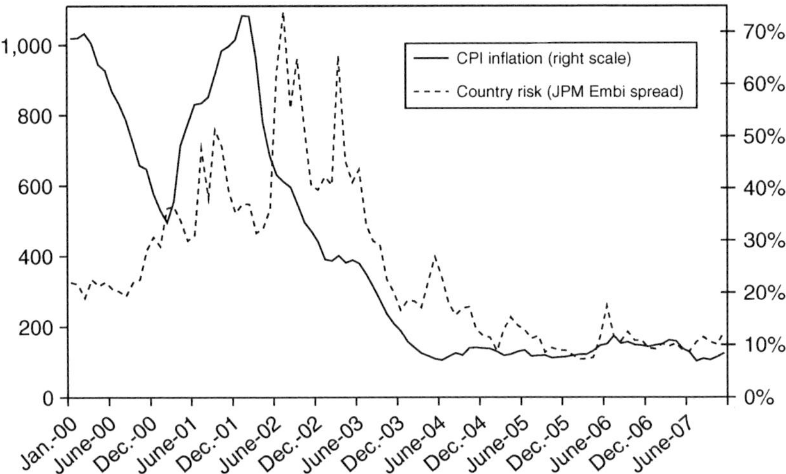

Figure 8.1   Country risk and disinflation process in Turkey
Source: Bloomberg, Turkstat.

all the economy. Only Koç, the largest accounts, according to some estimates, for 8 per cent of the country's GDP. Among the top 10 Turkish corporations, five belongs to the Koç's group.[11]

The size of the local market also makes Turkey interesting as a commercial and production base, in which the major Western enterprises are already investing substantially. Its 70 million population, with fast growing incomes, has no comparison at the European level. Turkey is the second largest country in Europe, after Germany, in terms of population, and with a favourable demographic trend: the Turkish citizens are younger than the European ones, with an average age around 29 years, ten years less with respect to the 'old continent'. The city of Istanbul, with a population around 11 million, is the main door through which to enter the local market. The Turkish income distribution is by far more unequal that any other European country (Eastern and Western), with a wide urban upper-class. Inequality is also visible at geographical level: the West side of the country is largely industrialised and service-oriented while the South and Eastern part is relatively underdeveloped (Aldan and Gaygisiz, 2006).

All in all, the recent evolution of the Turkish economy made possible that the characteristics of many emerging markets – high but very unstable growth, risky and difficult business environment, high inflation, complex political context – are leaving room to some qualities that make

Table 8.2 Turkey in comparison with other European countries

2006	Poland	Hungary	Czech Rep.	Slovakia	CEE-8	Romania	Bulgaria	Croatia	Turkey	EU 15
Population (m)	38.2	10.1	10.3	5.4	73.0	21.6	7.7	4.4	70.0	384.5
Average age, years[1]	37	39	39	37	38	38	41	40	29	39
Youth education attainment level, %[2]	69	60	59	52	65	47	49	55	27	59.1
Science and technology graduates[3]	9.4	5.1	7.4	9.2	8.9	9.8	8.5	5.4	5.6	13.6
GDP per capita €	7,107	8,919	11,066	8,145	8,254	4,501	3,268	7,704	4,525	27,700
Gross monthly average	636	642	713	503	638	245	181	906	815	3,513
Labour productivity per person (EU25 = 100)	61	75	69	69	64.5	37	34	62	42	106.3
R&D expenditure, % of GDP	0.6	0.9	1.4	0.5	0.8	0.4	0.5	1.2	0.7	1.91
Corporate tax (%)	19	16 (4)	24	19	19	16	10	20	20	29
FDI (in % of GDP, avg 2004–2006)	4.1	5.6	6.0	6.4	5.0	8.1	14.8	5.4	2.9	n.a.
GDP growth (avg. 2004–2006)	5.0	4.3	5.8	6.6	5.5	6.8	6.3	4.5	7.5	2.1

Notes: [1] 2005; [2] 2005, % of the population aged 20–24 having completed at least upper secondary education; [3] 2004, Tertiary graduates in science and technology per 1,000 of population aged 20–29 years; [4] +4% solidarity tax (slightly different tax base).
Source: Eurostat, EBRD, UniCredit New Europe Research Network.

Turkey similar to other Central Eastern European countries, some of them already EU members and not any more considered as emerging markets (see Table 8.2). A similar trend is visible in the financial sector.

The banking sector in Turkey: a deep change

Restructuring after the crisis

The recent financial history of Turkey is marked by frequent crises, with the last one, recorded in 2001. The financial crisis of 2001 has motivated the latest reforms that have shaped the actual banking system.

The banks' main fragilities stemmed from an inherent mismatch of maturity in their balance sheet: the stringent need to finance the public sector – via relatively longer-term securities – was not matched with the banking sector short-term funding (Özatay and Sak, 2003; Aktaş, Kaya and Özlale, 2005). Another major problem was the open foreign currency positions of banks which borrowed money in foreign currency and invested in high yielding government bonds in domestic currency (Özatay and Sak, 2003; Kasman, 2005; Kesriyeli, Özmen and Yigit, 2005). In 2001, currency depreciation, rising interest rates and the increase in non-performing loans (NPLs) – due to the difficulties of local enterprises on the back of the economic crisis – worsened the situation in an already structurally weak financial system (Kasman, 2005). The whole banking sector remained deeply affected, substantially disturbing the real side of the economy. One of the four state-owned commercial banks, Emlakbank, went bankrupt and has been submerged into Ziraat Bank, currently the biggest bank in Turkey, according to asset value. During the restructuring efforts, in the aftermath of 2001 crisis, many banks, state-owned and private, had to be recapitalised. On the private sector side, the situation looked even bleaker. Between 1997 and 2003, 21 privately owned banks were taken over by the banking authority. During the crisis, troubled private banks have obtained patronage from the Saving Deposit Insurance Fund (SDIF)[12] which managed their liquidity and NPLs. The initial cost of restructuring the state-owned banks and the banks taken over by the SDIF is estimated to be about US$44 billion, representing almost 30 per cent of the GDP in 2001. The fund is still working but its activity is now considerably reduced as banks taken over have either been sold out or liquidated. The remaining banks have been merged into a single bank; at the moment there is only one bank under the SDIF patronage.

Since this crisis, a deep change has been occurring. State owned banks' branches have been reduced by 24 per cent from 2000 to 2006;

meanwhile the number of their employees has been almost halved. However, today, the government Stake in the banking sector still stands at a level of around 30 per cent, both in terms of employees and branches, but it is expected to be further phased out. In the meantime, in 2001, the Turkish Banking Regulation and Supervision Agency (BRSA) introduced a more severe control system coupled with stricter rules and a more efficient accounting system. The Turkish government has been firmly committed to reform banking regulation and, inspired by the European legislation and by international standards, finalised its efforts in 2005. Making corporate governance rules more effective and risk control more accurate, this new legislation has fitted the Turkish banking system to the Basel II requirements, also setting out the rescue procedures in case of a difficulty.

The changes in the legislative framework, together with a radical change in the economic policy, both on the fiscal and monetary side, had reshaped in a couple of years the structure of the Turkish financial system.

The Turkish banking system and the participation of foreign players

Privately owned commercial banks – a total of 29 including local and foreign-owned, and excluding a bank that is still under the SDIF rule, as of December 2007, play an important role in the Turkish banking system: they hold roughly two-thirds of the total assets of the banking sector. The three state-owned banks, on the other hand, hold about 30 per cent of the banking sector assets. The residual 3 per cent of the assets is controlled by 13 'investment banks' (private, semi-private and public) that, in Turkey, contrary to the common definition at international level, support local administrations and non-profit institutions (Table 8.3).

The concentration of the banking system in Turkey is in line with the one in Central and Eastern Europe: the top five banks hold 62 per cent of the sector's asset[13] (85 per cent for the top ten).

Table 8.3   Banks in Turkey: December 2007

	Total	State-owned and SDIF	Private (including foreign)	Investment banks
No. of banks	46	4	29	13
No. of domestic branches	7,618	2,204	5,366	48
Employees	158,559	41,381	111,856	5,322

Source: Turkish Barkers' Association.

Before 2001, different to other transition countries in Central Eastern Europe, the presence of foreign capital was not significant in the Turkish financial system.[14] After 2001, as a result of the structural changes that took place, the banking system has become more attractive for foreign investors. Immediately after the crisis new opportunities did arise. For instance, late in 2001, HSBC, already present in Turkey at that time, bought Demirbank, a middle-sized bank, and this was the first relevant acquisition in the Turkish financial market at that time. In 2002 Uni-Credit entered the Turkish market through a 50 per cent joint venture (Koç Financial Service, KFS) with the local Koç Holding, the biggest Turkish conglomerate, which was the owner of a bank ranked among the top ten in the system.

However, it is between 2004 and 2006, during the economic consolidation of the country, that foreign interest in Turkey experienced a surge and not only in the banking sector. Many privatisation deals were achieved, particularly in 2005, including Tupraş (refinery), Erdemir (steel), Türk Telecom, Telsim (Telecommunications) and initial public offerings (IPOs) of financial institutions such as Halkbank, Vakifbank, and the flag-carrier airlines THY. The banking sector in particular saw record inflows of foreign investments and the sequence of local bank acquisitions by foreign banking groups has been one of the main determinants of restructuring in the Turkish financial framework.

In 2004 the French BNP Paribas set a joint venture with TEB (Türk Ekonomi Bankasi). In 2005, Fortis group, the Belgian–Dutch bank, bought a majority share in Dışbank and another middle-size bank, Denizbank, has been sold to the French–Belgian Dexia. KFS (the joint venture between UniCredit and Koç Holding) bought a majority stake in Yapi Kredi Bank, which is now, the fifth largest bank in the country. In 2006, the National Bank of Greece bought Finansbank (among the top ten banks), while the Greek Eurobank EFG did the same with the smaller Tekfenbank.[15] In 2007 the Dutch group ING acquired Oyakbank. Not only European banks entered the Turkish market in recent years: the American General Electric Consumer Finance, is now in joint venture with Doğuş Holding in Garanti Bank, the fourth Turkish bank in terms of assets; while the US giant Citibank entered the market with a 20 per cent participation in Akbank, the third largest Turkish bank.

Currently, among the top fifteen banks, four are state-owned or semi state-owned while the others are private. All the top10 private banks (with the only exception of IşBank, the second largest Turkish bank)[16] have already been involved in some kind of foreign investors participation, very often in tandem with local partners (Hagmayr and

Table 8.4   The top15 Turkish banks: September 2007

	Weight of total assets: (september 2007 (%))	Major shareholders
Ziraat Bank	14.7	State-owned
İş Bank	14.6	Pension fund of İşBank, CHP[17] and floating
Akbank	12.3	Sabanci Holding and Citibank
Garanti	11.3	Doğuş Holding and GECF
Yapı ve Kredi	9.1	Koç Holding and UniCredit
Vakıflar	7.6	State-owned and floating
Halk Bank	7.2	State-owned and floating
Finans Bank	3.6	National Bank of Greece
Denizbank	2.4	Dexia
Oyak	2.3	ING Group
HSBC	2.2	HSBC
TEB	2.1	Çolakoğlu Group and BNP Paribas
Fortis	1.7	Fortis
Şekerbank	1.0	Bank TuranAlem (Kazakhstan) and Pension Fund of Şekerbank
İller Bank	1.0	State-owned Investment Bank

Source: BRSA, UniCredit New Europe Research Network.

Haiss, 2006). From 2002 to 2006, in less than five years, the asset controlled by foreign banks has increased sharply to almost 30 per cent from a low 5 per cent.

The 'Copernican revolution' experienced by the banking system between 2004 and 2006 is set to continue along with the privatisation process, in which foreign investors are increasingly playing a role of primary importance. The privatisation of Vakifbank and Halkbank, which previously launched two different IPOs in 2005 and 2007, will be completed. Waiting in the privatisation agenda of the government is the probable IPO of Ziraatbank, the biggest Turkish bank, in 2009. The process of privatisation of the banking sector, which started after the 2001 crisis and is still continuing, is fostering the consolidation of the financial system, and also luring several foreign investors, most of which already operate in Central and Eastern Europe. To sum up, the wave of new foreign entries is due to the renewed stance of the business and governmental actors towards even more openness (the 2003 FDI legislation is an example among many), as well as the relative economic stability of the country and the EU prospects laying ahead.

Together with all the above-mentioned local factors, main international trends also need to be taken into consideration. The economies of many emerging markets, after the turbulence at the beginning of the decade,[18] benefited from a rather benign global scenario, with abundant liquidity and favourable monetary and growth conditions. Also the prosperous period of the Turkish economy took advantage from these factors. At the same time financial institutions at international level benefited from a rapid consolidation process. The economies of scale embedded into several activities (asset management, investment banking, insurance, credit cards, and so on) encouraged many European institutions to rethink their business along the lines of a pan-European one rather than a national one.[19] Large volumes and a multi-country approach are very often necessary to successfully compete on international markets. Many of the biggest international groups have a relevant presence in Central Eastern Europe: foreign banks play a leading role in most of the countries (Table 8.5), with Turkey being partially an exception. As mentioned, in Turkey international players hold less than 30 per cent of the banking assets (24 per cent in 2006); this share is higher than 90 per cent in many Central Eastern European countries. The vast local market and the relatively late opening of the market to foreigners have been supporting the creation of 'national champions' both in the financial and industrial sector. Koç, Sabanci and Doğuş, the three biggest national conglomerates, have a stake in three out of the five biggest Turkish banks. Despite the possible entry of other investors from abroad, the big local groups will maintain their qualified presence in the Turkish banking system in the near future.

Banking in Turkey: risks and opportunities

The current size of the Turkish banking system is amounting to 328 billion euro as of December 2007,[20] in terms of total assets (66 per cent of Turkish GDP). It represents only less than 2 per cent of the European banking market, but it is definitely not negligible if compared with other Central Eastern European countries. Just as an example, the size of the Turkish banking sector in terms of total assets, at the end of 2006, was as large as the sum of the banking assets in Czech Republic, Slovakia, Slovenia, Croatia, Romania, Bulgaria.

The Turkish banking total assets result as a mix of loans (48 per cent), asset under management (31 per cent), liquidity (13 per cent), and other assets[21] (8 per cent). On the liability side, deposits (62 per cent) and internal funds (14 per cent) play a major role. Since the corporate bonds market is virtually immature, issuing securities is still not a viable option for banks to raise funds. Therefore, they have been borrowing substantially from abroad, mostly via syndicated loan facilities. The liquidity and credit market concerns, following the sub-prime mortgage crisis in the

Table 8.5 Presence of top international financial institutions in Central Eastern Europe (ordered by total assets in the area)

2006	New EU members since 2004					New EU members since 2007		Western Balkans					
	Poland	*Czech Rep.*	*Slovakia*	*Hungary*	*Slovenia*	*Bulgaria*	*Romania*	*Croatia*	*Bosnia-H.*	*Serbia*	*Turkey*	*Russia*	*Ukraine*
UniCredit	Top5	Top5	Top5		Top5	Top5	Top5	Top5	Top5	Top5	Top5		Top5
Erste		Top5	Top5	Top5			Top5	Top5					
RZB			Top5			Top5	Top5	Top5	Top5	Top5			Top5
KBC		Top5	Top5	Top5									
SocGen		Top5			Top5		Top5	Top5					R
IntesaSanPaolo	R		Top5	Top5				Top5		Top5	R		
OTP				Top5		Top5							
Citigroup	Top5									R			
Market share of foreign-owned banks (%)	70	96	98	95	35	81	89	91	76	79	24	8	31

Notes: ⬜╱ Presence in the country; ⬜ R Representative office; ⬜ Top5 Among the top5 five banks interms of assets.

Source: UniCredit New Europe Research Network.

Table 8.6 Banking markets of Central Eastern Europe: a comparison with Turkey

€bn	Loans (bn €, 2007)			Deposits (bn €, 2007)			(Loans + deposits)/ GDP (%)
	Total	Retail	Corporate	Total	Retail	Corporate	
Russia	340	90	237	299	145	134	70
Turkey	159	54	94	198	126	52	72
Poland	131	73	48	139	78	40	83
Czech Rep.	63	27	28	89	51	26	114
Hungary	61	23	29	46	26	15	108
Ukraine	58	22	35	38	23	13	101
Romania	44	20	20	38	19	15	76
Croatia	29	15	12	26	17	7	150
Slovenia	27	7	17	19	13	4	136
Slovakia	25	8	12	31	14	10	102
Bulgaria	19	7	12	19	10	7	131
Serbia	11	4	6	11	5	4	71
Bosnia-H.	6	3	3	6	3	2	116

Source: UniCredit New Europe Research Network.

second half of 2007, are likely to create some problems for Turkish banks in raising funds from international markets both in terms of scarcity of available funds and higher prices. However, funding problems are on average less stringent than for other Central Eastern European banking systems: the latter have on average higher loans over deposits ratios[22] and are more dependent on foreign funding.

The sophistication of the Turkish banking market is high; nevertheless financial depth in Turkey is negligible compared to that of the Eurozone: At the end of 2007, the sum of loans and deposits was close to 72 per cent of GDP in Turkey far below the 250 per cent of GDP of the Eurozone. The same picture is also reflected in the number of branches: 573 every million inhabitants in Eurozone but just 94 in Turkey (195 in the new EU members, considering also Bulgaria and Romania[23]). Table 8.6 and Figure 8.2 show the different degree of financial penetration in various transition countries.

Structural factors (the catching-up process) and others issues pertaining to the economic situation have supported the fast development of the financial system (ECB, 2006). The reduction in interest rates, which went hand in hand with the disinflation process, has been a key element of the restructuring process: interest rates on loans and deposits have been more than halved in the last five years to the present levels.

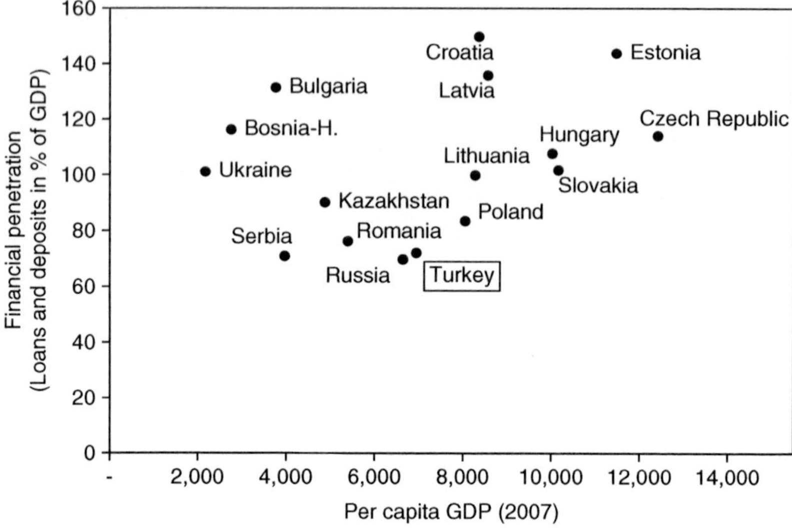

Source: UniCredit New Europe Research Network.
Figure 8.2   Financial penetration and per capita income: 2007

As of December 2007, the banking system loans amount to 158 billion euro 5.8 times the value as of the end of 2002, and about 32 per cent of the 2007 GDP. Household financing has been the more dynamic segment: in 2002 it represented 14 per cent of total loans (while 71 per cent were loans to non-financial corporations) with respect to the current 34 per cent (59 per cent to non-financial corporations). For example, the housing loans that registered triple-digit growth rates in 2004 and 2005 are still one of the fastest growing businesses with a growth rate of about 39 per cent in 2007. The new mortgage law that is in place since February 2007 will surely further boost the volumes in this segment.

Persistently high inflation rates and the volatility in the financial markets for almost two decades starting from early 1980s yielded very attractive real interest rates on deposits and hence resulted in avoidance of cash holdings by households and companies alike. Together with this, the interest of Turkish banks in technological novelties and resulting investments in credit cards boosted this business since the second half of 1990s. Although the rapid growth in mortgages, car loans and other individual loans in the last three years, credit card receivables still play an important role in Turkish banks' balance sheets. As of October 2007, credit card loans constitute about 29 per cent of all household loans.

Table 8.7   Turkey: trends in banking volumes

	2003	2004	2005	2006	2007
Total loans	66,743	101,578	153,101	215,000	271,867
y-o-y change	41.0%	52.2%	50.7%	40.4%	26.4%
– Retail	12,843	26,448	45,644	67,109	91,811
y-o-y change	94.4%	105.9%	72.6%	47.0%	36.8%
– Corporate	45,996	65,973	96,198	133,762	161,732
y-o-y change	36.3%	43.4%	45.8%	39.0%	20.9%
– Other (inv. banks loans, non-bank fin. inst.)	7,904	9,157	11,259	14,129	18,324
y-o-y change	13.4%	15.9%	23.0%	25.5%	29.7%
Total deposits	152,400	191,358	243,161	296,815	340,164
y-o-y change	12.5%	25.6%	27.1%	22.1%	14.6%
– Retail	100,868	124,615	147,845	185,353	215,504
y-o-y change	5.5%	23.5%	18.6%	25.4%	16.3%
– Corporate	33,779	45,551	64,233	75,956	88,570
y-o-y change	17.7%	34.8%	41.0%	18.3%	16.6%
– Other (non-bank fin. inst.)	17,752	21,192	31,083	35,506	36,090
y-o-y change	58.9%	19.4%	46.7%	14.2%	1.6%
Mutual Funds (AuM)	19,895	24,489	29,409	22,030	26,116
y-o-y change	98.9%	23.1%	20.1%	−25.1%	18.5%

Source: BRSA, UniCredit New Europe Research Network.

There are about 36 million credit cards in the banking system as a whole, meaning that 50 per cent of the Turkish population holds one.

Although deposits more than doubled between 2002 and 2006 the growth of loans has been more noticeable doubling the ratio between loans and deposits to 71 per cent from a low of 35 per cent in 2002. Two-thirds of the deposits derive from households and 25 per cent from companies, while the residual part involves to the public administration, investment banks and other non-banking financial institutions.

It is worthwhile mentioning the increasing confidence in local currency during the last years: the share of deposits and loans in foreign currencies, although still considerably high, has dropped in the last five years. In 2002, the share of foreign exchange deposits in total deposits, in a context of a previously almost 'dollarised' economy (Özatay, 2005), was about 60 per cent, and it fell to 36 per cent in 2007. Loans in foreign currency decreased to 24 per cent of total loans in 2007, from about 50 per cent.

Gross household financial wealth is about 2,676 euro per capita in 2007, a level that is almost 100 per cent higher than in 2002. Inequality

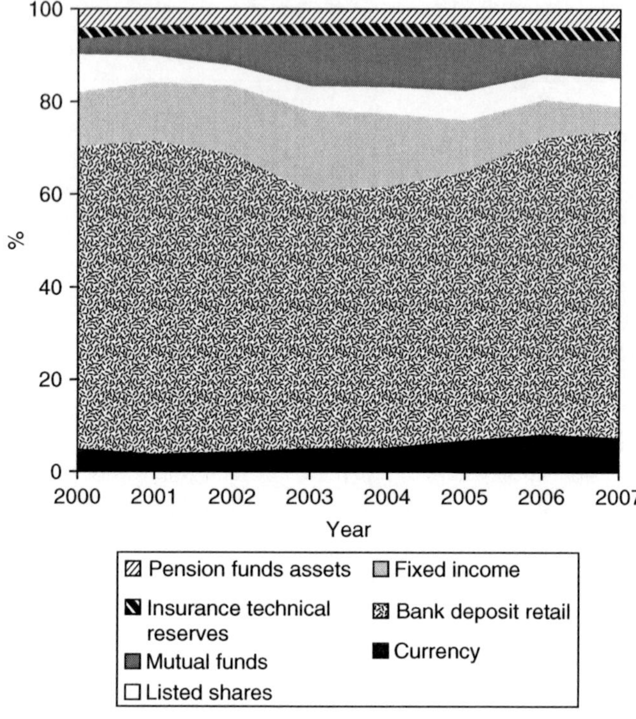

Source: UniCredit New Europe Research Network.
Figure 8.3   Turkey: allocation of Households' wealth (% of total)

remains an issue in Turkey leaving most of households financially inactive. From the active group the largest part of savings are held in the form of deposits (about 66 per cent of the total, see Figure 8.3) or invested in government bonds (usually short-term bonds) enjoying high interest rates. On the household portfolio, government debt instruments are roughly 5 per cent of the total. The shift to a more dare risk/return portfolio (towards shares, investment funds) is still not common: less than 15 per cent of the households' wealth is produced by in shares or mutual funds while the pension fund market is still in its infancy, playing a negligible role in the saving allocation process (see Figure 8.3).

The improved situation of the Turkish banking sector is particularly evident if we look at the trends in non performing loans (NPLs). Lower interest rates have supported the economic activity and, as a result of the increasing risk management practices, banks have been able to better

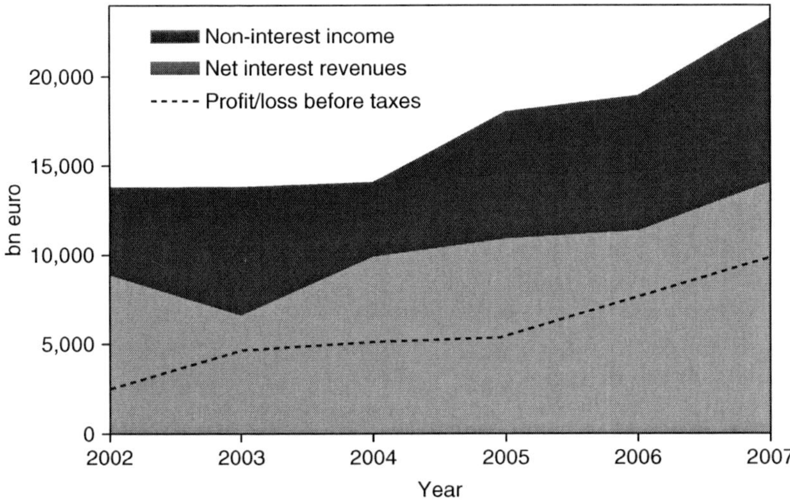

Source: BRSA, UniCredit New Europe Research Network.
Figure 8.4   Revenues and profits in the Turkish banking sector

handle problematic assets. The decrease in NPLs has been astonishing: they decreased to 3.6 per cent in December 2007 from 21.7 per cent in 2002.[24] This trend was driven, in particular, by the achieved financial solidity of the productive sector.

Things look different outside the corporate area: NPLs of households are on an upward trend. When consumer financing was less common, NPLs were below the total banking system average (under 5 per cent); however since 2006, the households NPLs surpassed the sector average.

A more competitive environment, in addition to narrower interest rate spreads, is forcing banks to extend their supply of new services, especially to retail customers, achieving revenues mainly from fees and commissions (Figure 8.4). After the 2001 crisis many banks were not very profitable if not actually making losses. The year 2002 represented a turning point towards an increasing profitability. In 2006 the banking sector profits (7.8 billion euro) were fourfold that of in 2002 as a result of an effective cost containment policy.

Conclusions

The Turkish economy and the Turkish financial sector are now completely different from a few years ago because of the massive overhauling

Table 8.8   Profitability and efficiency in the Turkish banking sector (%)

	2002	2003	2004	2005	2006	2007
ROE	14.7	22.2	19.8	16.8	24.4	24.0
ROA	1.8	3.2	3.0	2.3	2.9	3.1

Source: BRSA, UniCredit New Europe Research Network.

of the entire economic system. Supported by a period of immense economic growth, disinflation (and improvements in public finances since 2002, Turkey has been able to tackle the shortcomings in its financial system.

Nowadays the banking system is more modern and market-oriented. As in other Central Eastern European countries local banks are developing together with foreign partners, both from Europe (French, Italian, Greek, Dutch) and from the USA. Ten, out of the top 15 institutions, have already been involved, in recent years, in some kind of foreign investors' participation.

The rapid growth of total loans (they are now fourfold compared to 2002), especially from the households' side, has been the result of economic growth and decreasing interest rates. At the same time, the ratio of NPLs over total net loans is now lower than 4 per cent in comparison to an incredible high 20 per cent in 2003, while the sector is now producing profits almost fourfold the ones in 2002.[25]

After the rapid development of the last years, amid some turbulence (less significant than in the past and mainly stemming 'exogenously' from the international context), what's next for the Turkish financial system? Is there a risk to test again difficult times in the future?

The outlook for Turkey is quite positive and growth, reforms, privatisations and FDIs once again will support the activity of local and international players. A straighter path toward EU convergence would additionally help the country's economic recovery and its financial system. The European ambition has already been able to commit the political system and the civil society toward a common target as in the past for other continental countries. This particular 'external anchor' is an important element for Turkey; however, the speed of negotiations has been very slow in the last two years and the final aim of negotiations (the full EU membership) is still very far away.

The privatisation agenda is busy: highways, harbours, airlines (Turkish Airlines), electricity production and distribution facilities, mining industry, oil and chemistry companies, tobacco companies. Foreign investors will play a crucial role boosting the demand for sophisticated and cross-border banking services. The huge Turkish market,[26] still underpenetrated in terms of financial services, is set to be highly promising. The slowdown of EU accession process will not be able to stop the stride of the financial sector system.

Notes

1. Any opinions expressed here are those of the author(s) and not those of the institute(s). We thank Andrea Orame and our colleagues for their useful help.
2. Part of this ambiguity is stemming from the lack of consensus, in both the population and the elites of some countries (among them France and Austria), to the Turkish membership. On this topic, see Barysch (2007); World Economic Forum (2006), CirCaP (2007), Narbone and Tocci (2007) and Zucconi (2005).
3. For an analysis of the transition towards a flexible exchange rate regime in Turkey, see Ekinci and Erturk (2004) and Özatay (2005).
4. The very high rates of inflation, during long periods, had a very negative impact on the Turkish economy. In particular, in the past, inflation was considered the most problematic factor for doing business in the country, while it is considered not relevant now. See World Economic Forum (2006).
5. In the present chapter, 2007 data, if not final, are estimated by the UniCredit New Europe Research Network.
6. Turkey's ratings are Ba3/Stable (Moody's), BB-/negative (Standard & Poor's), BB-/stable (Fitch) as of September 2008.
7. Government instability was considered, after inflation, the most problematic factor for doing business in Turkey. See World Economic Forum (2006).
8. The Turkish voting system has set a barrier of 10% at national level preventing small parties to be represented in the parliament. This system is adding power to the biggest parties. In the 2002 elections the Akp received two-thirds of the seats having around 33% of the preferences by the voters.
9. The Cyprus issue is one of the main obstacles in Turkish–European relations. Cyprus, member of the European Union since 2004, is not recognised by Turkey, which gives political patronage only to the North part of the island (Turkish-Cypriot) while the custom union with EU would require Turkey to be opened also to the Greek-Cypriot part. The stop given by the 2004 referendum to reunification (the negative answers to the referendum, based on the Annan's plan, backed by UN, came from the Greek side, while the Turkish Cypriots were in favour of the agreement) postponed the resolution of the issue to the following years (Robins, 2007). This issue adds to the concerns related at EU level by any further enlargement (the so called 'enlargement fatigue'), after the entry of ten countries in 2004 and Bulgaria and Romania in 2007 (Barysch, 2007). Negative signals and discouraging comments coming from Europe, especially from the French Presidency, are also a source of

concern. Moreover support by the Turkish population for EU is declining, despite the support for the pro-EU policies by the ruling AKP.

10. The country risk in Figure 8.1 is defined as the spread between the Turkish bonds and a risk-free bond. The spread is the Jpm Embi (JP Morgan Emerging Market Bond Index).

11. Koç Group is actively involved in many activities, from automotive (joint ventures with Fiat and Ford) to home appliances, retail distribution, energy, tourism, real estate, banking and Finance. Koç Group is made of 120 companies, 21 of which are traded in the Istanbul Stock Exchange. The Group has around 93 thousands employees. It is the only Turkish company included in the top 500 companies around the world (Fortune 500). Sabanci Group, 52,000 employees and 70 companies, is the second largest family-owned conglomerate that characterised the Turkish economic structure: it is involved in media, financial sector, tyre industry, retail trade, cement, food, chemicals. Doğuş Group is the third one in terms of dimension, after Koç and Sabanci, of the big corporations, with 18,000 employees and 73 companies: it is involved in the financial sectors, construction, media, tourism, real estate, media and automotive.

12. In Turkey, Banking Regulatory and Supervisory Agency is in charge of the regulation and supervision of the banking sector, while the SDIF is the deposit insurance agency, who is also in charge of rehabilitating the banks taken over by the banking authorities, including managing asset collection efforts.

13. This value is below the ones in Czech Republic and Baltic States, roughly equal to Slovakia, Slovenia and Romania and above Bulgaria, Hungary and Poland.

14. Regarding the role of foreign banks in transition countries, see Claessens *et al.* (2001), Kraft (2002) Reininger *et al.* (2002), Uiboupin (2005), Lanine *et al.* (2006), Mucci and Revoltella (2006).

15. The recent involvement of Greek banks – and, in general, of the Greek business community in Turkey – is of particular interest: the Greek and Turkish diplomacies still have rather different views on the Cyprus issue, but the relation among the two countries are much better than in the past. This new era in Turkish–Greek relations started with the so-called earthquake diplomacy (with reciprocal assistance after two catastrophic earthquakes in Istanbul and Athens in 1999) and was developed in the following years. As a result, the support for Turkey's entry in EU among Greeks is rather high and rising. See World Economic Forum (2006).

16. 33% of IşBank is listed on Ise, the local stock exchange. Two-third of this 33% is foreign-owned. This figure is not as high as one could think, considering that two-thirds of the entire Ise floating is in the foreign investors' hands

17. Turkish Republican People's Party: traditionally secular and kemalist (it inherited the tradition of Mustafa Kemal Atatürk, founder of the Republic), the party belongs to the Socialist International. The party, the second one in Turkey in terms of votes according to the last elections (it represents now the main opposition to the ruling AKP), has not voting rights in the bank.

18. Before the Argentine crisis (2002), other countries/areas incurred in period of serious instability, such as Brazil (1999), Turkey (1999, 2001), Russia (1998), Far East (1997), Mexico (1994).

19. When referring to globalisation in the financial systems, we should mainly distinguish between wholesale and retail services. The former, including asset management, insurance, investment banking and credit card, take advantage of economies of scale and by the knowledge fully exploited by the largest international banks; the latter, mainly delivered through local branches, are still an asset of the local banks that succeed to be well rooted in the local society.
20. 261 billion euro at the end of 2006 (84% of Turkish GDP). Source: Brsa (supervision).
21. Including subsidiaries and fixed assets.
22. The loans/deposits ratio in 2007 is around 0.80 for Turkey, and around 1.06, on average, for CEE countries. The same ratio was 0.63 and 0.87 respectively for Turkey and CEE in 2005.
23. Data on branches are as of 2006.
24. The NPLs ratio is calculated as the ratio on non-payments on the previous period net loans. Source: Brsa (supervision). Data on household Npls are not available before October 2004.
25. In local currency. Almost four times bigger in Euro terms.
26. Turkey is the largest emerging market after the BRICs and the 17th economy in the world in terms of dimension.

References

Aldan, A. and Gaygisiz, E. (2006) 'Convergence Across Provinces of Turkey: A Spatial Analysis', CBRT Working Paper No. 06/09.

Aktaş, Z. Kaya, N. and Özlale, U. (2005) 'The Price Puzzle in Emerging Markets: Evidence from the Turkish Economy Using "Model Based" Risk Premium Derived from Domestic Fundamentals', Central Bank of the Republic of Turkey, WP No. 05/02.

Banking Regulation and Supervision Agency, 'Annual Report', various years.

Banks' Association of Turkey, 'Banks in Turkey', various years.

Barysch, K. (2007) 'What Europeans Think about Turkey and Why', Centre for European Reform briefing note.

Brooks, P. K. (2007) 'The Bank Lending Channel of Monetary Transmission: Does It Work in Turkey?', IMF Working Papers, WP 07/272.

Central Bank of Turkey (2006) 'Financial Stability Report', Vol. 2.

Centre for the Study of Political Change (CIRCaP) (2007) 'European Elites Survey'.

Cizre, Ü. and Çinar, M. (2007) 'Turkey Between Secularism and Islam: The Justice and Development Party Experience', ISPI WP 12.

Claessens, S., Demirguc-Kunt, A. and Huizinga, H. (2001) 'How Does Foreign Entry Affect Domestic Banking Markets?', *Journal of Banking and Finance*, Vol. 25, pp. 891–911.

Domaç, İ. (2003) 'Explaining and Forecasting Inflation in Turkey', Central Bank of the Republic of Turkey, WP no. 05/02.

European Central Bank (2006) 'Macroeconomic and Financial Stability Challenges For Acceding and Candidate Countries', ECB Occasional Paper Series, No. 48, 42–53.

European Commission (2006) *Attitudes towards European Enlargement*, Eurobarometer.

Ekinci, N.K. and Erturk, K. (2004) 'Turkish Currency Crisis of 2000–1, Revisted', CEPA Working Paper 2004-01.

Emre Alper, C. and Öni, Z. (2003) 'The Turkish Banking System, Financial Crises and the IMF in the Age of Capital Account Liberalization: A Political Economy Perspective'.

Ferrazzi, M. and Yucel, Y. (2007) 'Turkey, the Challenges of the Biggest European Market', *East Europe and Asia Strategy*, No. 14.

Hagmayr, B. and Haiss, P. (2006) 'Foreign Banks in Turkey and Other Eu Accession Countries – Does Minority vs. Majority Ownership Make the Difference?', Europainstitut Wirtschaftsuniversitat Wien.

Kasman, A. (2005) 'The Sources of Inefficiency in the Turkish Banking Industry', *Yapi Kredi Economic Review*, Vol. 16, No. 2, 3–19.

Kesriyeli, M., Özmen, E. and Yigit, S. (2005) 'Corporate Sector Debt Composition and Exchange Rate Balance Sheet Effect in Turkey', Central Bank of the Republic of Turkey, WP No. 05/16.

Kraft, E. (2002) 'Foreign Banks in Croatia: Another Look', Croatian National Bank Working Papers, W-10.

Lanine, G. and Vander Vennet, R. (2006) 'Microeconomic Determinants of Acquisitions of Eastern European banks by Western European banks', Universiteit Gent, WP 06-414.

Mucci, F. and Revoltella, D. (2006) 'Banking Systems in the New EU members and Acceding Countries', Bank of Slovenia WP, No. 11.

Narbone, L. and Tocci, N. (2007) 'Running Around in Circles? The Cyclical Relationship Between Turkey and the European Union', *South European society and politics*.

Özatay, F. (2005) 'Monetary Policy Challenges for Turkey in European Union Accession Process', CBRT Working Paper No. 05/11.

Özatay, F. and Sak, G. (2003) 'Banking Sector Fragility and Turkey's 2000–01 Financial Crisis', CBRT Working Paper.

Reininger, T., Schardax, F. and Summer, M. (2002) 'Financial System Transition in Central Europe: The First Decade', Suerf, Société Universitaire, Européenne de Recherches Financières, No.16.

Robins, P. (2007) 'Between the EU and the Middle East: Turkish Foreign Policy under the AKP Government, 2002–2007', ISPI Working Papers, WP – 11.

Uiboupin, J. (2005) 'Short-term Effects of Foreign Bank Entry on Bank Performance in Selected CEE Countries', Eesti Pank Working Papers No. 4.

World Economic Forum (2006) Global Risk Network, Europe@Risk, November.

Zucconi, M. (2005) 'The United States' and Europe's Turkish Connection. Europe's Turn To Manage It', CeSPI, Rome.

Index